GLOBAL COFFEE TOUR

CONTENTS

INTRODUCTION

From its discovery in Ethiopia, coffee has well and truly conquered the planet. Worldwide we drink around two billion cups a day, and for centuries it has shaped the way we live, driven national economies, kept us awake and some say even instigated artistic movements and helped win wars. And yet, ask any barista or coffee professional working today and they will tell you that in terms of flavour, we are living in a golden age of coffee. Farming practices have improved, coffee roasters have never before been so knowledgeable, and on high streets from Cape Town to Tokyo a new breed of coffee shop has arrived, serving only the best speciality coffee prepared with care. In the USA this revolution in producing high-quality coffee has been described as the third wave. Elsewhere it is known as the speciality coffee movement. Whatever you call it, most coffee experts agree: the best is yet to come.

WHAT IS SPECIALITY COFFEE?

The coffee shops and roasteries in this book are largely purveyors of speciality coffee. But what does this mean? According to the Specialty Coffee Association of America (SCAA), speciality coffee is that which scores 80 points or above out of a possible 100 when graded by a qualified coffee taster. Coffee that scores between 60 and 80 points is graded as commodity coffee – certainly still drinkable, but destined for the supermarket shelf or jars of instant. At these tasting sessions – a rigorous process known in the business as a 'cupping' – points are awarded for categories such as sweetness, flavour, balance and mouthfeel. To achieve such a high score, speciality coffee is generally grown in optimal soil, climate and altitude conditions, is harvested and processed at the right time and is roasted to perfection. In short, we're talking about very fine coffee – the cream of the crop.

Interest in speciality coffee has recently undergone a rapid expansion. The SCAA reports that in 1993 there were just 2850 speciality coffee shops in the whole of the USA. By 2013 the number was hovering around 30,000. As consumers become more demanding and palates more sophisticated, coffee producers, roasters and baristas are upping the ante with speciality coffee, and taking the so-called third wave to a possible fourth.

INTRODUCTION

WHAT IS THIRD WAVE COFFEE?

Love it or hate it, the term 'third wave' is useful in understanding where we are in the history of coffee making and appreciation. But what about the first and second waves? In countries such as the USA, the UK, New Zealand and Australia, the first wave of coffee usually describes the era when coffee became widely available to consumers as instant coffee, the second wave was when espresso drinks arrived on the high street (helped along by chains such as Starbucks) and better coffee became desirable. The third wave was coined in the USA in the late 1990s and describes a focus on coffee as a complex and artisanal food product, like wine.

Third wave coffee makers are innovators who are interested in how the whole journey from seed to cup affects the final outcome. They want to tweak and improve those steps to achieve better coffee. They value more than ever the relationship between the coffee farmer and the coffee roaster, and typically want to maintain the distinct flavours of the coffee's origin and variety, something they achieve with light roasting techniques. The role of the barista is also a key component. Precise control over coffee's preparation – the grinding, brew ratio, heating of milk or latte art, for example – is something to be honed and celebrated.

While most of the cafes and roasteries in this book will serve speciality coffee, they are not all third wave in style. In Italy, excellent dark-roasted shots of coffee have been served since the invention of the espresso machine in the late 19th century, while in Istanbul you can sip a drink which dates from the age of Suleyman the Magnificent: the wonderfully sweet and sludgy Turkish coffee. Third wave coffee pioneers are hardly responsible for all the great coffee in the world, but what they have introduced is a widespread sharing of knowledge about coffee. Through tasting notes, cupping sessions, barista classes, talks, festivals and sheer infectious passion, they have given us a language and understanding for what makes great coffee.

WHY GO COFFEE TOURING?

This book includes a huge range of coffee experiences, from the traditional coffee ceremonies of Ethiopia and *kissatens* of Japan, to vanguard studios that have more in common with a chemist's laboratory than a cafe. We've included both independents and coffee pioneers that have grown into corporate chains. What matters to us is the quality of the coffee and the visitor experience. In every place included you should learn something about coffee.

And why go coffee touring in the first place when great coffee is so widely available? There are a few reasons. The first is simple: time is the enemy of coffee; it tastes best when it has been freshly roasted and ground. You can buy speciality coffee online easily enough, but you are never going to get the same result as having it prepared for you by expert hands close to where it was roasted.

The second is that the story of coffee is intertwined with the history, economy and culture of so many different countries, that to understand it fully requires a coffee tour – whether that's to sip a flat white in Wellington or a *bicerin* in Turin. Excitingly, more coffee-producing countries are now enjoying the fruits of their best plants, meaning you can drink speciality coffee close to the field where it was grown.

Lastly, the world of coffee is filled with passionate people eager to share their obsession with you. To learn the most about coffee, you're just going to have to go and meet them.

And if you think you know a lot about coffee, we challenge you to tour one of the more unusual destinations in this book. Venture to Norway, Sweden or Hungary and you'll find exquisite coffee being prepared to the highest standards. Take a trip to Nicaragua or Colombia and you'll discover plantation owners keen to show you the possibilities of coffee grown in their countries. Elsewhere we reveal exciting cafes in Iceland, Cuba, Vietnam and Japan.

HOW TO USE THIS BOOK

For each of the 37 countries in this book we've included a profile of what you can expect from the coffee scene in that country. We have then organised the best coffee shops and roasteries to visit by city, or, in the case of the plantations, by region. In each entry we've suggested the coffee you should taste or buy while there, and have also recommended local sights and things to do so coffee tourers can make a day (or weekend) of their visit. There is a world of great coffee to try, now go and enjoy it! Dora Ball.

GLOSSARY

Types of Coffee

Americano Espresso and hot water

Cafe au lait Equal parts brewed coffee and steamed milk

Cafe mocha Espresso blended with chocolate syrup and topped with steamed milk or microfoam

Cappuccino One part espresso, one part milk and one part foam

Cold brew Coffee brewed using water at room temperature or colder. Usually steeped for 10 to 24 hours

Cortado From the Spanish verb 'to cut', a cortado is equal parts espresso and steamed milk

Crema A thin and desirable layer of foam found on top of an espresso

Doppio Or 'double' in Italian. Two shots of espresso pulled through the same filter and served as one

Drip/filter coffee Mechanized brew method using gravity to pull hot water through a bed of coffee grounds and a paper filter

Espresso A small, concentrated, syrupy shot of coffee that is achieved when pressure is used to force water through finely ground coffee

Flat white One part espresso to two parts steamed milk/microfoam

Latte One part espresso and three or more parts steamed milk

Latte art A design made in a drink using steamed milk/microfoam

Long black Espresso and hot water, a term popularised in Australia

Lungo Or 'long' in Italian. An espresso which is pulled longer or uses more water than a typical shot

Macchiato Or 'marked' in Italian. Is an espresso topped or – marked – with a small amount of steamed milk

Nitro cold brew Cold brew coffee infused with nitrogen and served on tap for a thicker, creamier texture

Piccolo Similar in espresso-to-milk ratio as the cortado, the piccolo is a drink made popular in Australia

Pour over A manual brew method that uses gravity to pull hot water through coffee grounds and a paper filter

Ristretto Or 'restricted' in Italian. An espresso that is pulled short or uses less water than a typical shot

Turkish coffee Brewed in a copper cezve or ibrik, Turkish coffee is unfiltered and made by boiling finely ground coffee beans in water

Technical Terms

Arabica Originally from Ethiopia, *Coffea arabica* is the world's most desired species of coffee plant

Blend When different coffees from different origins are mixed together to achieve a specific flavour profile

Brew ratio The proportion of coffee grounds to water used when brewing

Coffee cherry The fruit surrounding the coffee bean or seed

Cupping A method of coffee tasting used to determine quality, flavour attributes, and potential defects

Cup score A system of evaluating arabica coffee by assessing aroma, flavour, aftertaste, acidity, body, balance, sweetness, cleanliness, uniformity and defect each on a scale of 1-10. Coffees receive a total cup score out of 100

Green coffee After picking, processing, drying and before roasting, coffee seeds are known as green coffee

Microfoam When milk is steamed to a texture consisting of tiny bubbles

Natural/dry process Picked cherries are set out to dry naturally on raised beds or patios. As the fruit dries it imparts fruity flavours into the bean

Pulped natural or honey process After cherries are picked the skins are removed and beans are dried on beds with their sticky outer layer intact

Robusta Robusta or *Coffea canephora* is a species of coffee that is less desirable in flavour than arabica, has more caffeine, and is easier to grow

Single origin Coffee sourced from one geographic growing region which usually reflects the flavour attributes produced by a particular terroir

Speciality coffee Any coffee that acheives a cup score of 80 and above

Third wave Describes the overall trend of cafes and purveyors that source, prepare and serve speciality coffee

Washed or wet processing Picked cherries are hulled and put into fermentation tanks to remove the sticky outer layer. The beans are then washed before being set out to dry

THE B

What's in a bean? Quite a lot as it happens. These chemically complex little nuggets contain a whopping 1000-plus different aroma compounds (that's flavours and fragrance to you and me). Get to know your beans better by considering these four major factors in a coffee's flavour.

ORIGIN

Do you know your Kenyan from your Nicaraguan? Coffee is a fussy plant and only grows in countries found in the so-called Bean Belt, a strip around the globe between the Tropic of Cancer and the Tropic of Capricorn, with rich soil, warm temperatures and distinct rainy and dry seasons. Within these countries, a region's altitude, shade and soil make-up will dictate the varieties that can be grown and how delicious the outcome will be.

VARIETY

There are more than a hundred species and thousands of varieties of the coffee plant, of which only a few dozen are grown for consumption. In the speciality coffee world, the favoured species is Arabica (as opposed to the inferior quality Robusta), and – excitingly – varieties of this plant are being cultivated, cross-bred and discovered all the time. Some varieties, such as Java and Yirgacheffe, are only grown in their namesake regions, whereas varieties like Caturra are grown in many regions and produce different qualities and flavours depending on growing conditions.

EANS

PROCESSING METHOD

Look out for terms such as 'natural' or 'washed' on your next bag of beans. This refers to the method used to remove the fruit from the coffee seed. The natural method involves letting the coffee cherries dry in the sun before removing the dried fruit and outer husk. This process lends the coffee a fruity flavour. During the washed method, the fruit is removed in water before the bean is dried, giving the coffee a cleaner taste and increased complexity. Another hybrid method popular in Central America is the honey process: beans are dried with some of the fruit pulp attached. This process enhances the final product with notes of brown sugar.

ROAST PROFILE

After the coffee beans are processed, your local roaster can make their mark. Roasting coffee is a subtle art that transforms flavourless green beans into something (potentially) incredible. The roaster uses the heat, drum speed and airflow of the coffee machine to coax the inherent flavour from the beans and produce the desired level of acidity, bitterness and sweetness, also known as a 'roast profile'. Light and medium roasts allow the flavours of the beans' origin and variety to be more distinct. Dark roasts typically taste smoky and bitter.

GREEN BEANS

Measure out around 100g of green beans. Raw coffee beans are small, hard and have no discernible coffee flavour. Add them to a dry frying pan or wok on a medium heat and stir with a wooden spoon.

MINUTE 0

MINUTE 2

DRYING

After just a couple of minutes the beans will start to colour as they lose moisture content. Acids are developing, but there is still no coffee aroma.

At some point, any serious coffee hobbyist should try roasting beans at home. Raw beans can be sourced easily online or from a speciality coffee shop. Timings given here are a guide.

ROASTING

DARK ROAST

At the end of the second crack you will have a dark or espresso roast. The flavour should be chocolatey and bitter. Stop roasting! When you have reached the desired roast level, cool the beans then store them in an airtight container for a day before grinding.

MINUTE 19

MINUTE 18

SECOND CRACK

Snap! The beans will crack for a second time. Oils are forced to the surface and the beans will become very dark brown, glossy with oil and brittle. They will also emit a pungent smoke.

YELLOWING

Keep stirring as the coffee beans turn yellow through to light brown. Some toasty smells and steam will be coming off the beans as they continue to lose moisture. They will also start to swell with a build-up of gas.

MINUTE 5

MINUTE 8

FIRST CRACK

Pop! Around this time the coffee will start to pop or crack like popcorn due to the pressure of gas building up inside. Congratulations, you have reached the first crack! Your beans should be nearly double in size and will be leaving a flakey skin in the pan. Turn the heat down to low.

AT HOME

MEDIUM ROAST

Medium roast is also known as a city or American roast. It is a well-balanced roast, lower in acidity but with a fuller body. The beans should also be dark brown with a smooth surface.

LIGHT ROAST

Just a couple of minutes after the first crack you have reached a light roast. Brewed coffee will taste fruity or tangy with acidity. A light roast also emphasises the intrinsic flavour of the beans. You can stop roasting at any point from now on, or carry on to develop sweetness and body.

MINUTE 10

MINUTE 15

MINUTE 13

ROAST DEVELOPMENT

Keep stirring evenly on a low heat as you develop the roast. Sugars will be caramelising, and acids and other compounds are breaking down and developing flavour. Your kitchen will also fill with the smell of roasting coffee.

AFR
THE MID

TOP 3 *Coffee* TOWNS

CA &
OLE EAST

ADDIS ABABA

A sprawling city of over three million people and the capital of coffee's birthplace, Addis Ababa's bean scene is strong. Cafes run the gamut from stand-up Italian-style espresso bars to cozy coffee shops where wafts of roasting beans meet you in the street to modern spaces offering cold-brew.

CAPE TOWN

In just a decade, Cape Town has been transformed from a tea town with a bad instant coffee habit to a city of award-winning coffee shops. Origin Coffee can be credited with kick-starting the speciality coffee scene, and today palates and techniques are becoming as sophisticated as any.

ASMARA

Africa's 'Little Rome' combines the classic fire-roasted coffee ceremony of East Africa with the Italian *passeggiata* – a holdover of the colonial period that remains a central part of Asmaran life 80 years on. Head to Harnet Ave for cafes that have been hopping since before the war.

ERITREA

How to ask for a coffee in the local language? Hade bun, bejaka

Signature coffee style? Macchiato

What to order with your coffee? A homemade pastry at a cafe, or a plate of popcorn at a traditional tea ceremony

Don't: Leave a coffee ceremony without drinking all three of the glasses

Little Rome, Africa's Miami, the Art Deco City. Asmara is the heart of Eritrea's cultural scene, and coffee is the heart of Asmara. Throughout the day traditional coffee ceremonies give off the smell of beans roasted slowly over an open fire, ground with a mortar and pestle, and served with ginger in tiny cups. When the sun begins to set, the *passeggiata* heats up as locals take to the streets for an evening stroll to 'see and be seen', and there's nowhere better to see than from a cafe table over a macchiato.

Coffee culture in Eritrea stretches back to the drink's discovery in neighbouring Ethiopia. The two share a similar coffee tradition, with the drink a central part of social interaction across society. As beans are roasted, crushed, and served in three increasingly diluted pours around a communal table, so are stories shared, gossip exchanged, and relationships forged. But in Eritrea, an Italian colony from 1890 to 1947, the brew's history takes a unique colonial turn.

Under Italian rule the country saw an import that irrevocably changed its coffee scene: espresso. Steam-powered Italian machines still bear the workload, fuelled by Eritreans' love for the drink, and a respectable espresso or macchiato can be found in even the most out-of-the-way corners of the nation.

Get cosy with a group of friends or family, though, and it all goes back to the coffee ceremony ritual. From those tiny cups drink three rounds, known as *abol, kalayieti* and *bereka,* and you'll practically be an honorary Eritrean.

IMPERO BAR

45 Harnet Ave, Asmara; +291 112 0161

◆ Food ◆ Transport
◆ Cafe

At the heart of the art deco centre of Asmara, busy Bar Impero's exterior belies a cosy cafe attached to the grand Cinema Impero, built in 1937. Uniformed waitresses serve top-quality espressos and macchiatos to a constant flow of customers stopping in for a chat with friends or a quick caffeine recharge. Fronting busy Harnet ('Liberty') Avenue, the best seats in the house are at the row of outdoor tables, particularly during the daily *passeggiata* when the city takes to the streets to walk, talk and socialise. Grab a seat early and settle in for people-watching, as winding down the day with a coffee and friends in an old Art Deco cafe is perhaps the definitive Asmara experience.

THINGS TO DO NEARBY

Colonial-era Asmara
Art deco architecture across central Asmara defines the city's heritage, including the futuristic Fiat Tiagliero petrol station (opposite, far left), which serves as the unofficial tourism icon.

Tank Graveyard
Eritrea's long war with neighbouring Ethiopia casts a shadow over the outskirts of Asmara, where derelict military equipment gathers dust in the infamous tank graveyard.
Nr US Kagnew Station

ETHIOPIA

How to ask for a coffee in the local language?
Nē buna ibakiwo ifeligalehu
Signature coffee style? Strong espresso or macchiato
What to order with your coffee? Popcorn! Popcorn is often
served at the end of the coffee ceremony
Do: Always accept at least three coffees as part of the
coffee ceremony, especially in someone's home

Welcome to the birthplace of coffee.

According to legend, coffee's all-conquering march
dates back to a humble Ethiopian herder named Kaldi who,
in the ninth century, noticed that his sheep were particularly
energetic after chewing on what we now know as the coffee
plant, *Coffea arabica*. Whether the legend is true or not,
Ethiopia's claim to be the source of all coffee is no idle boast
– the *arabica* coffee plant is native to the southwestern
highlands of Ethiopia, and it was from here that the plant
(and coffee) colonised the world.

Ever since the brief and troubled occupation of the
country by the Italians in the mid-20th century, Ethiopians
have been among the most prolific coffee drinkers on
Earth and espresso bars serving macchiato seem to be
everywhere. It remains very much a part of the Ethiopian
day – especially in the morning at home, and again on the
way to work – to stop for a coffee in a dedicated coffee
shop. While things are slowly changing with the arrival of
contemporary cafes and new ways of drinking coffee in
what are essentially urban, middle-class venues, the typical
Ethiopian coffee is still an espresso ordered strong, and
drunk perched on a stool or standing up in a serious coffee
den where little else is served.

But the real way to drink coffee is rooted in ancient
rites of hospitality, and was designed to make coffee
a centrepiece of social and culinary traditions. Ethiopia's
renowned coffee ceremony follows a meal and is a central
element to any Ethiopian social gathering, whether for
family or business purposes. Seated on a low stool by
a tiny charcoal stove, the host scatters freshly cut grass,
which symbolises nature's gifts, as a nearby incense
burner smoking with *etan* (gum) adds fragrance and
solemnity. Over the stove, the host roasts the coffee beans
in a pan as guests draw near to inhale deeply and to
express their appreciation by saying *betam tiru no* (lovely).
Using a mortar and pestle, the host then grinds the beans
before brewing begins.

When the coffee is ready, and very much in the host's
own time, he or she serves the coffee in tiny china cups
with *at least* three spoonfuls of sugar. The final, or third
cup is key – it bestows a blessing and is known as the
berekha (blessing) cup.

CAFE TALK – ANDREW KELLY

Coffees from Ethiopia represent something of the holy grail for coffee drinkers: the flavours are surprising and delicious

TOP 5 COFFEES

- **Hunkute Cooperative** Wonsho District, Sidama
- **Duromina Cooperative** Agaro, Limu
- **Homacho Waeno Cooperative** Aleta Wondo, Sidama
- **Momora** Shakiso, Sidama
- **Hunda Oli Cooperative** Agaro, Limu

The espresso or macchiato may be Ethiopians' coffee staples, but cappuccino and a cafe latte known as *buna bewetet* (coffee with milk) are also popular. Sometimes the herb rue (known locally as *t'ena adam*, or health of Adam) is served with coffee, as is butter. In the western highlands, a layered drink of coffee and tea is also popular.

Ethiopia is the world's seventh-largest producer of coffee and employs an estimated 15 million Ethiopians. The industry is modernising with a number of formerly government plantations now in private hands – Tepi, for example, is now owned by a major supplier to Starbucks, although newly private suppliers also work closely with boutique coffee buyers across the globe as well as supplying to a local market.

It's all part of Ethiopia's coffee story, a remarkable tale born in legend and now very much a way of local life.

GALANI CAFE

Salite Mehret Rd, Nr JakRoss Villas, Addis Ababa;
www.galanicafe.com; +251 91 144 6265

◆ Food   ◆ Shop
◆ Classes   ◆ Cafe

Galani Cafe takes Ethiopian coffee into the 21st century in Addis Ababa. Galani wouldn't look out of place in New York City, a slick space peopled by baristas and knowledgeable coffee types, where you can learn how to be a barista, attend a cupping session or simply learn more about coffee, whether through a brew-guide course or spending an afternoon sampling the espresso, piccolo or cold coffees that make up the lengthy menu of coffee tastes and trends. The food here is the perfect complement and the coffees are all local, thereby enabling you to travel around the country on a coffee tour without ever leaving your Addis perch. Try one of the drip-filter coffees to taste Galani's coffees at their best.

THINGS TO DO NEARBY

Yod Abyssinia
With a rich combination of traditional food, traditional dance and a fine post-meal coffee ceremony, this restaurant is the perfect complement to Galani's contemporary cool.

Kategna
Another fine place for Ethiopian food, where the emphasis is very much on quality and tradition. The setting is something of a hybrid, with low wooden stools in a clean-lined space.
www.kategnaaddis.com

TOMOCA

Wavel St, Addis Ababa;
www.tomocacoffee.com; +251 11 111 1781

◆ Roastery   ◆ Cafe
◆ Shop

Tomoca is an Ethiopian classic. It's also a reminder that drinking coffee in Ethiopia is no passing fad, nor is it an arena for fancy variations on that most enduring of themes – the old-style espresso in an old-style cafe with precious little else to distract you from the serious business of coffee.

Built by the Italians in 1953, Tomoca has barely changed its look or ambience in the decades since – the period decor, the high stools, the Ethiopians quietly contemplating their morning brew. It's a marvellous introduction to the world of Ethiopian coffee, and, as is appropriate for the starting point of a journey, the map on the wall charts Ethiopia's coffee story in fascinating detail. Order an espresso – it's as simple as that.

THINGS TO DO NEARBY

St George Cathedral & Museum
A sacred centre of Ethiopian Orthodox Christianity, this imposing church is rich in murals, while the museum houses the coronation robes worn by Haile Selassie.

Itegue Taitu Hotel
This is one of the loveliest old mansions of Addis, where a good vegetarian lunchtime buffet, fine views and an old-world atmosphere are all thrown in to the mix.
taituhotel.com

FOUR SISTERS

Gonder; www.thefoursistersrestaurant.com;
+251 91 873 6510

◆ Food   ◆ Cafe
◆ Classes

The deeply traditional city of Gonder, former seat of kings, is the appropriate backdrop for one of Ethiopia's most traditional coffee ceremonies. Not far from the former royal compound, Four Sisters is indeed run by four sisters who place coffee in its rightful context, accompanied by deeply traditional food as well as cultural performances of music and dance in the evening.

The ceremony is as much about the rites of hospitality as the tastes themselves, and serves as a reminder that coffee stands at the centre of Ethiopian life in all its ancient complexity. As for the basics, they're remarkably simple – the coffee is strong, locally sourced and always of the highest quality. Plan to linger over a meal and leave time for the ceremony.

THINGS TO DO NEARBY

Royal Enclosure (Fasil Ghebbi)
The Unesco-listed seat of ancient Ethiopian kings is filled with echoes of King Solomon, and comprises an enormous complex of palaces and castles.

Senait Coffee Shop
Run by one of the Four Sisters, Senait, this little shop and internet cafe opposite the Royal Enclosure does fabulous coffee in a simple traditional setting.

© Xavier Gibert

KAFA COFFEE MUSEUM

Kafa Biosphere Reserve;
www.kafa-biosphere.com/coffee-museum; +251 47 331 0667

THINGS TO DO NEARBY

Kafa Biosphere Reserve
Hike through forested hillsides and look out for some 300 bird species as well as 300 species of mammal that could include spotted hyenas, hippos, lions and leopards.
www.kafa-biosphere.com

Mount Wellington
Lording it over the not-so-distant town of Jimma, this evocative hilltop castle delivers exceptional views and a genuine sense of living history.

For far too long, Ethiopia's coffee story went untold in the country itself. But the opening of the fine Kafa Coffee Museum in Ethiopia's coffee heartland of the Western Highlands is a long-overdue initiation into the story of coffee in the land of its birthplace. At one level, this is about the history of coffee in Ethiopia. Look a little closer, though, and you'll find explanations of the different types of Ethiopian coffee production (from wild to plantation-grown). The museum illuminates everything from natural growing techniques and small-scale subsistence coffee production to the compromises (eg the use of chemical fertilisers) required for mass production. It's a fascinating story, and one to linger over... though sadly not with a coffee as none is served here!

BEBEKA COFFEE PLANTATION

Mizan Tefari, southwest Ethiopia;
+251 47 111 8621

If you've made it this far, you've probably already had the good fortune to sample the pleasures of Ethiopian coffee. Well, here, in the southwest of Ethiopia, is where much of it comes from. One of numerous plantations in this, the wellspring of Ethiopian coffee, Bebeka can complete a cafe-to-source journey by taking you to the very soil that gave rise to one of the world's greatest culinary passions. At 93 sq km, it is Ethiopia's largest coffee farm – and also its oldest. You'll need your own vehicle and the guards at the gate will give you a guide, after which the story of Ethiopian coffee will take on a whole new (or actually, a rather old) dimension.

THINGS TO DO NEARBY

Tepi Coffee Plantation
Not far from Bebeka, Tepi is another accessible coffee plantation with tours and a real sense of serious coffee at every turn.

Southwest Omo Valley
Experience tribal Africa at its most fascinating by immersing yourself in the remote villages and wild landscapes here.

LEBANON

How to ask for a coffee in the local language?
Marhaba, beddeh kahweh menfadlak
Signature coffee style? Traditional Lebanese coffee is boiled continuously, making it intensely strong, and is prepared and served in a small rakweh metal pot so you can drink more than one cup
What to order with your coffee? Traditional Lebanese sweet pastries; maamoul stuffed with dates and pistachio or baklawa
Do: Flavour your coffee with cardamom grains

Coffee touches every element of daily life in Lebanon, traversing the fragile barriers of the population's different religions that have defined the Cedar Republic's turbulent history. Whether you are in a remote mountain village or refugee camp, in edgy Tripoli or fashionable Beirut, the ritual of offering, serving and drinking coffee remains a reassuring constant for everyone.

The roots of Lebanese coffee stretch back centuries to the village tradition of families roasting Arabica beans themselves, then finely grinding them and boiling up a seriously strong brew. Visit a Lebanese family today and you will be immediately offered a tiny glass of scalding, bitter coffee. Out on the street, there is both traditional and modern, from Starbucks to street vendors who pour thick black coffee from metal jugs with a built-in heating element. In the old-fashioned cafes, habitues enveloped by clouds of *narghile* smoke spend hours over a small copper pot of coffee, while in contemporary barista bars aficionados choose between beans from Brazil, Ethiopia, Colombia, Vietnam, Kenya or Indonesia, then ask the brewmaster to prepare an AeroPress or flat white.

Watch out for two very special Lebanese coffee customs. When your coffee is served and the froth has a hole, sip it immediately and legend has it that you will soon get an *abda* – a money payment. Never drink the thick grounds at the bottom of a coffee cup; tip them out onto the plate and someone will interpret the shapes and read your fortune.

CAFE YOUNES

Neemat Yafet St, Beirut;
+961 1 750 975

◆ Food   ◆ Shop   ◆ Transport
◆ Roastery   ◆ Cafe

Tucked away off the grand Rue Hamra, known as Beirut's Champs-Élysées, the Younes roastery has been providing Lebanon's finest coffee since 1935, with the family behind it having lived through French colonialism, civil wars and invading armies. Today's third-generation owner, Amin, claims the reason for the characteristic taste and aroma of its artisan coffee is the continued use since 1960 of a vintage Probat drum roaster, allowing every bean to roast perfectly. The Probat used to be in Younes's downtown cafe, which was bombed and abandoned in 1975 during the Lebanese Civil War. Miraculously it was still there three years later, bolted to the ground to thwart looters, when Amin and his father transported it during a break in fighting to its present location.

When Cafe Younes opened a casual coffee shop next to the roastery in 2008, it immediately became everyone's favourite hangout in the bohemian Hamra neighbourhood, offering its fans not just the famous coffee but tasty food, art exhibitions, occasional poetry readings and concerts.

The shady terrace is a favourite people-watching spot for Beiruti fashion stylists, interior designers, artists and actors. Be warned though; if you order the popular Lebanese 'white coffee' – a *café blanc* – instead of some variation on a latte you'll get a glass of hot water with a drop of orange or rose blossom. For a great coffee, try the Yemen Anesi instead; when freshly roasted and brewed the flavours are fruity and spicy. It comes served in a traditional *rakweh* coffee pot.

THINGS TO DO NEARBY

Amal Bohsali
Amal Bohsali has been baking irresistible pastries since 1878. Watch the master-pâtissiers at work in their Hamra showroom and taste delicious *baklawa* and *knefe*.
www.abohsali.com.lb

Mohammed Al-Amin Mosque
Known as the Blue Mosque, and opened in 2008, this immense blue-tiled structure with 65m-high minarets symbolises Beirut's rebirth, surrounded by ancient Roman ruins, Greek Orthodox and Maronite churches.

La Corniche
Join the crowds for a sunset stroll along Beirut's historic Corniche promenade, wandering past the glamorous Sporting Club's beach to the famous Pigeon Rocks cliffs.

Sursock Museum
This sumptuous museum of Lebanese contemporary art is housed in an extravagant white mansion that mixes Ottoman and Venetian influences. It was recently reopened after a multi-million dollar renovation.
sursock.museum

MALAWI

How to ask for a coffee in the local language?
Kapu ya khofi chonde

Signature coffee style? Arabica filter coffee

What to order with your coffee? Nthochi (banana bread)

Do: If you're trying a cup of the potent beans grown by local cooperatives, order it with plenty of milk to avoid being blown across Lake Malawi

Tobacco and tea are Malawi's main crops, but coffee's been around a while too; the country has been growing Arabica since its introduction by missionaries in the 1800s. And while some neighbouring countries are better-known producers, coffee is nonetheless one of Malawi's major exports, with six coffee cooperatives representing thousands of smallholders who receive donor support. The subtropical climate and nutrient-rich soil they enjoy should prove rich coffee ground, but recurrent droughts and unpredictable rainfall restrict its production, resulting in quality over quantity.

Malawian coffee is typically characterised by its medium acidity and light body, but despite the local crop a good cup of coffee is often hard to find, as most locals prefer to accompany the Lake Malawi views with a cold Carlsberg. However, there are a few good restaurants and cafes serving a passable cappuccino in Lilongwe and Blantyre. Out of town, the top park lodges and beach hotels are your best bet for a palatable caffeine fix, while in spots such as Mzuzu and Zomba, Italian-run guesthouses are havens of quality.

To learn about – and taste – Malawi's Arabica output, head to the hills of Livingstonia, the village that has grown up around the Free Church of Scotland's mission station named after Dr David Livingstone. It's reached via a bone-jarringly bumpy switchback with 20 hairpin bends, but you'll be rewarded with a cup of local coffee in the Craft Coffee Shop at the historic hilltop village. If you like what you see, you can stay at either the Lukwe or Mushroom Farm permaculture eco-lodges, where coffee buffs can organise tours to local growers, best undertaken during the harvest season between May and August.

MZUZU COFFEE DEN

M5, Mzuzu, Northern Malawi;
coffeeden.mzuzucoffee.org; +265 1 320 899

◆ Food   ◆ Shop   ◆ Transport
◆ Roastery   ◆ Cafe

With its two-tone furniture and wi-fi, this buzzy cafe in the dusty capital of Malawi's Northern Region is a favourite with young locals, aid workers and travellers escaping the heat. It serves reviving cups of the strong sweet beans grown by Mzuzu Coffee (a cooperative of some 3000 local farmers), probably best enjoyed in a milky cappuccino or latte given the potency of Mzuzu coffee. You can buy bags of this Malawian black gold in the gift shop.

The multifaceted cafe, which also serves breakfast and dishes such as Lake Malawi chambo fish, hosts art exhibitions and musical evenings, and even has a computer room offering photocopying and printing to the laptop-touting clientele. Ask about accommodation at Mzuzu Coffee Suites, and tours of the coffee farms.

THINGS TO DO NEARBY

Livingstonia
If you've made it to Mzuzu, don't miss this historic mountain village, where you can stay in an eco-lodge and tour the local coffee farms.

Nyika National Park
Located at 2000m, this breathtaking slice of highland scenery is the place to snap antelopes standing in rolling grasslands and tour the coffee plantations around Chakaka and Nkota.

SATEMWA COFFEE TOUR

Thyolo, Southern Malawi;
www.satemwa.com; +265 1473 500

◆ Food   ◆ Classes   ◆ Cafe
◆ Roastery   ◆ Shop

THINGS TO DO NEARBY

Mt Mulanje
Fringed by tea plantations, this massif of some 20 peaks reaching over 2500m offers hiking among green, waterfall-fed valleys, with black eagles and endemic Mulanje cedars to spot.
www.mcm.org.mw/ mulanje.php

Huntingdon House
Spend a night or stop for lunch at Satemwa's atmospheric colonial guesthouse with its wraparound veranda and croquet lawn. Afternoon tea is also available, natch.
www.huntingdon- malawi.com

The historic Satemwa tea estate in the mountainous Shire Highlands has been cultivating coffee since 1971, with 45 hectares of the stuff including old and rare varietals such as Geisha. Drop by en route between Blantyre and Mt Mulanje, take a guided tour of the farm and learn, for example, that they plant trees in the coffee fields to offer shade and improve soil quality. With its emerald-green plantations and riverine forests at around 1000m, Satemwa is a stunningly beautiful estate established by Scots in 1924, where the environmental practices include protecting indigenous flora and fauna. Coffee is hand-picked to ensure the cherries are ripe, then sun-dried for two weeks, with sweet, aromatic results. Take a tour between May and August, when the coffee harvest takes place.

SOUTH AFRICA

How to ask for a coffee in the local language?
Kan ek asseblief 'n koffie bestel (Afrikaans); Ndicela
ikofi (Xhosa)
Signature coffee style? Cappuccino
What to order with your coffee? Milk tart (if you can
find one, a chocolate brownie if you can't)
Do: Keep an eye out for moerkoffie in small-town South
Africa. This strong cuppa is traditionally brewed over
an open fire and served with condensed milk and
a rusk — a rock-hard biscuit that's perfect for dunking

There was a time, not too long ago, when ordering
a coffee in South Africa might well have meant
sipping a cup of Ricoffy – an instant brew made up of coffee
and chicory. With heritage that dates back to the French
Huguenot settlers who arrived in the 17th century, it's still
popular today. But luckily there are plenty of alternatives.
The South African coffee renaissance began at the dawn of
the 21st century, when a cafe called Vida e Caffe opened on

Cape Town's Kloof Street. Vida soon became a nationwide
chain and its reliable flat whites are found in airports, malls
and high streets across the country. A few years later the
real revolution began, again in Cape Town. Micro-roasteries
started to appear, the first South African baristas emerged
and ordering a coffee became something of an art form.

Since then coffee culture has boomed. There are
hundreds of roasteries around the country, an association
dedicated to speciality coffee, national barista
championships held annually and, in 2012, South Africa got
its own coffee magazine filled with news on the local brews.
In 2016, the first Starbucks opened, and there are now four
branches, all in Johannesburg and Pretoria. Somehow
though, it feels as if Starbucks missed the boat here – coffee

CAFE TALK – WAYNE OBERHOLZER

While the speciality coffee industry in South Africa is young, its growth in both size and knowledge has been rapid. The range of coffees on offer, the styles of cafes and the general coffee drinker's knowledge is vast and growing

TOP 5 COFFEES

- **Origin** Seasonal Blend
- **Espresso Lab** Christmas Blend
- **Bean There** Olga's Reserve
- **Rosetta** Kenya Blends
- **Portland Project** Renegade

lovers are hooked on their micro-roasted espressos and proudly support their home-grown coffee shops.

Most of these coffee shops are in larger cities – notably Cape Town, Johannesburg, Durban and Pretoria – but you will find occasional gems in smaller towns too. Elsewhere, the days of opting between Ricoffy and Nescafé with your slice of milk tart are long gone, save for in the smallest of towns. Don't be surprised if you're asked 'cream or foam?' when you order a cappuccino – it's a local quirk to squirt whipped cream atop the milky brew in old-school cafes.

Most of the coffee beans you'll find are imported from South America, Asia and other parts of Africa, although there are a few coffee estates in South Africa. Assagay Coffee near Durban, Sabie Valley Coffee in Mpumalanga

and Beaver Creek Estate in Port Edward all offer plantation tours, followed up with a cupping of the brews. And if you're looking for a little schooling, you can get an education along with your caffeine fix. Select cafes throughout the big cities offer cupping sessions, home barista classes or longer, fully fledged courses. Or if you're more into the sipping side of things, pull up a stool and toast the remarkably fast-moving scene with a decaf AeroPress, a Hario V60 pour-over, a nitro cold-brewed coffee or just a simple flat white.

KAFFA HOIST

Washington St, Langa, Cape Town;
www.kaffahoist.yolasite.com; +27 71 120 6345

◆ Food
◆ Cafe

Take a short detour off the N2 highway to visit this friendly open-air cafe – the first of its kind in the Langa township. Zimbabwean born co-owner Chris Bangira worked in the coffee industry for almost a decade before opening the cafe in 2016 at the Guga S'Thebe Arts Centre, Langa's community centre. He serves a lot of tourists, here to explore Cape Town's oldest township, but the hope is that Langa locals will make Kaffa Hoist their go-to for lunch, coffee or homemade ice tea. Chris is working on a plan to add a roastery, but for the moment you can sip his signature flat white in the courtyard or at quiet times lean on the counter and chat to the affable owner.

THINGS TO DO NEARBY

Mzansi
This hugely popular restaurant dishes up a traditional African feast while owner Nomonde shares insight into life in Langa, past and present.
mzansi45.co.za

Hoghouse Brewing Company
It's an odd location, tucked away in a business park, but the beers here come with magnificent food, all smoked or slow-cooked over hot coals.
hhbc.co.za

ORIGIN

28 Hudson St, Cape Town;
www.originroasting.co.za; +27 21 421 1000

◆ Food   ◆ Classes   ◆ Cafe
◆ Roastery ◆ Shop   ◆ Transport

place filled with brunching families, young creatives tapping out emails on their Macs and, of course, coffee enthusiasts back for the latest seasonal espresso blend.

The food is what you'd expect – free range, pasture-raised and locally sourced, with an inventive breakfast menu and bagels boiled and baked in-house. And of course there's the coffee menu. Pick from a range of single-origin beans or take the latest blend either in espresso form or one of the many slow-brewed styles.

For those who just can't decide, order the tasting board, featuring three different coffees from the menu. While you wait for your brew, nip upstairs to see the roasters at work, or stick around on the shop floor to watch the spectacle of a siphon coffee in progress.

THINGS TO DO NEARBY

V&A Waterfront
African art, restaurants galore, museums for all the family, bars, boat trips... it's easy to see why the Waterfront is one of Cape Town's most enduringly poplar attractions.
www.waterfront.co.za

Bree Street
Cape Town's coolest street is awash with boutique clothes stores, artisanal bakeries, bustling bars and an ever-changing roster of cutting-edge restaurants.

Green Point Park
This top park offers kids' play areas, an open-air gym, a labyrinth and plenty of paved paths for strolling or cycling, all within sniffing distance of the ocean.

Lion's Head
Scrambling atop this mini mountain (and at times hoisting yourself up with ladders and chains) gives a magnificent view of Table Mountain and the city beneath.

In the mid-2000s, Cape Town had a dearth of decent coffee shops. Then Origin launched its first roastery and, along with a few other cafes around town, is largely credited with the birth of the South African coffee revolution. Since then, the convivial cafe's on-site academy has trained thousands of baristas and fielded four South African national barista champions. Today, it's a welcoming

TRUTH COFFEE

36 Buitenkant St, Cape Town;
https://truth.coffee; +27 21 200 0440

◆ Food ◆ Classes ◆ Cafe
◆ Roastery ◆ Shop ◆ Transport

THINGS TO DO NEARBY

District Six Museum
This deeply moving museum
documents the forced
removals of the apartheid
era, when non-white
citizens were evicted,
homes bulldozed and
communities ripped apart.
www.districtsix.co.za

Company's Garden
Flanked by museums and
galleries and criss-crossed
by wide pathways, Cape
Town's city park will
comfortably keep you busy
for an entire day.

Roeland Liquors
A short hop from Truth,
Roeland offers one of
the best selections of
boutique booze in the
city, including craft beer,
micro-distilled gin and
plenty of pinotage.
www.roelandliquors.co.za

Mount Nelson
If you tire of coffee, head
to this 19th-century hotel
(named after Horatio, not
Mandela) for the most
sumptuous high tea in town.
*www.belmond.com/mount-
nelson-hotel-cape-town*

However hip you think you are, you never feel quite
cool enough for Truth. This place is the mad-
scientist-in-an-antique-shop embodiment of steampunk
chic. Exposed bulbs and extension cords dangle from bare
ceilings; ornate, empty frames hang on the walls; cogs and
pipes dominate a decor that looks as if it was created by
Tim Burton. The staff are decked out in top hats, bustles
and flying goggles and you keep expecting Johnny Depp
and Helena Bonham Carter to walk down the stairs in full
Victorian get-up. And at the centre of it all is Colossus,
a vintage Probat coffee roaster hailing from the 1940s that
offers the real reason this place has been voted the best
coffee shop in the world.

The on-site barista academy offers everything from half-
day coffee appreciation classes to week-long professional
courses. But if you're here to simply enjoy the coffee, grab
a stool at the massive communal table and order a cup of
the 18-hour cold-brewed 'potion' or a shot of the signature
Resurrection blend – or drink outside the box with a Sunrise
Espresso, a single shot laced with orange juice for the
perfect morning kick-starter.

DOUBLESHOT COFFEE & TEA

Cnr Juta & Melle Sts, Braamfontein, Johannesburg;
www.doubleshot.co.za; +27 83 380 4127

◆ Food   ◆ Shop   ◆ Transport
◆ Roastery ◆ Cafe

Johannesburg is experiencing a remarkable revival, with former no-go areas being revitalised by restaurants, bars and coffee shops. Doubleshot is anchored in one of those very neighbourhoods – Braamfontein, which is a student-filled district wedged between the university campus and the city centre. Stools lined up along a counter-top looking out onto the street are the perfect place for a spot of Jozi people-watching while you nibble on a pastry and sip your chosen brew.

The minimalist decor serves to focus the attention on the coffee shop's remarkable showpiece, known as Luigi – the veteran GW Barth roaster dating back to 1916. At its helm is Alain Rosa, who also specialises in blending loose-leaf tea. The selection of these is remarkable, and for those just-too-hot-for-a-cuppa days, there's also a line of hand-crafted ice teas. The roasts vary weekly, keeping the coffee nerds coming back for more, but for the quintessential Doubleshot experience, try to grab yourself a double shot of the Malawian roast from Satemwa Estate (see p27), whose owner, Alex Kay, is a partner in the coffee shop.

THINGS TO DO NEARBY

Constitution Hill
Serving as a prison for just under a century, Constitution Hill is now home to the constitutional court, in addition to a poignant and excellently laid-out museum. *www.constitutionhill.org.za*

Neighbourgoods Market
The heart of artisanal culinary culture in South Africa, the Neighbourgoods Market is open on Saturday mornings for locally sourced goodies and, of course, great coffee. *www.neighbourgoodsmarket.co.za*

Origins Centre
As well as its exhibits that trace the origins of mankind, this museum has plenty of marvellous information on indigenous San culture, with a focus on rock art. *www.wits.ac.za/origins*

Wits Art Museum
Entrance is free to this exceptional museum, operated by the university, which features an astonishing array of historical and contemporary African art. *www.wits.ac.za*

KOFI AFRIKA

7166 Vilakazi St, Orlando West, Soweto, Gauteng;
www.facebook.com/pg/kofiafrika.sa: +27 84 665 2400

◆ Food
◆ Cafe

When Soweto-born-and-raised coffee veterans Mpumelelo Zulu and Lawrence Murothela launched Kofi Afrika in 2016, it was the first true coffee shop in Soweto – a city that's home to a million people – and it's settled in nicely. Set on famous Vilakazi St, 500m from Nelson Mandela's former home (see opposite), Kofi Afrika sees a steady trickle of travellers joining the locals for a taste of live jazz or some world-class people-watching while sipping a flat white brewed with specially selected Ethiopian and Tanzanian beans.

Downstairs, The Box Shop is an incubator for young designers and local entrepreneurs looking to kick-start their businesses. Browse a changing selection of clothing, custom furniture and handmade cosmetics before heading up for a coffee.

THINGS TO DO NEARBY

Mandela House
The humble home that the late and great Nelson Mandela once lived in is a shrine to his memory and a must-visit for any visitor to Soweto.
www.mandelahouse.com

Chaf Pozi
Sitting at the base of the Orlando Towers (see below), you can watch bungee jumpers hurtle into the void as you chow down on *shisa nyama* – barbecued meat.

© Klaus Lang / Getty Images

Soaking, pressing, pouring, squeezing – there's a world of ways to coax flavour from the bean, and they all have their own quirks (and loyal following).

I. THE PRESS

This immersion method involves letting coffee grounds soak in hot water before straining or pressing the brew through a metal filter. Pressed coffee is usually thick in texture due to the sediment that remains in the brew.

BREWING

5. CEZVE

Also known as an ibrik, a cezve is a Turkish coffee pot. This small vessel is typically made of copper and is used to heat finely ground coffee and water over a flame or on a hob resulting in a thick, rich, concentrated brew.

4. SIPHON

Invented in Europe in the mid-19th century, the siphon, or vacuum coffee maker, is an elaborate immersion brewing device made of glass that uses vapour pressure to force hot water into ground coffee.

Illustration: Jon Dicus

2. ESPRESSO MACHINE

A typical espresso machine uses nine bars of pressure to force water through a bed of finely ground coffee and a filter. The resulting shot of coffee is syrupy and highly concentrated.

3. MOKA POT

Invented in Italy, the moka pot is an aluminium stove-top brewer popular in Europe that uses pressure to force hot water through finely ground coffee. The unfiltered brew is highly concentrated like espresso and often has crema.

METHODS

6. POUR-OVER

Hot water is hand poured over a bed of coffee grounds and drips through a paper filter using gravity. This single-cup manual method is popular with baristas who are keen on controlling every aspect of the brew.

7. JEBENA

A traditional clay jebena is used in an Ethiopian coffee ceremony. The coffee is roasted immediately before brewing, hand-ground using a pestle and mortar, and then brewed directly in a jebena over hot coals.

THE AM

TOP 5 Coffee TOWNS

ERICAS

PORTLAND

The signs may read 'Keep Portland Weird,' but make no mistake, when it comes to coffee, this Oregon town is deadly serious. Home to third wave pioneers Stumptown, it's hard to find a second-rate cup here, and baristas are as well-qualified as they are coiffured.

SAN FRANCISCO

Maybe it's the boost needed to climb all those hills, but San Franciscans are obsessive about their brews, and the city has been buzzing with speciality coffee for decades. Coffee tourists can also check out the flagship cafes of Peet's and Blue Bottle.

SEATTLE

The home of Starbucks loves coffee, and not just served by the vanilla-scented bucketload. The city has an exciting crop of roasters keeping a population of demanding palates happy. Carry your take-out down to Pike Place Market to find the eclectic soul of the city.

MEXICO CITY

Cute spots to enjoy a quality cup are popping up all over the place in the Latin mega-city. Lying on the doorstep of the country's coffee-growing regions, the city is proud to champion its local producers and baristas will likely know the farmer who produced your very cup.

VANCOUVER

Just like its Pacific Northwestern cousins south of the border, Vancouver will do you right by coffee. Beautiful independent cafes abound, especially in the Commercial Drive and Main St 'hoods. Be sure to pick up some beans from 49th Parallel.

BRAZIL

How to ask for a coffee in the local language?
Um cafezinho, por favor!
Signature coffee style? Espresso
What to order with your coffee? Pão de queijo (tapioca cheese bread)
Don't: Just order a cappuccino – Brazilians love to add chocolate, sugar or even colourful syrups to it. Go with a café com leite to be on the safe side

Think Brazil, think sun, sand and samba, yes? Coffee? Not so much. Yet coffee practically seeps through the pores of South America's biggest country, be it exquisite speciality espresso or cheap, sickly sweet thermos-cradled swill.

The country's ferocious consumption of cupped lightning is fuelled by a long, intimate – and, at times, rocky – seed-to-cup relationship that has historically played itself out like a dramatic *telenovela*. Once a land of ruling coffee barons, Brazil's bond with coffee goes back to the French settlers who lugged coffee plants over from Ethiopia in the early 18th century, but the bottom fell out in the late 19th century due to the abolition of slavery. It's rebounded so much since that today Brazil is the largest producer of coffee in the world, controlling more than 30% of international production.

As is often the case with coffee-producing nations, most of the good stuff was traditionally exported; however, the economic boom of the early 2010s boosted speciality-coffee consumption domestically, and today Brazil's biggest cities are a mighty fine place for a cup of joe. 'A new-found supply of complex coffees, along with a better income for regular Brazilians created by the economic boom, allowed for the appearance of a booming speciality coffee scene in Brazil,' explains coffee farmer and roast master Mariano Martins. 'It's no longer hard to find a place in São Paulo, Curitiba or Brasília where you can ask for a double ristretto, or an AeroPress shot, without being looked at as if you've just stepped out of an alien spaceship!'

FAZENDA SANTA MARGARIDA

São Manuel, SP;
www.martinscafe.com; +55 11 4301 8848

◆ Food ◆ Classes ◆ Cafe
◆ Roastery ◆ Shop

Founded in 1860, the family-run Santa Margarida Estate, 262km east of central São Paulo, is one of Brazil's top coffee getaways. Tours run during harvest season (July and August) on Mondays (in Portuguese) and Wednesdays (in English), when caffeine aficionados can follow the farm's agronomist and roast master Mariano Martins on a tree-to-cup tour. Hands-on practice with the farm's roasting operation is included as is the sampling of eight different coffee lots, so visitors can taste the difference between varieties and processing methods.

THINGS TO DO NEARBY

Brotas
Some 98km north of Fazenda Santa Margarida, the charming town of Brotas is a Brazilian adventure-tourism hotbed, with some of the country's best white-water rafting.

Pedra Do Índio
This 100m-high viewpoint located on a private farm 27km southeast of São Manuel offers a stunning view of the region's postcard-perfect Tres Pedras rock formations.
+55 14 99679 0724

COFFEE LAB

R Fradique Coutinho, São Paulo, SP;
www.raposeiras.com.br; +55 11 3375 7400

◆ Food ◆ Classes ◆ Cafe
◆ Roastery ◆ Shop ◆ Transport

At first glance, Coffee Lab is true to its name: an industrial-vibed space more suited to laboratory work than an exquisite cafe experience. And that's just the way owner (and one of Brazil's top baristas) Isabela Raposeiras wants it. It's about the coffee and its quality – not the cool factor. As a result, this part cafe/part barista school is the go-to caffeine venue in São Paulo for single-origin varieties from far-flung speciality Brazilian lots and (domestically speaking, anyway) outside-the-box preparations. If you visit, treat yourself to the rare Brazilian microlot tasting.

THINGS TO DO NEARBY

Beco de Batman
Vila Madelena is Sampa's most artistically inclined district and there's no better canvas to illustrate that than Beco de Batman (or Batman's Alley), which harbours a living museum of street art.

Feira Benedito Calixto
This good-time open-air Saturday market is a rousing mélange of handicrafts, antiques, superb food stalls and live music (usually *chorinho*, a type of samba).
pracabenedito calixto.com.br

SANTO GRÃO

Rua Oscar Freire 413, Jardins, São Paulo, SP;
www.santograo.com.br; +55 11 3062 9294

◆ Food ◆ Classes ◆ Cafe
◆ Roastery ◆ Shop ◆ Transport

Chic Santo Grão was one of the city's first speciality coffee cafes, and the first of six branches opened by founder Marco Kerkmeester around São Paolo. This flagship's location in Jardins remains a can't-miss São Paulo destination for three key single-origin coffees: dark, full-bodied and chocolatey Cerrado de Minas; lighter, fruitier and acidic Sul de Minas, and sweet, smooth and rich Mogiana – which represent the best of three key growing regions.

If you're spoilt for choice, opt for the signature Blend Santo Grão and take it out on to the large, airy terrace; it's a great spot from which to people-watch.

THINGS TO DO NEARBY

MASP
Latin America's most comprehensive collection of Western art is housed in this iconic Modernist beast designed by architect Lina Bo Bardi along Av Paulista in 1968. *www.masp.art.br*

Casa Amarela
This crafts shop/museum houses a terrific collection of artefacts from the Villas-Bôas brothers, the first white men to encounter the upper Xingu river indigenous communities of the Amazon. *www.casaamarela.art.br*

CANADA

How to ask for a coffee in the local language?
May I please have a coffee?
Signature coffee style? Double Double: drip coffee
with two creams and two sugars
What to order with your coffee? A doughnut
Do: Be sure to say please and thank you; Canadians
are known for their politeness. And don't order
a double double in an independent cafe

When it comes to coffee, nothing is more Canadian
than a double double. Served in a red take-away
cup, and comprised of drip coffee with two dollops of cream
and two spoonfuls of sugar, the double double is as typically
Canadian as a maple leaf, a canoe, or the mounted police.
It is not surprising to learn then that the double double was
made famous through a doughnut shop co-founded in 1964
by an ice hockey player named Tim Horton. These days, Tim
Horton's is one of the largest fast food chains in Canada.
Over the years, Timmy's, as it became affectionately known,
has been successful at simultaneously paying homage to
the country's favourite sport while inscribing the sweet,
creamy and caffeinated double double into the Canadian
cultural lexicon.

However, in recent years the country has seen the
emergence of a burgeoning speciality coffee scene that
has been gradually shaped from the outside in by more
established and quality-focused coffee drinking cultures.
Most notably, over the past two decades, second and
third wave influences from Seattle and Portland migrated
over the US–Canada border to Vancouver and began to
take hold.

These days you can find a thriving independent coffee
scene in almost every major city in the country, with
purveyors committed to sourcing, roasting and brewing
the best coffee beans their money can buy. In the context
of the world, Canada's speciality coffee culture is still in its
infancy, but as more and more Canadians are beginning to
take an interest in quality over convenience, the future of
Canadian coffee is promising.

PHIL & SEBASTIAN COFFEE ROASTERS

Simmons Building, 618 Confluence Way SE, Calgary, Alberta; www.philsebastian.com; +1 587 353 2268

- ◆ Food
- ◆ Classes
- ◆ Cafe
- ◆ Roastery
- ◆ Shop
- ◆ Transport

Phil Robertson and Sebastian Sztabzyb have been firm caffeine buddies for more than 20 years, having met at university in the 1990s when they were both studying to become engineers. After Phil's uncle introduced him to espresso, and a subsequent coffee-tasting road trip to Seattle, where they sampled cappuccinos that they described as 'life altering', the duo decided that their new life's mission was to bring great coffee to Calgary.

In 2007, Phil and Sebastian launched a coffee stand at the Calgary Farmers' Market. Since then, they have opened additional locations, begun sourcing their own beans from Central America, South America and Africa, and launched a roastery. A decade on from that one market stand, they now operate a flagship cafe with exposed brick walls, high ceilings, and sturdy wood beams in the restored Simmons Building, once a bedding manufacturer's warehouse, in the up-and-coming East Village, where you can stop in for a cup or a coffee-tasting flight.

If you're keen to learn more, you can take introductory classes in espresso making or brewing coffee using three different techniques (french press, AeroPress and pour-over). Then, move on to seamless milk steaming and latte art-making, an inventive way to enhance your coffee experience at home. As Phil and Sebastian found, drinking better coffee might even change your life.

© Johannes Hulsch / 500px

THINGS TO DO NEARBY

Glenbow Museum
This contemporary museum in downtown Calgary showcases the region's stories, past and present, with a focus on Western Canadian art, history and culture. *www.glenbow.org*

Sidewalk Citizen
Savour some seriously tasty breads and baked goods at this Simmons Building cafe. Try a *bureka* (flaky Israeli-style pastry), cheese stick or anything sweet. *sidewalkcitizenbakery.com*

Studio Bell
Nine interconnected towers house the National Music Centre, with exhibitions celebrating Canadian music, performance spaces, and three Canadian Music Halls of Fame. *studiobell.ca*

Banff National Park
A 90-minute drive from Calgary, Canada's first national park offers glacier-topped mountains, turquoise lakes, and more than 1600km of hiking trails. *pc.gc.ca/en*

KICKING HORSE COFFEE

491 Arrow Rd, Invermere, British Columbia;
www.kickinghorsecoffee.com; +1 250 342 3634

◆ Food   ◆ Shop
◆ Roastery   ◆ Cafe

In 1996, Elana Rosenfeld and her then partner Leo Johnson began roasting coffee in their garage in the Canadian Rockies town of Invermere. Today, the company they founded has become Canada's largest brand of organic fair-trade coffee. Their bright, casual cafe, located outside their roasting plant and within an easy drive of Kootenay, Yoho and Banff National Parks, is a popular stopping point for Rocky Mountain road-trippers.

The company shares its name with the nearby Kicking Horse River, so named, legend has it, for a runaway horse that kicked a British explorer and nearly sent him to his grave. While the company's claim that a 'kick-ass' cup of java brought the poor adventurer back to life is clearly apocryphal, Kicking Horse Coffee adopted the name for its brand and the Kick Ass moniker for its dark roasted beans

THINGS TO DO NEARBY

Lussier Hot Springs
Explore mountain peaks, rock canyons and grasslands in this diverse park. Soaking in the mineral pools at Radium Hot Springs is a highlight. *www.env.gov.bc.ca/ bcparks*

Cross River Wilderness Centre
Experience First Nations culture as well as the outdoors at this family-run off-the-grid lodging. Go hiking, join a wilderness workshop or arrange a sweat-lodge ceremony. *www.crossriver.ca*

Columbia Wetlands
Canoe or kayak through the serene marshy wetlands around the Columbia River. Columbia Wetlands Outpost rents boats and offers guided float tours. *www.columbiawet landsoutpost.com*

Kootenay National Park
Explore mountain peaks, rock canyons and grasslands in this park. Soaking in the mineral pools at Radium Hot Springs is a highlight. *pc.gc.ca/en*

and a recently introduced cold brew called Kick Ass Kooler.

Stop for a brewed coffee or a variety of espresso drinks, including a 'Canadiano' (the cafe's take on an Americano), along with a wrap, sandwich, muffins or pastry, before heading back out onto the rocky road. And maybe pick up one of the fun souvenirs on the way out; T-shirts and coffee mug proclaim the brand's kick-ass awesomeness.

CAFÉ MYRIADE

1432 Rue Mackay, Montréal, Québec;
www.cafemyriade.com; +1 514 939 1717

◆ Food ◆ Cafe
◆ Shop ◆ Transport

Serving coffee from Vancouver-based roasters 49th Parallel (see p49), along with beans from guest roasters from across North America and Europe, this cafe in downtown Montréal's Golden Square Mile is known for the precision with which staff prepare espresso drinks, filtered coffee and hot chocolate.

Equal care is taken over the milk, which isn't ordinary grocery-store carton stuff, but sourced from a consortium of Québec family farms. Pair your latte or *chocolat chaud* with a croissant, scone or other pastry. Although the cafe has no wi-fi, you can sit either in the window-lined interior or out on the sidewalk terrace to sip your drinks in the sun. They have two other Montréal locations.

THINGS TO DO NEARBY

Montréal Museum of Fine Arts
The city's main art museum sprawls across five pavilions, housing 40,000-plus paintings, photographs, sculptures and other works, from ancient times to the present day. *www.mbam.qc.ca*

McCord Museum
At this engaging museum about Montréal's history and culture, explore everything from Aboriginal clothing to urban society. Check the calendar for summer concerts or other activities. *www.musee-mccord.qc.ca*

BOXCAR SOCIAL HARBOURFRONT

235 Queens Quay West, Toronto, Ontario;
www.boxcarsocial.ca; +1 416 203 2999

◆ Food ◆ Cafe
◆ Shop ◆ Transport

Boxcar Social is a multi-roaster cafe that carries a rotating selection of beans from some of the most well-regarded roasters in North America and Europe. Order the single-origin coffee flight to sample the same coffee prepared as espresso, macchiato and a pour-over, and stay late into the evening to enjoy a full food menu as well as an extensive selection of wines, beers, bourbons and scotch.

Founded in 2014 by entrepreneurs Joe Papik, John Baker, Chris Ioannu and Alex Castellani, the mini-chain now spans six sites in the city – each distinctively conceptualised, designed and built by its clearly multi-talented owners. The expansive harbourfront site, housed next to artists' studios and galleries, is possibly the nicest, with a whopping 200 seats inside and a patio overlooking Lake Ontario.

THINGS TO DO NEARBY

Harbourfront Center
The Harbourfront Center is home to festivals, theatre, galleries, exhibitions, and tons of special events. Be sure to check out what's on when you visit. *www.harbourfrontcentre.com*

Toronto Island
Hop on the ferry at the Jack Layton Terminal and escape the city for an afternoon. Relax in nature, take in the views and explore the Toronto Islands. *www.torontoisland.com*

PILOT COFFEE ROASTERY & TASTING BAR

50 Wagstaff Dr, Toronto, Ontario;
www.pilotcoffeeroasters.com; +1 416 546 4006

◆ Roastery   ◆ Shop   ◆ Transport
◆ Classes   ◆ Cafe

Pilot Coffee was founded in 2009 by husband and wife duo Andy and Jessie Wilkin, who had the idea of introducing some of the coffee culture that was prevalent in Australia and New Zealand (Andy's home) to the city of Toronto. The resulting cafe and roastery, called Te Aro (after the suburb of Wellington, NZ, where the couple met), became so successful that they eventually moved the roaster out and expanded their business to this new venture. If you drop by the family-owned Pilot Roastery during its short hours, order a Trust the Barista and allow whoever is manning the pumps to curate a seasonal flight of coffees using a variety of brew methods just for you.

THINGS TO DO NEARBY

Maha's Brunch
Take a short walk to Maha's for its famous Egyptian brunch. No reservations, and long queues at the weekend, but it's well worth the wait.
www.mahasbrunch.com

Left Field Brewery
Drop in for a pint, take a tour of this baseball-themed craft brewery, and keep an eye out for upcoming pop-ups and special events.
www.leftfieldbrewery.ca

49TH PARALLEL COFFEE ROASTERS

2902 Main St, Vancouver, British Columbia;
www.49thcoffee.com; +1 604 872 4901

◆ Food ◆ Cafe
◆ Shop ◆ Transport

At 49th Parallel Coffee Roasters, coffee and doughnuts are paired together like wine and cheese. The company's micro-roasted coffee, carefully sourced from farms in Africa and Latin America, is a revered product in numerous culinary establishments across Canada, while its doughnuts (called 'Lucky's'), including exotic flavours such as crème brûlée and Earl Grey/lavender, are the pièce de résistance.

49th Parallel began as a small-scale coffee roaster in 2004, expanded into a cafe in the Kitsilano neighbourhood in 2007 and began making its own doughnuts at a second cafe on Vancouver's trendy Main St in 2012. In the latter establishment, with its streamlined art deco design aesthetics, you can sip on rich, caramel-coloured lattes while watching the doughnut-making exploits of the staff through a glass partition.

THINGS TO DO NEARBY

False Creek Seawall
You can access 28km of waterside paths by strolling down Main St to False Creek, Vancouver's busy bay surrounded by parks, public art and the erstwhile Olympic Village.

Telus World of Science
Built for the 1986 Expo and recently upgraded, this sparkling silver orb overlooking False Creek stimulates young scientific minds with educational shows and an IMAX cinema. ***www.scienceworld.ca***

AUBADE COFFEE

230 E Pender St, Vancouver, British Columbia;
www.aubadecoffee.info; +1 604 219 9247

◆ Shop ◆ Transport
◆ Cafe

This small cafe founded by Eldric Stuart shares a space with an antique store in Vancouver's Chinatown neighbourhood, and features a small but well-curated selection of beans from a rotating list of world-renowned roasters. The focus is on quality and approachability with precisely brewed beverages served across an intimate kitchen-like counter. Coffee is brewed on the AeroPress using Aesir paper filters designed by Stuart himself, and when you visit, be sure to order one of his signature seasonal AeroPress brews. A nice touch is the residency programme that allows baristas interested in learning the ins and outs of running a coffee shop to take over the space for a day.

THINGS TO DO NEARBY

The Keefer Bar
Start your evening with cocktails at The Keefer Bar. This apothecary-themed and eclectic Chinatown bar also serves Asian-inspired small plates. ***www. thekeeferbar.com***

Oyster Express
Visit this casual Chinatown spot for fresh local oysters, seafood and cocktails. Drop by its cosy space during the happy hour (5-7pm) for cheap pre-dinner bivalves. ***www.oysterexpress.ca***

MILANO COFFEE ROASTERS

156 West 8th Ave, Vancouver, British Columbia;
www.milanocoffee.ca; +1 604 879 4468

◆ Food   ◆ Classes (on request) ◆ Cafe
◆ Roastery ◆ Shop   ◆ Transport

First things first, Milano isn't in Milan, or even Italy. It's in Mount Pleasant, Vancouver, although the business was founded by an Italian in Vancouver's Little Italy neighbourhood way back in 1984. What sets Milano apart are its bean mixes. Rather than offering single-origin coffee, it concocts blends that can contain up to a dozen different varieties of bean, all roasted on-site.

There are various coffee styles to enjoy in the cafe's spacious woody interior overlooking a lively park, everything from pour-overs to French press to drip, although, with its Italian roots, Milano's tour de force is its espresso. On any given day, the cafe offers a menu of six different espressos. All of them go down remarkably well with a sweet cannoli.

THINGS TO DO NEARBY

Granville Island
The epicentre of Vancouver's arts, crafts and small business community (see below) is awash with street performers, market banter and the laidback rhythms of west coast life. *www.granvilleisland.com*

Museum of Vancouver
A small museum in a lovely setting in waterside Vanier Park that offers a concise overview of Vancouver's short history. *www.museumofvancouver.ca*

COLOMBIA

How to ask for a coffee in the local language?
Me puede regalar un tinto/café, por favor
Signature coffee style? Tinto (black)
What to order with your coffee? Arepas (corn flatbread);
buñeulos (fried dough balls)
Do: Ditch frothy expectations of a grand cafe
experience, and order your tinto from one of the
Thermos-toting carts you'll see roaming the streets

Colombia and coffee go hand in mug, and the figures are impressive: the country is the world's third-largest coffee producer and ships out more than 800,000 tonnes of beans each year. It is also the largest pure exporter of Arabica beans, with more than 500,000 coffee producers in the country growing the beans that are thought to have first arrived in Colombia back in the 18th century, brought across from Venezuela by Jesuit priests.

Today coffee is Colombia's largest export, accounting for approximately 7% of the country's GDP, with its major coffee-growing region – the so-called Coffee Triangle – now even listed as a Unesco World Heritage Site because of its 'coffee cultural landscape'.

Coffee is truly king here, and suitably accorded almost regal status by the fact that all of Colombia's beans are handpicked. But as you sit down to your morning joe in Colombia, so often the bitter flavour you experience isn't so much the drink as the disappointment.

The paradox concerning Colombian coffee is that the overwhelming majority of the high-quality beans are exported, leaving only the poorest beans for domestic consumption. That's not to say there isn't good coffee to be found in Colombia, but it can be a bit of a treasure hunt. It comes in its rawest and most basic form from the street carts that serve *tinto* ('ink', or black coffee) or *perico*

('painted'; coffee with milk) from Thermos flasks, while the Oma and Juan Valdez chains are ubiquitous in cities throughout Colombia (the fictional, mule-accompanied Juan Valdez character was once named one the world's most recognisable advertising icons).

CAFÉ JESÚS MARTÍN

Carrera 6A No 6-14, Salento, Quindio;
www.cafejesusmartin.com; +57 300 735 5679

◆ Food ◆ Cafe
◆ Shop ◆ Transport

© Kris Davidson / Lonely Planet; © age fotostock / Alamy Stock Photo

THINGS TO DO NEARBY

Cocora Valley

Walk or ride a horse through this beautiful valley, spiked with the world's tallest palm trees (and Colombia's national tree): wax palms.

National Coffee Park

What's not to love about a theme park based on coffee? This park in Montenegro has the usuals – waterslide, rollercoaster – but also a coffee museum and plantation.
www.parquedelcafe.co

San Vicente thermal springs

Soak up the 37°C bliss of five thermal pools; stay the night and you can grab a cabin with private thermal pool.
sanvicente.com.co

Los Nevados Natural National Park

The reason for the Coffee Triangle's fertile soil is the snowcapped volcanoes of Los Nevados. Volcanic activity closes hiking trails here, so check ahead. **www. parquesnacionales.gov.co**

If the bland reality of Colombian coffee in situ has you hanging out for a decent cuppa, head straight to its source in the Coffee Triangle, which is where the bulk of the nation's coffee is produced. Here, in the region's oldest town, Salento, where colourful buildings spill down the streets like rows of sweets, Café Jesús Martín is fighting the good fight on behalf of all coffee lovers.

Opened in 2008 by the son of a local coffee farmer, the cafe's mission is largely to show Colombians what it is they're missing – to educate and inspire by illustrating what coffee can really be. Beans are sourced from Jesús Martín's own plantations and other small producers (always single-origin), roasted in the Jesús Martín factory and then served in the cafe.

The tone is Colombian casual, with colourful murals swirling across the cafe walls, coffee sacks as cushion covers, a few tables on a landing above the bar, and coffee art featuring the likes of bears and dogs. A big part of the experience comes in a show of difference, with baristas lining up ground beans for comparison – those you'll be drinking in the cafe, and those being drunk by the rest of the country. Be sure to take the taste test and all will become clear...

COSTA RICA

How to ask for a coffee in the local language?
Un cafécito, por favor
Signature coffee style? Café chorreado
What to order with your coffee? A tasty snack such as
one of the local cakes (queques), biscuits (galletas),
pastries (pasteles) or empanadas
Don't: Order instant or percolator coffee, as it is not
considered to be good style. It's also best not to ask
for an espresso if you don't see an espresso machine.
Go with a cafécito

To talk about coffee in Costa Rica is to sing the
praises of the *chorreador*. Consisting of a *bolsita*
(fine-cloth sock-like 'little bag'), often held open and
upright by a wooden stand, the *chorreador* allows poured
hot water to filtrate through coffee grounds and into
a receptacle. It is the precursor to the pour-over coffee
practices now so expensively in vogue wherever quality
baristas hold court.

The *chorreador*, however, has been in use for a long time
in Costa Rica – certainly since the 1830s, when laws required
families to plant at least two coffee bushes on their land
and coffee became the country's number one export. (It has
since been surpassed by other products.) As a result, coffee
is a deeply embedded, extremely popular part of the culture.

To this day, *Ticos* (Costa Ricans) drink lots of java from the
nation's eight coffee regions and 80,000-plus producers,
most of whom cultivate plots smaller than five hectares. But
not all *café chorreados* are equal, of course. Costa Rican
gourmet beans – the fabled *granos de oro* (golden beans),
with a well-deserved reputation as some of the world's best
– have largely bypassed local markets. Even today, about
90% of coffee production is exported, leaving most Ticos to
brew from a reduced selection, sometimes of lower quality.

All things are relative, though; there is almost always
a great cup of joe to be found wherever you are in the
country. All the more so as artisanal cafes and coffee
impresarios have begun to find a strong domestic audience.

55

FINCA ROSA BLANCA
COFFEE PLANTATION RESORT

Santa Bárbara, Heredia;
www.fincarosablanca.com; +506 2269 9392

◆ Food   ◆ Classes   ◆ Cafe
◆ Roastery   ◆ Shop

In order to appreciate the many purposely and modestly hidden layers of the Finca Rosa Blanca Coffee Plantation Resort (FRB), one must first unwind beneath the canopy of indigenous trees and luxuriously thick undergrowth that provides privacy to its hotel guests, a rich habitat for birds and ideal conditions for some of Costa Rica's best organic, sustainably managed, shade-grown, single-origin coffee.

The end goal for FRB's owners and staff is always quality. They see it as a symbiosis of refined hospitality, environmental sensitivity (FRB has 'five-leaf' sustainable certification) and devotion to creating superb coffee which, says co-owner Glenn Jampol, 'touches base with the core values of the people consuming it.'

FRB produces one of the country's few estate coffees, meaning it owns and controls the entire production process. In pursuit of excellence, its coffee wizards can – and do – improvise and innovate at every step of the way, including sustainably reusing the organic materials added to and resulting from the process.

Coffee and coffee-inspired food are served at FRB's El Buho Bar and El Tigre Vestido Restaurant. And the in-depth, educational, 2½-hour coffee plantation tour, followed by coffee cupping and tasting, is, like everything at FRB, one of the best in the world.

THINGS TO DO NEARBY

Braulio Carillo National Park
Easily accessible via hiking trails, this extensive protected area spans seven ecological zones and habitats that are home to hundreds of animal species. *www.sinac.go.cr*

Museo de Cultura Popular
Set in the home of a former president, this museum devotes displays to the popular culture of 19th-century Costa Rica. *www.museo.una.ac.cr*

Rainforest Adventures Atlantic Park
Families love the zip lines, aerial tram ride, guided nature hikes and more in this private eco-reserve abutting Braulio Carillo National Park. *www.rainforestadventure. com/costa-rica-atlantic*

Toucan Rescue Ranch
Rehabilitation and release back into the wild is the goal in this safe home for rescued toucans and other wildlife. *toucanrescueranch.org*

CUBA

How to ask for a coffee in the local language?
Póngame un cafecito, por favor
Signature coffee style? Café Cubano (also called cafecito)
What to order with your coffee? Flan (the standard Cuban dessert)
Do: Opt for black coffee in small traditional cafes, as Cuban milk is usually powdered and not ideal for making lattes or cappuccinos

In Cuba, you're not going to find many homes without a *cafetera* (Italian style espresso-maker) poised on the hob, ready for action at a moment's notice.

It's as ubiquitous as the bottle of dark rum hidden in the 1950s drinks cabinet, or the photo of Che Guevara hung above the TV set. Coffee is Cuba's great social leveller. Put half a foot inside a Cuban house and you'll promptly be invited in for a *cafecito*, the customary short espresso, brewed fresh and usually served with a large slice of local gossip. The sugar is default, added during preparation, creating a strong, sweet, intense drink.

Cuba has long been one of the world's great coffee growers. Ruins of old coffee plantations around Santiago de Cuba dating from the early 19th century are listed as a Unesco World Heritage Site. The first farmers were French immigrants escaping from a slave rebellion in Haiti and, for a time in the mid-19th century, coffee production exceeded that of sugar.

The 1959 revolution and the resulting US embargo ripped a large hole in Cuba's coffee industry but, after years in the doldrums, coffee culture is making a comeback. A flurry of new cafes has recently opened in Havana following a relaxation in private business laws. Between them, they serve the two popular Cuban brands – Cubita and Serrano – mainly to tourists. Pure coffee is still out of reach to average Cubans who have to make do with *café mezclado*, an inferior blend of coffee beans mixed with dried peas.

EL CAFÉ

Amargura #358 btwn Villegas and Aguacate St, Havana;
www.facebook.com/elcafehavana; +53 7861 3817

◆ Food　　◆ Transport
◆ Cafe

El Café is a triumphant story of procuring produce
in a country still beset by baffling bureaucracy
and mind-bending rules. Industrial engineer-turned-chef
Nelson Rodríguez Tamayo's mission to serve espressos,
along with sourdough and fried egg breakfasts, is, as the
Cubans say, a *película* (film).

Returning to Cuba from London in 2014 with his young
family, and failing to find a decent breakfast in Havana,
Nelson began to percolate his plans. Beans, sourced
from the Escambray Mountains, are roasted off-site, and
delivered still warm to the touch. At the busy caffeine refuge

he opened in 2016 with Marinella Abbondati, tables and
mismatched chairs are clustered on pretty Spanish tiles.
Order the *café frappe*, served in a chunky American diner
glass, before pacing the humid streets of Havana.

THINGS TO DO NEARBY

Clandestina
Cuban designer Idania del
Río sells cheeky T-shirts,
cloth bags and souvenirs
which humorously play on
Cuban conundrums and
history. The silk-screen
posters are a gorgeous
must-buy. ***www.facebook.
com/clandestinacuba***

Experimental Gallery
Collector Arley's eclectic
colonial corner space sells
quirky memorabilia, the
Pop Art of artist Ares,
street photography by
Sahara Habana (FB), and
vintage Cuban posters.
***Corner of Amargura
and Aguacate***

EL DANDY

Brasil cnr Villegas, Habana Vieja, Havana;
www.bareldandy.com; +53 7867 6463

◆ Food　　◆ Transport
◆ Cafe

The dandiest player in Havana's emerging cafe
scene inhabits a typically dishevelled tenement in
the city's Old Town overlooking the once-forgotten, but now
trendy, Plaza del Cristo. With its retro photo art, intriguing
jumble of keepsakes and noisy slice of Havana streetlife
visible through the arched doorway, this is surely the best
place in the city to linger over an aromatic coffee.

The Cuban/Swedish-run cafe opened in 2014 and uses
local Cuban beans specially ground for every cup. To satisfy

a growing army of curious tourists, Dandy's coffee menu
incorporates far more than the standard *café cubano*. Try
the *café el Dandy*, a kick-filled blend of condensed milk,
espresso, cinnamon and Havana Club rum.

THINGS TO DO NEARBY

**Museo Nacional de
Bellas Artes**
The finest art gallery
in the Caribbean offers
a feast of Cuban art (with
some international cameos)
across two sites. ***www.
bellasartes.cult.cu***

Museo de la Revolución
The rebellious story of
Cuba's past laid out in
one of Havana's most
opulent palaces (the old
presidential palace) and
gleefully told with *mucho*
propaganda.

JAMAICA

How to ask for a coffee in the local language?
Me need fi full up pon sum kaffee
Signature coffee style? Drip coffee
What to order with your coffee? Meat patty
Don't: Waste your time searching for hip micro-roasters or latte artists; Jamaica's best coffee often appears out of beach shacks that look like they'll blow away in the next hurricane

Jamaica produces the Ferraris of the coffee world. But, rather like the supersonic cars, not a lot of people get to try them. Instead, most of the country's low-yield, high-end coffee is earmarked for export, with more than 80% of it going to Japan.

Jamaica's best beans come from the Blue Mountains, whose cobalt slopes rise abruptly behind the steamy capital, Kingston. Here, their growth, harvest and processing is meticulously overseen by the Coffee Industry Board of Jamaica. According to local lore, the coffee's superior quality is a by-product of the mountains' damp mists, steep lofty slopes (certified Blue Mountain Coffee must be grown

between 3000ft and 5500ft) and excellent drainage. As a result, the coffee cherries mature slowly to ensure a rich, nutty brew that is low in acidity. Above all, Jamaican coffee is wonderfully smooth.

Coffee culture in Jamaica doesn't enjoy the historical intrigue of Italy or the hipster affiliations of the US. But that's not to say you can't find a decent cup here. In fact, Jamaica is one of the few countries in the world where you'll rarely suffer a bad brew. Cappuccinos aren't the norm. Rather, locals tend to drink their coffee piping hot out of large ceramic mugs with a little added milk. With Blue Mountain set aside for souvenir-hunting tourists and five-star Tokyo hotels, locals are left to sup on High Mountain, a smooth chocolatey coffee that's long played second fiddle to the premier blend. Then again, there's no shame in being runner-up to a Ferrari.

59

OLD TAVERN COFFEE ESTATE

1.5km southwest of Section Village, Blue Mountains;
+1 876 865 2978

◆ Roastery ◆ Cafe
◆ Shop

The Twyman family has been responsible for producing some of the world's best Blue Mountain Coffee for decades. High up in Jamaica's longest range and reachable by 4WD only, the family's estate is run by David, the son of late owner Alex, who emigrated to Jamaica from England in 1958 and persevered for a decade to secure a Coffee Board License, which allowed him to sell the beans directly to clients under the coveted 'Blue Mountain Coffee' trademark. His persistence ensured the bean's impressive heritage continues; Jamaica's Blue Mountain Coffee dates back to 1730, when the first Arabica plants were introduced to the island from Saint-Dominque (present-day Haiti).

© Mark Bassett / Alamy Stock Photo

THINGS TO DO NEARBY

Blue Mountain Peak
Starting from Penlyne Castle hamlet, hikers make night-time ascents of Jamaica's tallest peak. At sunrise on a clear day you can see Cuba.

Strawberry Hill
Swim in the infinity pool, sample the sumptuous Sunday brunch or relax in the Caribbean-style cottages at this luxury hotel in the foothills of the Blue Mountains. *www. strawberryhillhotel.com*

Downhill Cycling
Blue Mountain Bicycle Tours offer exhilarating guided descents past coffee plantations clinging to steep slopes. *www. bmtoursja.com*

Holywell Recreation Area
Well-maintained hiking trails thread their way through the unique ecosystems of primary montane forest, cloud forest and elfin woodland. Beautiful waterfalls and excellent birdwatching.

The Twymans make good use of traditional fermentation and sun-drying processes while keeping the use of chemical fertilisers and pesticides to a minimum in their single-estate beans. Visitors are welcome by prior arrangement and treated to lessons on coffee growing and production, with a tasting session at the end. The rare peaberry beans grown here are mild-flavoured and prized by coffee connoisseurs. You can buy the Old Tavern Coffee Estate beans directly from the farm or at the Kingston office; the brew itself is served in Kingston's top restaurants and cafes.

SMURF'S CAFE

Ocean View Hill Drive, Treasure Beach, St Elizabeth Parish;
+1 876 504 7814

◆ Food   ◆ Shop
◆ Roastery ◆ Cafe

Forget pretentious pour-overs and Monet-worthy latte art. Smurf's Cafe is unashamedly old-school, a simple breeze-block breakfast joint set back 200m from the sand in the mellow Jamaican community of Treasure Beach. The self-service coffee comes out of a smudged silver urn next to the kitchen and is made (legend has it) from a mix of various local beans that are home-roasted by the owner, Dawn. But never mind the recipe; this stuff is divine, a smooth, dangerously addictive brew that goes down like melted chocolate. Imbibe it in the morning over a generous plate of Jamaica's signature breakfast, ackee and saltfish, and you'll feel like you've died and ascended to the big coffee roaster in the sky.

THINGS TO DO NEARBY

Frenchman's Bay
On Treasure Beach's best strip of sand (see opposite), in the shadow of the Santa Cruz mountains, the worst hassle you'll get is when a local fisherman asks you to help pull the boat ashore.

Jakes Hotel
Way more than a mere hotel, bohemian Jakes holds mosaic classes and rents bicycles – perfect for exploring the disparate necklace of beach hamlets hereabouts.
www.jakeshotel.com

MEXICO

How to ask for a coffee in the local language?
Un café, por favor
Signature coffee style? Café de olla
What to order with your coffee? Tres leches cake
Don't: Be a lap-top camper. Mexico's best coffee bars
are extrovert places where you can enjoy chatter, life
and people rather than hiding behind the walls of the
worldwide web

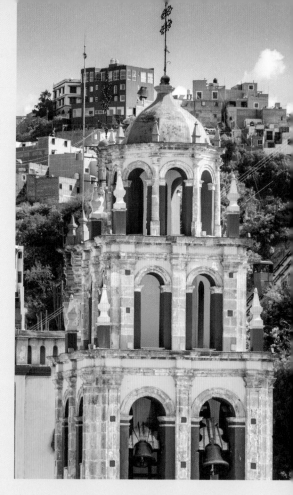

Although rarely mentioned in global top-ten lists, Mexico is actually the world's eighth-largest coffee producer, with a strong bias towards organic fair-trade beans. Its coffee is largely a tale of three states: Veracruz on the Atlantic coast, Oaxaca in the central south and Chiapas wedged up against the border with Guatemala.

Chiapas harvests Mexico's biggest crops, producing high-quality Arabica beans that are masterfully blended into brews endowed with a rich chocolatey flavour. Oaxaca's coffee is a little milder, while in Veracruz – the state where the coffee plant was first introduced to Mexico in the late 1700s – the joe is milder still.

Hunt down one of the country's historic cafes and you're likely to find that the caffeine comes with delicious

complementary snacks such as sweetbreads and *tres leches* cake. One of the oldest is the legendary Gran Café de la Parroquia (see p67) in the port city of Veracruz. Conceived in 1808, it later made its name by inventing the *café lechero*, a frothy milky coffee served in a tall glass by waiting staff dressed in starched white jackets. Veracruz State is also home to Mexico's ultimate coffee town, Coatepec, where the crop is grown, roasted and served in a multitude of rustic cafes, each and every one of them thick with the aroma of freshly ground beans.

The most traditional Mexican coffee confection is the distinctive but hard-to-find *café de olla*, traditionally served at home in small earthenware mugs. The rich and spicy concoction is made by mixing ground coffee, *piloncillo* (raw cane sugar) and cinnamon sticks in a clay pot. Aficionados call it 'Mexican chai'.

CAFÉ TAL

Temezcuitate 4, Guanajuato;
www.cafetal.com.mx; +52 473 732 6212

◆ Roastery ◆ Cafe
◆ Shop   ◆ Transport

Run by an American expat, Café Tal is named after the cat that adopted this place as home, enticed perhaps by the attention of many of Guanajuato's 20,000 students who use this as their homework and caffeine *casa*. Wander past and you'll be lured in by the aroma of beans, all sourced from Mexico, that are roasting in a retro Primo roaster. As for the cafe? It's grungy. But it's all part of the image. And who cares if a lamp doesn't work. Here, it's all about the coffee, and Tal's cappuccino is the best in town. Oh, and if you get the cafe's logo – a cat on a cup silhouette – tattooed anywhere on your bod, you'll get free filter coffee for life.

THINGS TO DO NEARBY

Monumento a El Pípila
Work off your buzz by taking the steep funicular to Monumento a El Pípila, the massive statue dedicated to a hero of the War of Independence, and walking back down.

Mercado Hidalgo
Wander through the main plaza to Mercado Hidalgo, a massive food market housed in a building whose incongruous design is based on an old French railway station.

FINCA LAS NIEVES

Café Cafetal, Calle del Morro S/N Col. Marinero, Puerto Escondido;
fincalasnieves.mx; +52 954 582 2414

◆ Food   ◆ Classes   ◆ Cafe
◆ Roastery   ◆ Shop

If you're a real coffee lover then visiting a coffee farm must surely hover near the top of your bucket list. And what better one to visit than an organic plantation run by a hilarious half-Dutch, half-Swedish Mexican-born man?

Located in the Sierra Madre del Sur, just 90 minutes from surfers' paradise Puerto Escondido, visits to Finca las Nieves are organised by the farm's beachfront Café Cafetal and can be done as day trips, overnight stays, or even working holidays if the coffee bug really bites.

The finca originally began producing coffee in 1880, but mismanagement and economic woes almost drove it to ruin. Under Gustavo Boltjes' guidance it has returned to glory and now produces a variety of different coffees, including a small set of highly sought-after Geishas that fetch top dollar at auctions. The finca's setting is no less impressive. Despite its proximity to the beach, cooler temperatures and a lush natural setting complete with its own waterfalls offer ideal conditions for growing high-quality Arabica coffees.

THINGS TO DO NEARBY

Playa Zicatela
This wonderfully hippy beach is famed for the great surfing waves of the Mexican Pipeline, but at three kilometres long there's plenty of room for non-surfers too.

Bar Fly
Is dancing to great electronic sounds under the night sky with a cold beer in hand your thing? Then you'll love this open-air beach bar.
www.facebook.com/ BarflyClub

Casa Wabi
This unexpected artists' retreat (see below left) just north of Puerto was designed by famed Japanese architect Tadao Ando and is a must for architecture fans.
casawabi.org

Temazcalli
A local take on the sauna, this spiritual experience takes up to one and a half hours and is accompanied with chants intended to purify your soul.
www.temazcalli.com

To help the plants along, Boltjes has created his very own 100% organic fertilisers and makes sure that even waste doesn't go to waste. The results have been so great that green coffee buyers from all over the world are now buying his coffees, helping to keep the farm alive and offering employment to many locals. And the best part? After returning to Puerto Escondido, you can watch an amazing sunset while sipping on a cold beer. Heaven!

HEY BREW BAR

Texas 81, Nápoles, Mexico City;
www.facebook.com/heybrewbar; +52 55 7158 5381

◆ Food   ◆ Cafe
◆ Shop   ◆ Transport

THINGS TO DO NEARBY

Lucha Libre at Arena México
The quintessential Mexican wrestling experience (see left) is an absolute must for anyone visiting the capital. It's wild, colourful and incredibly fun.
www.ticketmaster.com.mx

Castillo de Chapultepec
This relatively modern castle was built to house the short-lived Mexican monarchy and offers sweeping views of Avenida Reforma and El Parque de Chapultepec.

Museo Tamayo
Mexico has many fantastic museums, but this one in particular is a great choice for contemporary art.
www.museotamayo.art

El Farolito Mesa Népoles
A top spot for traditional Mexican tacos, with a great choice of barbecued meat. *taqueriaselfarolito. com.mx*

At first glance Mexico City may not seem like the kind of place you'd find a fine coffee bar whose focus is the simple promotion and supply of freshly brewed filter coffees – especially in a city where the numerous American coffee chains don't even have filter coffee on the menu. A big welcome, then, to Hey Brew Bar.

Located in the up-and-coming Colonia Nápoles, where a smattering of nice coffee bars, great eateries and cute craft beer stores combine to create a youthful vibe, Hey Brew Bar wouldn't look out of place in New York or Tokyo. Its clinically clean look and an entirely white bar intentionally put the colours of the fine coffees used here firmly to the fore, in a space that founder Rodrigo Moreno created as a place where people could sample carefully picked single-origin coffees from select farms in Nayarit, Oaxaca, Veracruz and Chiapas states. And by highlighting

a different brew method every day, he also successfully demonstrates how the same coffee can taste completely different when prepared with a V60 or an AeroPress.

All the coffees are carefully roasted by Café Sublime in Guadalajara, and by working only with Mexican growers, Hey Brew Bar takes advantage of the rich variety and high quality of fine single-origin coffees that are almost literally grown on its doorstep.

In the teeming mass that is Mexico City, Colonia Nápoles is a relatively quiet neighbourhood, making it rather pleasant to just sit on the terrace, reading a book and slurping away on that freshly brewed coffee.

DOSIS

Av Álvaro Obregón 24B, Roma Norte, Mexico City;
www.dosiscafe.com; +52 55 6840 6941

◆ Food   ◆ Shop   ◆ Transport
◆ Classes   ◆ Cafe

This friendly coffee bar towards the end of beautiful Avenida Alvaro Obregón has taken a great deal of inspiration from legendary coffee shops on Valencia Street in San Francisco and successfully combined it with a distinctly Mexican experience.

The baristas at Dosis are wonderfully friendly and always have great recommendations up their sleeves. On a hot sunny day, you may want to try their velvety cold brew with almond milk or a shot of espresso made with beans of the Xilotepec variety grown in Oaxaca state.

A large cultural space at the back hosts markets, cinema nights and workshops, so check the cafe's Facebook page for upcoming listings.

THINGS TO DO NEARBY

The historic centre
One of the most beautiful and best-preserved colonial cities in the world, Mexico City's remarkable centre offers a wealth of top sights.

Tráfico Bazar
This indie shop is the best place to find great things from up-and-coming designers and makers, including fashion, accessories and souvenirs.
www.facebook.com/ traficobazarmx

GRAN CAFÉ DE LA PARROQUIA

Av Gómez Farias 34, Veracruz;
www.laparroquia.com; +52 229 322 584

◆ Food   ◆ Cafe
◆ Shop   ◆ Transport

The Gran Parroquia is more than a mere cafe; it's an historic monument, an animated piece of theatre and one of the city of Veracruz's most famous sights. In operation since 1808 and still serving around 3000 customers a day, this spirited Mexican institution lures every element of the city's diverse personality into its huge, non-showy interior. Some come to gossip, others to daydream, still more to dig into doorstep-sized slices of *tres leches* cake. But one thing binds them together. They all, periodically, tap their spoon on the side of their coffee glass. The spoon-tapping is a peculiar tradition that relates to the cafe's de rigueur drink. When you order a *café lechero*

in the Parroquia, a waiter in a starched white coat brings you an espresso in a glass. If you require milk, you have to tap your spoon on your glass to attract the attention of another waiter who deftly navigates around the tables with a steaming jug of *leche*. On being summoned, they will hold the jug high in the air and dispatch an aerated measure of milk skilfully into your glass.

It's practically heresy to leave the Parroquia before you've downed at least one *café lechero*. Don't resist.

THINGS TO DO NEARBY

Zócalo
The centre of Veracruz's urban life is this buzzing square ringed by lines of colonial porches, and filled with the amateur theatrics of Mexican life.

Malecón
Wrapped around the Caribbean coastline, this breezy sea wall is where locals go to *dar un paseo* (take a walk) when the heat and humidity of Veracruz becomes too much.

San Juan de Ulúa
This significant colonial fort hums with maritime history; its passageways, staircases, bridges and battlements are best explored with a guide.

Museo Histórico Naval
Veracruz's best museum has been brought up to date with some recent refurbishments that have made its maritime exhibits documenting old naval spats more interactive and interesting. **www.gob.mx/ semar**

NICARAGUA

How to ask for a coffee in the local language?
Un café, por favor

Signature coffee style? Café con leche (coffee with milk) is the breakfast standard

What to order with your coffee? Coffee is typically served with breakfast and in Nicaragua, that's gallo pinto, or rice and beans, with eggs and plantains or a tortilla. In modern coffee shops, coffee may be served with a slice of cake or a pastry

Do: Steer clear of coffee chains in favour of smaller, locally owned coffee shops who are more likely to work closely with Nicaraguan farmers and roasters

These days, it's not unusual to find organic, shade-grown, Fairtrade-certified Nicaraguan coffee sold by the bean – or by the carefully prepared cup – at cafes in New York or San Francisco. But that wasn't always the case. Nicaragua is a country that's been ravaged by political unrest and economic hardship for most of its modern history. So despite the fact that its northern highlands are the ideal terroir for coffee production, Nicaraguan beans weren't always on the market: during the Cold War era, exportation to the US was banned altogether.

Nicaragua still has problems, but coffee isn't one of them. The world is awakening to the particular appeal of coffee – fragrant, fruity, and moderately acidic – harvested in the regions of Jinotega, Matagalpa and Segovia. As coffee exportation has picked up in recent years, Nicaraguan people have started drinking more (and better) coffee, too. Today, more than 40,000 families are working in coffee cultivation in rural communities throughout the country. And in busy cities like Managua, León and Granada, Nicaraguan people aren't just having the standard coffee with breakfast: they're meeting friends and family in cafes after work.

Sadly, higher demand doesn't necessarily mean better coffee quality. For every smooth, bold cup with notes of nut and vanilla, there's both a watery instant coffee being brewed in someone's kitchen, and a sugary flavoured coffee being served inside a shopping mall. But the overall scene *is* improving, and coffee farmers are getting in on the game, too, welcoming visitors to witness harvest and production – and, of course, to buy some whole beans to take home.

PAN Y PAZ

Esquina de los Bancos, una Cuadra y Media al Este, 1ra Calle NE, León;
www.panypaz.com; +505 2311 0949

◆ Food   ◆ Classes   ◆ Cafe
◆ Roastery   ◆ Shop   ◆ Transport

Nicaragua's coffee-growing regions produce some of the finest beans in the world. But the good stuff, at least until recently, has been produced mostly for export. A pair of Europeans in search of a good cup of coffee – and a great baguette to go with it – are changing that reality in León, a Spanish colonial city near the Pacific coast.

Christian (from France) and Miranda (from the Netherlands) founded Pan y Paz, an artisan bakery specialising in traditional French bread and pastries, in 2010. They started working with local coffee providers, ultimately partnering with Twin Engine Coffee. It's the only coffee company in Nicaragua that exclusively roasts 100% speciality-grade Nicaraguan Arabica beans. After opening their original outlet here, two blocks from the city's central park and featuring outdoor seating in a peaceful courtyard, they've opened a second, coffee-focused location half a block from León's cathedral; a cafe and tasting room where visitors can sample coffees from all over the country.

THINGS TO DO NEARBY

Catedral de la Asunción de María de León

León's striking neoclassical cathedral (see left), the largest in Central America, was built to withstand earthquakes. It contains the tomb of Ruben Darío, Nicaragua's celebrated Modernist poet. *www. catedraldeleon.org*

Museo Histórico de la Revolución

León is the heart of liberal Nicaragua. This museum, just off the plaza, traces modern history from the Managua earthquake of 1972 to the Sandinista revolution. *www. nicaragua.com/museums*

Nicaragüita Restaurante & Cafe

Icy mojitos, crispy tostones (fried plantains), and live music are just a few of the highlights at this friendly little cafe and restaurant. *www.facebook.com/ nicaraguitacafe*

Las Peñitas

Catch the bus to the beach and explore this quiet coastal village and the Isla Juan Venado Nature Reserve, a key nesting ground for sea turtles. *www.laspenitas.com*

Whichever location you visit, it's essential to pair a coffee with something fresh out of the oven. Miranda recommends a simple coffee with a chocolate croissant in the morning, and in the afternoon, a mocha (made with Nicaraguan cocoa) and a pastry made with coffee cream and locally grown cashews.

USA

How to ask for a coffee in the local language? I'd like a ____ coffee, please (fill in with ultra-specific ordering details, ie 'half-caff, no foam, almond milk')

Signature coffee style? Drip coffee in a to-go cup, or a latte with designer fixings

What to order with your coffee? Something sweet, such as a homemade cookie or cheesecake

Don't: Get your tipping wrong! When ordering at a cafe counter no tip is necessary if you're taking your beverage to go; it's customary to offer a small tip (round up to the next dollar) if you're sticking around

America has always called itself the 'melting pot', and the swirling together of disparate cultures has had a direct and significant impact on the country's approach to coffee over the years. From the Italians' intense predilection for all things espresso to Australia's laid-back coffee lifestyle, the US's current coffee scene is a mosaic of choice united by a desire for transparency, traceability, and – most importantly – flavour. But it's been a slow century of evolution from bland, burnt crystals to today's bright and fruity beans.

First came the era of the 1950s housewife, who cooked for her family with chemically enhanced foods (hello minute-rice!) and introduced coffee-esque powder into her larder and daily routine.

Clever marketing made speciality flavours the next must-have, with coffee shops joining the McDonald's chain gang nationwide. And since little ceremony is placed upon the American mealtime, the travelling cup of joe quickly became as important an accessory as a purse. For the last few decades the 'have it your way' mantra largely dictated the way Americans consumed their morning jolt, headlined by java juggernaut Starbucks. The brewing process became a very personalised experience, contrary to the democratisation of coffee during the first wave, with speciality coffees gussied up with foam, cream, and extra syrups, toppings and flavours.

Today, the customer isn't always quite right, as America's baristas and roasters are moving deeper down the speciality coffee rabbit hole and emphasising the product instead of the marketing techniques. Now, beans are being treated like wine grapes or chocolate – their flavour and roast profiles are dutifully documented and blended to create tastes that run the gamut from puckery, lemony brews, to deep

TOP 5 COFFEES

Stumptown Hair Bender
Intelligentsia Black Cat Classic Espresso
Counter Culture Apollo
Devoción Wild Forest
Blue Bottle Three Africans

CAFE TALK – DARLEEN SCHERER

The state of the coffee scene in America is strong – the quality of our product at every step continues to improve, from data logging in roasting to the expert preparation by the barista. This is a very exciting time in coffee

chocolatey notes. Everything is small-batch, and counter workers are keen to match their selection of flavours to their customers' tastes rather than having to decorate a to-go frappucino. And as for size, in America's coffee culture, at least, bigger is no longer better.

So what's next? Well, with a relatively short turnaround between the second and third waves of coffee, customers and entrepreneurs alike are eager to discuss what's next. The narrowing divide between corporate and craft roasteries would suggest that the industry will drill deeper down to further illuminate the differences of each single-

origin bean and variety, and how to best prepare them for the inevitable cup.

Even Duane Sorensen, the founder of boutique brand Stumptown – which he sold to coffee conglomerate JAB Holdings (Peet's parent company) in 2015 – has made his anticipated return to the heavily saturated market of small-shop bean dispensers he essentially created. Puff opened its doors in Portland in November 2017, founded on the same passion for the 'have it your way' roasting that sparked Stumptown's inception.

As it turns out, America's melting pot is more of a mug.

BOXCAR COFFEE ROASTERS

1825 Pearl St B, Boulder, Colorado;
boxcarcoffeeroasters.com; +1 720 486 7575

◆ Food ◆ Shop ◆ Transport
◆ Roastery ◆ Cafe

Boxcar Coffee Roasters has a unique brewing technique for the high elevation of Colorado's Boulder city, which is about a mile above sea level. Conceived over a campfire in the Rocky Mountains, the 'Boilermakr' is brewed by boiling coffee grounds in a flask. The high altitude lowers water's boiling point to the perfect extraction temperature of 202°F (94°C). Baristas boil the grounds for only a few seconds before putting the flask on ice to slow extraction. The grounds are strained and then your cowboy-style coffee is ready to drink. Boxcar's cafe has brick walls, marble tables, skylights and plants, making it perfect for coffee dates and Instagram photoshoots. It shares the space with gourmet grocery Cured, so you can happily stock up on charcuterie, cheese and wine while your Boilermakr bubbles.

THINGS TO DO NEARBY

Pearl Street Mall
This charismatic four-block-long pedestrian mall is filled with shops and restaurants for both kids and adults to enjoy, and also hosts street performers, concerts and beer festivals. *www.boulderdowntown.com*

Sanitas Brewing Co
A delicious brewery that's perfect for a sunny day outside on a big deck where you can challenge your friends to games of cornhole and bocce ball. *www.sanitasbrewing.com*

INTELLIGENTSIA

3123 North Broadway, Chicago, Illinois;
www.intelligentsiacoffee.com; +1 773 348 8058

◆ Food   ◆ Cafe
◆ Shop   ◆ Transport

THINGS TO DO NEARBY

Wrigley Field
Home of the Chicago Cubs, Wrigley Field is an iconic baseball stadium that is named after the famous Wrigley's chewing gum magnate, William Wrigley Jr.
www.mlb.com/cubs

Mortar & Pestle
This globally inspired breakfast, lunch and brunch restaurant serves an eclectic menu of dishes, including funnel cake, fried green tomatoes and foie gras eggs.
www.mortarand pestlechicago.com

Wilde Bar & Restaurant
Named after the infamous Irish writer Oscar Wilde, this pub has a classic Chicago aesthetic with big leather chairs and a fireplace surrounded by bookshelves.
wildechicago.com

Laugh Factory
Enjoy a night of stand-up and cocktails at one of Chicago's famous comedy clubs. This one features seasoned and upcoming comedians, and the occasional celebrity guest.
www.laughfactory.com/ clubs/chicago

Intelligentsia introduced the concept of direct trade to the coffee industry and is a pioneer of the third wave movement. Founders Doug Zell and Emily Mange launched their luxury empire at this location in Chicago as a way to connect with the coffee community. At the beginning, they roasted beans in-house, experimented with different blends on older machines and built strong relationships with sustainable farmers abroad. They are meticulous about the way their coffee is crafted and sourced, paying well-above fair-trade prices for their hand-selected beans. Fast-forward over 20 years and they own coffee bars all over the country, with teams of award-winning baristas; they have to earn their place at the bar by taking a 30-page test and proving their chops during extensive trainings.

The original coffee bar in Chicago stays busy and is known for its efficiency, although baristas will still take time to add the finishing touches to your latte art. It's located in a bustling part of town where 9-to-5ers come for a quick fix in the morning or an afternoon pick-me-up, but it's nice to stay a while and take in the industrial vibe; the assortment of seating makes this a great place to come with a laptop or enjoy conversations over the latest single-origin roasts.

AVOCA COFFEE

1311 West Magnolia Ave, Fort Worth, Texas;
www.avocacoffee.com; +1 682 233 0957

◆ Food ◆ Classes ◆ Cafe
◆ Roastery ◆ Shop

It's not overstating the case to say the bean scene in Fort Worth exists thanks to Garold LaRue, a fifth-generation coffee farmer, and Jimmy Story, who opened Avoca Coffee in a former auto-mechanic workshop in Fort Worth's trendy Southside. Along with running one of the best cafes in the area, they supply and educate numerous cafes, restaurants and groceries in Fort Worth and Dallas.

The cafe doubles as a micro-roastery and you can watch as beans, sourced from Central America and Africa, are roasted and packaged (a second cafe is in the city's museum district). Elsewhere, at communal tables, eager coffee hounds (an eclectic mix of students, tradespeople and businessfolk) sip on their lattes... or espressos, cold-brews, cappuccinos and yes, even mocha lattes.

Be sure to buy some beans: the Mogwai Blend is smooth, with lingering chocolate and cherry overtones.

THINGS TO DO NEARBY

Kimbell Art Museum
Get a non-caffeinated kick from the works of Rembrandt, Goya and Picasso in this Louis Kahn-designed museum, located near Avoca Coffee's Foch St branch.
www.kimbellart.org

The Southside
Wander down Fort Worth's rehabilitated and hipster-chic Magnolia Avenue, Southside, for great eats, crafts and a glass-blowing gallery. *www. nearsouthsidefw.org*

GREENWELL FARMS

Kealakekua, Hawaii;
www.greenwellfarms.com; +1 808 323 2295

◆ Roastery ◆ Cafe
◆ Shop

From January through May, the volcanic slopes of West Hawaii are dusted by 'Kona snow' – the local nickname for the showy white blossoms of coffee trees. Introduced to the Hawaiian islands by Christian missionaries in the early 19th century, coffee began a boom in small plantations across the Kona district. Today, a patchwork of hundreds of small family farms still grows coffee on these rugged, mineral-rich slopes drenched by tropical rain showers and sunshine. Though 100% Kona coffee is hardly inexpensive, it's justifiably famous for its rich, medium-bodied and mellow flavour profile.

Among a handful of Kona coffee farms open to the public, none is more historic than Greenwell Farms, established in the 1850s. Friendly tour guides at this family-owned farm

THINGS TO DO NEARBY

Kona Coffee Living History Farm
Step back into the 1920s and experience Japanese immigrant life on this heritage coffee farm, where all the work is still undertaken by hand.
www.konahistorical.org

Kona Coffee Festival
For 10 days in November, the Kona district celebrates its coffee with parades, musical concerts, arts and cultural exhibits, coffee-picking contests, cupping competitions and more.
konacoffeefest.com

Ka'aloa's Super J's Authentic Hawaiian Food
Dive into Hawaiian soul food at this family-owned roadside kitchen serving heaped plate lunches. Don't leave without tasting the *poi* (mashed taro).
+1 (808) 328-9566

Kealakekua Bay State Historical Park
Snorkel, kayak or dive with brilliant tropical fish and turtles at the aquamarine bay (see above left) where Captain Cook and ancient Hawaiians first met.
hawaiistateparks.org

will patiently explain the entire process from harvesting and pulping coffee cherries to drying and roasting the beans. This is your chance to get up close and smell a coffee tree, as well as to taste free samples of freshly brewed coffee. Don't leave without nabbing a bag of 100% Kona coffee beans to stash in your suitcase. Want to take home something special? Buy the Elizabeth J limited-edition coffee made with bright, fruity Pacamara beans.

G&B

317 S Broadway Ste C19, Los Angeles, California;
gandb.coffee; +1 213 265 7718

◆ Food   ◆ Cafe
◆ Shop   ◆ Transport

G&B is what happens when two Intelligentsia (see p75) employees decide to start a high-end coffee concept bar. Kyle Glanville (G) and Charles Babinski (B) are both champion baristas and held positions at Intelligentsia as VP of strategy and Intelligentsia Venice lead trainer, respectively. To fulfill their coffee-bar dream in their own cafe, they built a 360° marble countertop so that patrons could order at the bar, rather than waiting in line. They've also made it easy to skip the wait completely by enabling you to order via text. If you're lucky, you can snag one of the 19 stools, but if they're all taken, enjoy an Iced Almond Macadamia Cappuccino (vegan, of course), while wandering through Downtown Los Angeles' historic Grand Central Market.

THINGS TO DO NEARBY

Grand Central Market
This Downtown LA gem has a variety of food stalls and jewellery shops. The bright colours and bustling aisles here are reminiscent of a European market. *www. grandcentralmarket.com*

The Broad
A contemporary art museum with free admission. Advance tickets are available on the first of each month for the following month, and sell out quickly. *thebroad.org*

ABRAÇO

81 East 7th St, New York City, NY;
www.abraconyc.com

◆ Food   ◆ Cafe
◆ Shop   ◆ Transport

What would quintessential New York cafe service be without a slightly curt greeting from the barista? Monosyllabic remarks notwithstanding, everything else at Abraço does indeed feel a like hug, from the locals huddled together in the no-frills space to the warm, rich brews swirling around in your mug.

Inspired by the espresso bars of southern Europe, this East Village haunt is a family-run affair, and a refreshing departure from the more corporate cafes that have been creeping into the city as of late. A recent move across the street to a larger space means there's more room to linger over your latte for a little while longer – don't miss the olive oil cake that perfectly sops up the dregs, or the moreish chocolate babka.

THINGS TO DO NEARBY

Tenement Museum
A detailed recounting of the harsh conditions that immigrants faced upon their arrival in New York in the mid-19th century set in a real-deal tenement building that formerly housed those new arrivals. *www.tenement.org*

Katz's Delicatessen
Famously orgasmic sandwiches – ask Meg Ryan's Sally – have been served here for almost 150 years. Partner a pastrami sandwich with a bowl of matzo ball soup for the ultimate in Jewish comfort food. *www. katzsdelicatessen.com*

CAFFE REGGIO

119 Macdougal St, New York City, NY;
www.caffereggio.com; +1 212 475 9557

◆ Food ◆ Transport
◆ Cafe

Caffe Reggio served the first cappuccino in the United States, and proudly exhibits the enormous espresso machine that crafted its inaugural cup in 1927. The Italian gem has been a haunt of New York City college students for decades and is a top spot for a leisurely afternoon of espresso, tiramisu and people-watching. But it's also a must-visit mecca for espresso aficionados, and its setting, in Greenwich Village, is one of the most vibrant parts of NYC, so all the more reason not to miss out on it. The cafe plays classical music and is filled with antique curios that hang over intimate nooks perfect for late-night dates – if you're on one, the best seat in the house for snuggling up with a loved one and a cappuccino is in the alcove under a bust of Queen Nefertiti.

THINGS TO DO NEARBY

IFC Center
The IFC Center is an independent movie theater around the corner from Caffe Reggio. They have midnight screenings of cult classics on Fridays and Saturdays.
www.ifccenter.com

Washington Square Park
Famous for its marble arch, fountain, demonstrations and built-in chess tables, Washington Square Park is an icon located in the middle of the NYU campus.

DEVOCIÓN

69 Grand St, Brooklyn, NY;
www.devocion.com; +1 718 285 6180

◆ Food   ◆ Classes   ◆ Cafe
◆ Roastery   ◆ Shop   ◆ Transport

THINGS TO DO NEARBY

Smorgasburg
Williamsburg's collection of food carts and satellite vendors congregate along the water during the warmer months to serve Brooklynites tasty snacks and killer city views. *www.smorgasburg.com*

Maison Premiere
A Big Easy lifestyle permeates the Speakeasy-like cocktail house, where the roster of fastidiously mixed cocktails and fresh oysters have a distinctive Louisiana feel. *www.maisonpremiere.com*

Buttermilk Channel
Down in Carroll Gardens, the ultra-hip Brooklyn hood, lurks this must-try brunch spot dispensing comfort food to the masses. *www.buttermilkchannelnyc.com*

Jane's Carousel
Fun for kids and adults, the fully restored merry-go-round is a blast from the past (the 1920s, to be exact) along the waterfront in Brooklyn Bridge Park. *www.janescarousel.org*

Devoción seeks to superimpose the tenets of the modern food movement – freshness, quality and transparency – on coffee by shipping in its beans directly from the source. The focus is squarely on Colombia, with a network of sustainably maintained haciendas sending fresh-from-the-farm produce directly to the brick-lined cafe and roasting space in Williamsburg. It's the first cafe operation of its kind in regards to total traceability: sourcing, purchasing, transporting and serving all under one umbrella.

And boy what a difference fresh beans make. The speciality house blends – known around the city for being especially citrussy and bright – are so sought after that they are the preferred beans of Eleven Madison Park, the upscale Manhattan eatery which, at the time of writing, commands pole position on the annual list of the World's 50 Best Restaurants.

As well as an assortment of baked goods and espresso-based beverages that will convince you never to go back to old beans again, the cafe and roastery also vends *cascara* – an effervescent beverage made from the pulp of the coffee cherry that's high in antioxidants but low in caffeine.

© Olee March

HAPPY BONES

394 Broome St, New York City, NY;
www.happybonesnyc.com; +1 212 673 3754

◆ Food   ◆ Cafe
◆ Shop   ◆ Transport

Stark is the word that comes to mind when you enter Happy Bones, a black-and-white-brick space in trendy SoHo that feels shockingly minimal save for the scatter of design magazines on the counter. Even the cafe dwellers are clad in New York's classic variations of a grey-toned get-up. The real shock, however, is the assortment of intensely robust espresso-based drinks – a colourful jolt to the system after entering the monochromatic world.

Originally from New Zealand, the founders mix their homeland's coffee culture with elements inspired by Italy's world-renowned espresso bars; a typical New York beast bred from diametrically different backgrounds. Go for the cortado or the flat white to really see the baristas work their magic.

THINGS TO DO NEARBY

New Museum of Contemporary Art
Rising above the street, the New Museum is a sight to behold: a seven-storey stack of off-kilter, white boxes. The museum's mission is simple: 'New art, new ideas.'
www.newmuseum.org

Barbuto
Celebrity chef Jonathan Waxman marries rugged Tuscan flavours with American comfort food at this West Village favourite.
www.barbutonyc.com

SUPERCROWN

8 Wilson Ave, Brooklyn, NY;
www.supercrown.coffee;

◆ Food ◆ Classes ◆ Cafe
◆ Roastery ◆ Shop ◆ Transport

THINGS TO DO NEARBY

Roberta's
Whisper-thin pizza dough gets the royal treatment. Despite its unassuming façade it's a place of pilgrimage for foodies. **www.robertaspizza.com**

Chess and the Sphinx
All your Brooklyn hipster dreams will come true at this Bushwick fashion mainstay, which proffers vintage designer wear to street gear. **www.chessand thesphinx.com**

Prospect Park
Brooklyn's answer to Central Park is a marvel of landscape architecture that's often considered to be a more successful space than its neighbour.

The Royal Palms Shuffleboard Club
The throwback sport offers more than ironic intrigue. Pushing stones across the floor, tiki punch in hand, is good honest fun. **www. royalpalmsshuffle.com**

Housed in a light-filled industrial space in Bushwick, New York City's unofficial streetwear capital, Supercrown is the brainchild of Darleen Scherer, a coffee savant whose decades of curiosity have led her to earn an unofficial PhD in roasting. Intimately familiar with the chain of progress, from the plant to the cup, Darleen has an extensive network of farmers and importers, and creates unique bean blends with the precision of a sommelier.

Full transparency is given to her process, with an unassuming cafe upfront and a collection of well-built grinders and roasters in the rear, backed by an eye-catching pink accent wall. Regular cuppings keep the employees up to date on the last batches and brewing styles.

But don't misinterpret the staff's encyclopedic knowledge of the bean for unbridled pretension – the roasters also know how to have fun, and find ways to playfully include coffee in the on-site cafe's offerings. You will taste a hint of java in the vinaigrette for the kale salad, and make sure you don't miss the coffee soft-serve ice cream; a more recent addition to the menu after several months of taste-testing. Each tangy-sweet slurp is worth a thousand brain-freezes.

BLUE BOTTLE COFFEE

300 Webster St, Oakland, California;
http://bluebottlecoffee.com; +1 510 653 3394

◆ Food   ◆ Classes   ◆ Cafe
◆ Roastery ◆ Shop   ◆ Transport

Named after Vienna's first coffeehouse, Blue Bottle Coffee is fanatical about freshness. At this third wave roaster, serious baristas combine the precision science of brewing for peak flavour with foam art. Most importantly, they want *you* to appreciate what you're tasting. That's why Blue Bottle's original brick warehouse offers free cupping and brewing classes every weekend. Learn to taste, smell and savour the difference between Ethiopian, Peruvian and Colombian beans sustainably sourced directly from coffee farmers, then sip magical blends. Once class is finished, sidle up to the coffee bar and order Blue Bottle's own signature drink, the Gibraltar – a double shot of espresso served with a little steamed milk in a glass tumbler.

THINGS TO DO NEARBY

Jack London Square
Join the crowds promenading outdoors in the sunshine or swing by for sunset drinks with waterfront views after paddling Oakland's estuary in a rental kayak. *www. jacklondonsquare.com*

Old Kan Beer & Co
Follow railroad tracks west to this craft brewery serving upscale pub grub by Michelin-starred chef James Syhabout. *old-kan.com*

© Lindsey Swedick; © Bella Donovan

LA COLOMBE COFFEE ROASTERS

1335 Frankford Ave, Fishtown, Philadelphia, Pennsylvania;
www.lacolombe.com; +1 267 479 1600

◆ Food ◆ Classes ◆ Cafe
◆ Roastery ◆ Shop ◆ Transport

'America Deserves Better Coffee' was the guiding principle of co-founders Todd Carmichael and JP Iberti back in 1994 when the duo started La Colombe, so it stands to reason that their coffee empire has expanded to include cafes in cities from New York to Los Angeles. But it's here in Philadelphia that the magic got started. La Colombe's flagship cafe, located in the hipster-friendly neighbourhood of Fishtown, is a soaring industrial space where the coffee beans have been carefully sourced and roasted. To celebrate 20 years in the business, the owners set up a micro-distillery in the back, so there's not just one but two things you can't miss here: Different Drum, La Colombe's coffee-infused craft rum, and the Draft Latte, a frothy iced coffee served on tap.

THINGS TO DO NEARBY

Jinxed Philadelphia
Next door to La Colombe, this antiques emporium is the place to pick up a vintage Polaroid or an old screenprint of the Ben Franklin Bridge. *www. jinxedphiladelphia.com*

Wm Mulherin's Sons
Wood-fired pizzas and elegant craft cocktails are the house speciality at this gorgeously restored Fishtown landmark, once the HQ of an Irish-owned whiskey business. *www. wmmulherinssons.com*

COAVA

1015 SE Main St, Portland, Oregon;
www.coavacoffee.com

◆ Food   ◆ Classes   ◆ Cafe
◆ Roastery   ◆ Shop   ◆ Transport

Small-batch fanatics might believe that although Stumptown's mission was altruistic, it has long since become overexposed and corporate – so purists are flocking to Coava, which has several locations around Portland in various disused industrial spaces.

As of 2017, Coava has paired its central roasting facility with its HQ in a custom-built spot that promises public cuppings every day at 1pm (except Sunday). The general messaging at Coava promises to take coffee to the next level – and maybe even the next so-called 'wave' – as the transparency of bean procurement and roasting practices continues to increase. In farming, the company's reputation is underpinned by the idea that an in-depth understanding of each partner farm will legitimise its single-origin credo. And the aromatic flavours crammed into each cup of joe are a testament to the success of the painstaking analysis of each cherry type over the past 10 years.

No matter which location you decide to try, you'll be treated to at least a couple of pour-over options and espresso flavours. Don't forget to sip your brew with a pastry from Little T American Baker, one of the best sweetshops in the American West.

THINGS TO DO NEARBY

Salt & Straw

The famed cone shop made its name by blending strange flavours (bone marrow ice-cream anyone?), but these days the long lines of lip-lickers come for the gamut of more traditional icy snacks too.
www.saltandstraw.com

Cargo

Thousands of knick-knacks and trinkets from Morocco to India are assembled in a massive hangar-like space but without that massive importer mark-up.
www.cargoinc.com

Langbaan

A super-secret chow house tucked within another restaurant, Langbaan does high-end Thai dishes arranged in a prix fixe parade – it will stretch your understanding of Southeast Asian flavours.
www.langbaanpdx.com

Kachka

If there were such a thing as 'Russki chic' it would be Kachka – a restaurant dedicated to the fresh revival of Soviet classics. Don't forget the vodka!
www.kachkapdx.com

STUMPTOWN

4525 SE Division St, Portland, Oregon;
www.stumptowncoffee.com; +1 855 711 3385

◆ Food   ◆ Classes   ◆ Cafe
◆ Roastery   ◆ Shop   ◆ Transport

THINGS TO DO NEARBY

Powell's City of Books
The ultimate independent bookstore takes up a full city block (with a few spin-off locations too) and is full of every new and used tome imaginable, plus a chill cafe.
www.powells.com

Portland Japanese Garden
Take a moment of Zen amid the pines and pagodas of an imported Japanese garden – often considered one of the best outside the Land of the Rising Sun.
www.japanesegarden.org

Voodoo Doughnut
This sweets vendor pushes the envelope when it comes to unique flavours – our favourites are generously wrapped in chunks of kid-approved cereal.
www.voodoodoughnut. com

Bible Club
In a nondescript house in a suburban neighbourhood south of the city's central core, this cocktail bar fully embraces the Prohibition Era with period antiques and dishware, not to mention excellent drinks.
www.bibleclubpdx.com

How do you out-Starbucks Starbucks? That's the million-dollar question in a billion-dollar industry that the founders of Stumptown attempted to answer. And wouldn't you know it, they succeeded.

Stumptown, along with a couple of other American roasteries, pushed coffee's third wave movement into the collective consciousness – cafe-goers could finally appreciate the complexities of the bean beyond how it was brewed and blended with milk. And that coffee-like-wine attitude still permeates and pushes the legendary brand forwards in its ever-evolving philosophy.

Today, the company has cemented its reputation as a pillar of modern American coffee, and there are a handful of locations around Portland and beyond – even one at the airport if you want to initiate yourself immediately upon arrival. Coffee enthusiasts can grab a cuppa all over town, but the truly inquisitive should head to Stumptown's headquarters, housed in a converted lumber factory, for

a dedicated hour of eye-opening cupping. This is the site of the original location, where Duane Sorenson opened the very first Stumptown in 1999 in an old beauty salon.

Whether or not you end up at the HQ, or simply grab an espresso to go, the Stumptown staff are properly equipped to school patrons on the myriad ways that bean provenance and roasting practices create a spectrum of tasting notes.

PHILZ COFFEE

3101 24th St, San Francisco, California;
www.philzcoffee.com; +1 415 875 9370

◆ Food   ◆ Cafe
◆ Shop   ◆ Transport

One cup at a time. That's Philz Coffee's motto. The brand is relatively unknown outside of the Bay Area, but has a cult following with those who drink it. Founder Phil Jaber started out running a mini supermarket in the Mission District of San Francisco. Not wanting his legacy to be cigarettes and convenience food, he set out on a quest to create the most delicious coffee he could. After visiting thousands of cafes, drinking gallons of coffee and spending seven years on his first blend, he now proudly owns a family-run business with his CEO son, Jacob, and serves a loyal community of Philz lovers. Phil regards himself as being in the people business, not the coffee business. Each location puts people first by giving baristas their own drip station at the counter. This makes every brew an intimate hand-crafted coffee experience.

THINGS TO DO NEARBY

Balmy Alley
Artists depict themes ranging from human rights to local gentrification and natural disasters in various styles on this historic block-long alley with an ever-changing collection of murals. *balmyalley.com*

Urban Putt
The first and only indoor miniature-golf range in San Francisco has 14 uniquely crafted holes, a full bar and restaurant serving American food. *urbanputt.com*

Humphry Slocombe
Find funky flavours such as Pumpkin Hazelnut, Blue Bottle Vietnamese Coffee and Elvis (the Fat Years) at this innovative ice-cream shop named after British sitcom characters. *www. humphryslocombe.com*

Southern Exposure
This alternative art space whose rotating exhibitions have included a giant golden egg sauna and ceramic waterfall is always worth a visit, especially during the annual live drawing rally. *www.soex.org*

This flagship Mission cafe has big windows, bright colours and lots of seating in which to relax and enjoy your cup of love. My favourite roast? Ambrosia, known as the 'Coffee of God', but the Iced Mint Mojito is by far the most popular order. There's nothing like fresh mint over Philz iced coffee on a sunny San Francisco day.

RITUAL ROASTERS

1026 Valencia Street, San Francisco, California;
www.ritualroasters.com; +1 415 641 1011

◆ Food ◆ Shop ◆ Transport
◆ Classes ◆ Cafe

THINGS TO DO NEARBY

826 Valencia
Pick up a new hook hand or spyglass at 'San Francisco's Only Independent Pirate Supply Store'. Purchases support the free creative writing classes held here.

The Chapel
Stay 'til night time and catch a show underneath the 40ft arched ceiling of this gorgeous mortuary-turned-music-venue.
www.thechapelsf.com

Mission Dolores Park
A favourite spot for lounging on fog-free days, this 16-acre 'Leave no trace' park is perennially populated by locals of all stripes. *sfrecpark.org*

Bar Tartine
Widely believed to offer the best baked goods in San Francisco, brave the queue to pick up a few of its unparalleled pastries.
www.bartartine.com

Often credited with being one of the first ventures to bring third wave coffee to the Bay Area, Ritual Roasters was founded in 2005 and remains a San Francisco favourite for the many coffee geeks in the city. The Valencia location is its flagship store, and it's a beauty; the stark-white south wall features local art, while the light wood panelling that makes up the floor climbs the north wall, framing the baristas behind the angular, dark stone counter they work at. This area is illuminated by windows out front, as well as ropes of light that loop down from the ceiling.

Of the six locations, several boast bespoke brews. If you're feeling adventurous, the Flora Grubb Gardens location is tucked away in a jungle-like plant nursery and features the refreshing Cherry Bomb, a mix of maraschino cherry syrup, tonic water and cold brew that tastes like a light cocktail, with slight sweetness rounding out complex citrus and herbal flavours.

Wherever you go, be sure to try out the ever-changing seasonal espresso: a carefully selected blend of the most exciting flavours of the moment promoted with eye-catching local art and cheeky titles. I tried a shot of Acid Test, a psychedelic blend with a fresh grapefruit flavour resting on a creamy chocolate base, Ritual's tribute to the 50th anniversary of the Summer of Love.

SIGHTGLASS COFFEE

270 7th St, San Francisco, California;
sightglasscoffee.com; +1 415 861 1313

◆ Food   ◆ Classes   ◆ Cafe
◆ Roastery ◆ Shop   ◆ Transport

A visit to Sightglass Coffee isn't your average trip to get your caffeine fix. Standing in its queue with the sights, smells and sounds around you, you can't help but be stimulated by this elevated coffee experience.

Brothers Jerad and Justin Morrison opened the doors to their flagship shop back in 2009. Home to Sightglass Coffee's biggest work-horse, their cast-iron production roaster, the site exposes the entire process that brings you a cup of coffee. Whether you're looking for a stellar espresso, drip coffee or 'quick cup' (batch brew), Sightglass has a single-origin or curated-blend option for you. Other offerings include its affogato bar in partnership with the well-known Pacific Northwest creamery Salt & Straw, and the Sparkling Cascara Shrub, a drink made from the dried skins of the coffee cherries.

Unsurprisingly for such a vibrant neighbourhood filled with factory buildings, nightclubs and industrial apartments, SoMa (South of Market) has become the epicentre for tech startups in the city, which makes it a great area to explore, especially when you factor in its wealth of museums, distinguished restaurants, bars, music venues and, at its eastern end, the AT&T Park baseball stadium, home to the San Francisco Giants. Not for you? Sightglass has three other outposts in the city, and their beans are served in a variety of well-regarded restaurants throughout the Bay Area.

THINGS TO DO NEARBY

San Francisco Museum of Modern Art
On the same block as a few other museums worth visiting – the Museum of African Diaspora, the Contemporary Jewish Museum and the Yerba Buena Center for the Arts. *www.sfmoma.org*

Slim's
One of San Francisco's more intimate venues, Slim's gets a variety of live music acts, from blues to electronic, indie rock to rockabilly, and more. *www.slimspresents.com*

Una Pizza Napoletana
Carved out of an old garage, these wood-fired 100% handmade Neapolitan pizzas sell like hot cakes. Doors close when the dough runs out... and they do run out. *www.unapizza.com*

City Beer Store
Hundreds of different kinds of bottled craft beers with rotating brews on tap and nice takeaway options, including a mix-n-match 6-pack. *citybeerstore.com*

© Michael O'Neal

WRECKING BALL COFFEE ROASTERS

2271 Union St, San Francisco, California;
www.wreckingballcoffee.com; +1 415 638-9227

◆ Food   ◆ Cafe

◆ Roastery   ◆ Transport

Created by married couple Trish Rothgeb (30-year coffee veteran and founding member of the Barista Guild of America) and Nicholas Cho (international coffee lecturer and founder of the esteemed, but now defunct Murky Coffee), Wrecking Ball's Union Street location represents what Cho calls an 'evolved coffee experience'. The claim sounds grandiose, but a glimpse of the shop's interior will tell you that Wrecking Ball intends to deliver on that promise. The decor evokes the spaceport from *2001: A Space Odyssey* – clean, modern utilitarianism softened with homeliness.

Wrecking Ball focuses on roasts that emphasise a bean's inherent flavour. Coffees sourced from certain areas tend to taste a certain way, and instead of complicating that in the search of something new, Wrecking Ball seeks to highlight and celebrate the flavours that made great coffees famous in the first place.

A favourite offering in the shop, the iced cappuccino, was described by Cho as 'fleeting, ephemeral', and 'not supposed to exist'. I half expected to see the Loch Ness

THINGS TO DO NEARBY

McElroy Octagon House
This eight-sided architectural oddity is an artifact of a short-lived trend from over 150 years ago. Have a look around the museum inside and well-kept garden outside. *nscda-ca.org/octagon-house*

Blackwood
Hit up this hip restaurant for a fusion of Thai and American flavours. Go for brunch to try its famous smoky-sweet 'Millionaire's Bacon'. *blackwoodsf.com*

Gamine
A small neighbourhood-favourite authentic French restaurant open for brunch, lunch and dinner. Try the escargots or the grilled flat-iron steak. *gaminesf.com*

Fort Mason Center
What was once a shipyard and embarkation point for WWII troops is now a vast cultural center and gathering place for events, drinking and eating. *www.fortmason.org*

monster swimming in my glass, but the fleeting nature of the drink has more to do with temperature than mythical beasts. You're encouraged to start drinking as soon as the drink comes out: a hot, silky layer of steamed milk sitting upon the ice-cold, creamy coffee base. The sensation is akin to jumping out of a hot tub and into a pool. The effect only lasts the first couple of minutes, but the smooth, rich flavour is there to stay.

COFFEE

VICTROLA COFFEE

310 E Pike St, Seattle, Washington;
www.victrolacoffee.com; +1 206 624 1725

◆ Food   ◆ Classes   ◆ Cafe
◆ Roastery   ◆ Shop   ◆ Transport

sits strategically next to the company's roastery, a room full of heavy sacks and handsome machinery that looks a little like a science lab, complete with bearded boffins with ear muffs and clipboards. If that doesn't intrigue you, the regular Wednesday morning cuppings should. Here, you get to smell, sip and taste unusual single-origin coffees from places like Rwanda and Burundi while learning about the subtle elements that make them so good.

If you stick around to relax, the atmosphere is quiet, bookish and local, especially compared to the tourist frenzy that inhabits the showcase Starbucks Reserve Roastery half a block away. There's usually good art on the walls too, best pondered over with a fruity muffin and a bottle of Victrola's new, super-cool Lake Party Cold Brew.

THINGS TO DO NEARBY

Optimism Brewing Co
Switch from micro-roasted coffee to micro-brewed beer in this large, family-friendly taproom overshadowed by huge beer vats and permeated by the hop-heavy aromas of good craft-brewed suds.
www.optimismbrewing. com

Lost Lake Cafe & Lounge
You'll find a damned fine cup o' coffee in this *Twin Peaks*-themed diner and, if you're lucky, cherry pie too.
www.lostlakecafe.com

Elliott Bay Book Company
The best independent book shop in Seattle is a large but cosy emporium of erudite writing which, with its flop-down chairs and on-site cafe, encourages lingering.
www.elliottbaybook.com

Wall of Sound
A bedroom-sized vinyl shop staffed by experts and dedicated to esoteric subgenres you'd struggle to find anywhere else.
www.wosound.com

Seattle's Victrola cafes are like a rare vinyl record by your favourite band. There are only three of them, but they are all worth crossing town for. Even better, two of them are in the city's fashionable Capitol Hill neighbourhood.

The East Pike Street establishment, the second Victrola cafe to open, in 2007, is housed in a former car showroom with picture windows and a large streamlined interior. It

ZEITGEIST COFFEE

171 S Jackson St, Seattle, Washington;
www.zeitgeistcoffee.com; +1 206 583 0497

◆ Food ◆ Cafe
◆ Shop ◆ Transport

THINGS TO DO NEARBY

Klondike Gold Rush National Historical Park
Before hipster stubble, the beards in these streets belonged to feverish stampeders embarking on the 1898 Klondike Gold Rush. This museum relates their story.
www.nps.gov/klse

Smith Tower
Once Seattle's tallest building but a mere dwarf amid today's skyscrapers, this 1914-vintage tower is still an architectural beauty inside and out, and was recently reopened after a renovation.
www.smithtower.com

Occidental Square
Lovely red-bricked square with creeping ivy, resident food carts, noble statues and a liberal smattering of games, including cornhole and table tennis, available for public use.

CenturyLink Field
This massive stadium hosts American football in the winter and soccer in the summer, and is known nationwide for the decibel level of its fans.
www.centurylinkfield.com

Possibly the best indie coffee bar in the city that practically invented them, Zeitgeist brews up some of Seattle's smoothest cups of joe to go with its luscious baked goods. The atmosphere is trendy industrial, with exposed brick walls and large windows ideal for observing the rich-meets-poor toing and froing of Seattle's historic Pioneer Square neighbourhood outside. Not that Zeitgeist is overtly fashion-conscious. With more than 20 years in the business, the cafe easily predates 21st-century hipsters with their Klondike-era beards and tattoos.

Zeitgeist's staying power is in its genes. Several of the cafe's founders went on to create other successful Seattle brands including Top Pot Doughnuts, now a small national chain with 18 outlets, and Sun Liquor, one of Seattle's first micro-distilleries. But perhaps the best thing about Zeitgeist is that it has spawned no copyists. It remains loftily unique.

Zeitgeist doesn't roast its own beans on-site. Instead, it sources them from a reliable local roaster and then lets its baristas grind and press them into the finest cuppings. Equally tasteful are the surroundings. The cafe acts as a de facto art gallery and is a major hub in Pioneer Square's monthly Art Walk.

For the full Zeitgeist experience, savour a doppio macchiato with a sweet almond croissant.

ONYX COFFEE LAB

7058 W Sunset Ave, Springdale, Arizona;
onyxcoffeelab.com; +1 479 419 5739

◆ Food ◆ Cafe
◆ Shop

Onyx Coffee Lab has a farm-to-cup mantra and a scientific method to its brews, both testaments to its third wave coffee ethos. Husband-and-wife owners Jon and Andrea Allen built the brand by creating one of the lightest brews in the region – roasting small batches of green beans with delicate notes, rather than extracting bold flavours. The original location in Springdale features a siphon bar, Kyoto cold-brew towers, a meeting room and a drive-through coffee bar for when it's too hot to leave the car. There are caffeinated cocktails on-site too, such as the Matcha Dark and Stormy, but the most popular order to sit and sip at the reclaimed wood tables is still a classic latte.

THINGS TO DO NEARBY

Tontitown Winery
Family-owned Italian style winery with free wine tastings every day of the week. It hosts live music on Fridays and Saturdays on its outdoor patio.
tontitownwinery.com

Waterside walk
Behind Onyx Coffee Lab is a lovely walkway that goes around a lake – perfect for a leisurely stroll post-coffee, or coffee in hand.

KALADI BROTHERS

315 South Kobuk St, Soldotna, Alaska;
kaladi.com; +1 907 262 5980

◆ Food ◆ Cafe
◆ Shop

This Alaskan classic enjoyed humble beginnings as a summer-only coffee cart in Anchorage. Despite the name, there are no brothers behind Kaladi Brothers' brew, but the company maintains a family atmosphere throughout its cafes, and has stayed true to classic coffee techniques rather than delving into third wave culture. The South Kobuk St coffee shop is a local favourite, with a ceiling covered in an eclectic array of artworks including Kaladi-inspired takes on Michelangelo's *Creation of Adam*, Andy Warhol's *Campbell's Soup Cans* and SpongeBob SquarePants. In addition to monthly art shows, it has music events on weekend evenings, which pair perfectly with cold-brew that you can take home in a growler after the show.

THINGS TO DO NEARBY

Soldotna Creek Park
Find breathtaking scenery of the natural Alaskan countryside at this park equipped with a kids' playground, plus events and live music year-round for everyone.

Bridge Lounge
Take a seat on the deck and light up a fireplace for a great night under the stars at this trendy lounge overlooking Kenai River.
www.facebook.com/ bridgelounge1

PRESTA

2502 N 1st Ave, Tucson, Arizona;
www.prestacoffee.com; +1 520 333 7146

◆ Roastery   ◆ Cafe
◆ Shop   ◆ Transport

It's difficult to believe Presta began life as a humble mobile coffee cart (known as Stella Java) parked at Tucson's St Mary's Hospital in 2012. What's more apparent from the moment you step into this sleek, minimalist, industrial building is owner Curtis Zimmerman's enthusiasm for cycling. Racing bikes line the walls of this airy space, accessed via a paved walkway along a nondescript rockery dotted with a few green desert plants. It's a studiously low-key welcome after the buzz of nearby 1st Ave; only the sandwich-board signage is a clue that you're close.

THINGS TO DO NEARBY

The Grill, Hacienda del Sol
See why Tucson is America's first Unesco world city of gastronomy at this romantic restaurant, once a hideaway of Tracy and Hepburn. *www.haciendadelsol.com*

Mission San Xavier del Bac
Known as the 'white dove of the desert', this blend of Moorish, Byzantine and Mexican Renaissance architecture glows amid its remote surroundings (see opposite).

Saguaro National Park
If you watched cartoons of roadrunners and coyotes as a child, the enormous cacti in this sprawling park will feel oddly familiar. Sunsets here are otherworldly. *www.nps.gov/sagu*

El Guero Canelo
Don't leave Tucson without an infamous Sonoran Hot Dog experience! Check out the hype at one of the four El Guero Canelo branches in town. *www.elguerocanelo.com*

Presta started roasting its own beans in late 2014 and moved into this site in 2015. (A second location that's more cafe than roastery, serving craft beer and wine, opened in the Mercado San Agustin in late 2016.) Take a seat at the communal table overlooking the patio and inhale the aromas from the blue Joper roaster as tunes from the record player compete with the hiss of steam. You might be tempted with the cold-brew from the nitrogenated tap, but a latte allows you to appreciate the art of the barista as well as the handmade rustic mugs in which it's served.

ESPRESSO MARTINI (UK)

Contemporary as far as classics go, the queen of coffee cocktails was invented by London bartender Dick Bradsell in the 1980s when a well-known model asked him for something to 'wake me up and f*** me up'.

60ml (2fl oz) vodka
35ml (1¼fl oz) fresh espresso
30ml (1fl oz) coffee liqueur
10ml (⅓fl oz) sugar syrup
coffee beans, to garnish

Shake all ingredients vigorously with ice then strain into a chilled martini glass. Garnish with a few coffee beans.

Hot, cold, tall, short – however you like them, coffee cocktails are the perfect excuse for a caffeine hit. Some are embedded in the history books while others are more recent creations, but they all have a story.

CAFFEINATED

CAFÉ BRULOT DIABOLIQUE (USA)

Translating to 'devilishly burnt coffee', this cocktail was invented at Arnaud's in New Orleans as a way to hide alcohol during Prohibition.

2 cinnamon sticks
10 whole cloves
peel of 1 lemon
1 orange, quartered
3 tbsp sugar
90ml (3fl oz) brandy
750ml (25fl oz) coffee

Simmer cinnamon, cloves, lemon peel, orange, sugar and brandy. Before it boils over, place in a bowl in front of guests and carefully ignite, stirring slowly until flames die out. Pour coffee into brandy and ladle mixture into demitasse or espresso cups.

WHITE RUSSIAN (Belgium)

Adding cream to a Black Russian, first made in 1949, creates this cocktail. Invented by a Belgian barman, the only thing Russian about this drink is the liberal use of vodka. It rose to fame in 1998 when cult film *The Big Lebowski* made it popular. Unlike The Dude's recipe, this version uses fresh coffee, as well as coffee liqueur.

ice cubes
60ml (2fl oz) vodka
60ml (2fl oz) Kahlua or other coffee liqueur
180ml (6fl oz) cooled coffee
180ml (6fl oz) single cream

Fill a tumbler with ice. Pour in vodka, liqueur and coffee and stir. Slowly add cream and serve.

COCKTAILS

MARIA THERESIA (Austria)

A Viennese speciality named in honour of Marie Antoinette's mother, the only female head of the Habsburg Dynasty, perhaps because she encouraged making schnapps to create tax revenue for the government.

3 tbsp orange liqueur
1 tbsp sugar
250ml (8½fl oz) coffee
whipped cream
zest from 1 orange, to garnish
grated dark chocolate, to garnish

Warm a coffee cup or glass with boiling water and discard after two minutes. Add liqueur and sugar to the cup and stir until dissolved. Stir in coffee, top with cream and sprinkle with orange zest and chocolate.

KAFFEPUNCH (Denmark)

Popular with Danes for staying awake during the festive season, *kaffepunch* comes from Fano, a tiny island off the Danish coast. The meaning is twofold: *kaffepunch* is served in punch glasses but it also packs a punch!

500ml (17fl oz) coffee
schnapps, to taste
2 tbsp sugar
peel from 1 orange

The instructions for *kaffepunch* are simple: place a coin in a coffee cup and add coffee until it's no longer visible. Then add schnapps until you can see the coin again. Alternatively, stir sugar into hot coffee until dissolved then top with schnapps and orange peel.

TOKYO

Japan has always embraced new trends, and coffee is no exception. Its capital is the place to go for the highest proliferation of third wave-style coffee shops, but be sure to round out your education with a visit to a traditional *kissaten*.

CHIANG MAI

Thailand's northern city of temples has exploded with coffee shops, many having the added bonus of serving single-origin roasts grown within just an hour or two of the coffee shop itself. Coffee tourists will be spoiled for great music, food and street life.

IPOH

Ipoh's signature white coffee is famously hot, sweet and almost buttery in taste, and has spawned a chain of cafes that has found its way around Malaysia. For the authentic stuff, Sin Yoon Loong is adored for following the traditional recipe.

INDONESIA

How to ask for a coffee in the local language?
Boleh minta kopi satu

Signature coffee style? Kopi Tubruk – finely ground coffee beans or powder are mixed directly in a cup of boiling water, with sugar often added automatically

What to order with your coffee? Sweet, sticky multi-coloured kue lapis rice cakes such as klepon (green rice balls filled with liquid palm sugar and coated with grated coconut)

Don't: Be surprised if your coffee is served in a cup with a lid – it's to stop flies and insects falling in

The island of Java's name has been transformed into a popular generic for any kind of coffee, but few people realise the importance of this sprawling equatorial archipelago in the story of what locals call *kopi*. Indonesia was one of the first places outside Ethiopia and Arabia to grow coffee, introduced by the Dutch colonial administration in the early 1800s. Today it is the world's fourth-largest producer, with more than a million sq km of plantations and organic smallholdings, spread across not just Java but Sumatra, Papua, Flores and Sulawesi.

Each island's beans are known to baristas across the globe for their particular personality; from Sulawesi's nutty, warm spicy flavour to intense Sumatran coffee, with cocoa and tobacco notes, and the rare Old Java, an aged coffee made from beans stored for up to five years. For the most part, all these specialist gourmet varieties head straight for the export market.

Until recently, most locals have been happy sipping a tiny glass of their favourite *Tubruk*, a muddy, sweet brew, in one of the murky *Warung Kopi* that sit on every street corner. But third wave barista-led speciality coffee bars are finally opening up in all the major cities, promoting Indonesia's distinctive home-grown varieties. We'd suggest avoiding the controversial *Kopi Luwak*, though. Hyped as the world's most expensive and finest coffee, *Luwak* get its distinctive earthy, smooth taste from beans that have passed through the systems of sadly exploited palm civet cats, which love to eat the coffee berries. Fine when these animals live in the wild, but today many are kept in atrocious conditions or used for tourist sightseeing. Fortunately Indonesia boasts a host of other wonderful brews to choose from.

SENIMAN COFFEE STUDIO

5 Jalan Sriwedari, Ubud, Bali;
www.senimancoffee.com; +62 361 972 085

◆ Food   ◆ Classes   ◆ Cafe
◆ Roastery ◆ Shop   ◆ Transport

Bali's cultural capital Ubud has become the island's foodie and coffee capital, and Seniman Coffee Studio, behind Ubud Palace, is the real seed-to-cup deal when it comes to craft coffee. The cafe has the feel of a bohemian clubhouse where animated baristas pull espressos for curious tourists, locals and expats, and coffee professionals and barmen hang out with restaurant chefs. Across the road is a cold-brew bar where brewing and cupping workshops are held, while the Diedrich roaster is overseen by Balinese I Kadek Edi, who brings the same creativity to his roasting as he did to his former woodcarving profession.

Seniman's reputation has been forged by promoting plantations across the islands of the Indonesian archipelago, and particularly by encouraging the coffee growing right here in Bali. What makes the cafe so cool is that everyone is made to feel at home, from committed coffee connoisseurs who come to try a speciality Bali Karana Kintamani, grown in the highlands, to streetfood lovers who adore the *soto ayam* chicken broth and crème brûlée espresso, or the cocktail crowd ordering Espresso Martinis. Grab one of the reclaimed teak rocking chairs, check out the current art exhibition, explore the tempting store filled with upcycled glassware and coffee tasting trays. With free wi-fi and magazines to browse, don't be surprised to spend half the day here. And do try the Ice Black, where a blend of Sumatra Gayo, Bali Pulp Natural and Fully Washed beans is brewed for 8 to 10 hours using cold water and ice.

THINGS TO DO NEARBY

Museum Puri Lukisan
On Ubud's main street, the island's oldest museum exhibits an unparalleled collection of traditional and modern Balinese paintings, set in lush gardens with a lotus pond.

Ubud Royal Palace
Still the official residence of the ruler of Ubud, the grounds and temple are open to the public, a magical venue for Balinese dance and gamelan performances.

Ubud Market
Before 9am this is a teeming food market packed with live chickens, exotic fruit spices and streetfood stalls. Then everything disappears, to be replaced by tourist souvenir stalls.

John Hardy Ubud Workshop
Book ahead for the free tour of this workshop, where skilled local artisans design and craft intricate jewellery in a lush compound of bamboo and adobe buildings.
www.johnhardy.com/bali-boutique

JAPAN

How to ask for a coffee in the local language?
Kōhī o kudasai
Signature coffee style? Pour-over
What to order with your coffee? Toast
Do: Be patient. Coffee-pouring in Japan is an exacting
and invariably slow process

When people in Japan talk about 'first wave',
they're most likely referring to *kissaten*, which
was the word for coffee shop long before the foreign
'cafe' entered the national lexicon. When they first began
appearing in the early 20th century, *kissaten* were portals
into an exotic world and carried a whiff of the demi-
monde. Today the word is used to describe a coffee shop
that embraces an aesthetic and taste that predates the
arrival of mass-market chains.

In a *kissaten*, the interior may have art deco or
mid-century touches (often because it's that old). The
coffee is prepared one cup at a time, by a measured pour-
over (or sometimes a siphon). The house blend (*burendo
kōhī* in Japanese) will likely be a dark roast, served in
a small, dainty cup, always with a saucer, teaspoon and a
dollhouse-sized pitcher of cream that holds just enough to
turn your single serving into that perfect shade of caramel.

Another *kissaten* staple is the 'morning set' (*mōningu
setto*), which usually includes a hardboiled egg and fluffy,
thick-sliced toast with a cup of coffee – for around the
same price as a cup any other time of the day. Served from
opening until 11am, this set is one of Japan's great bargains.

But it's never just about the food and drink. *Kissaten* are
individually owned and the personality of the 'master' or
'mama' (as the proprietors are called) is always on show; to
run a coffee shop in Japan is an act of creative expression,
and one to which many aspire. James Freeman, founder of

California's wildly successful Blue Bottle Coffee, has often
credited Japanese *kissaten* as an inspiration.

Inversely, Japan has embraced the third wave coffee
movement with great enthusiasm. Every city now has an
indie roaster, even though, in a typically tiny shop, the
roaster might take up a third of the square footage. Many
roasters and baristas come to Tokyo to study and practise
and then return to their hometowns to spread the gospel
of coffee as a way of life.

The second wave has been a success here, too; the
country has more than 1200 Starbucks as well as half-a-
dozen local chains, like Doutor, that are equally ubiquitous.
In urban Japan, where families live in tight quarters with
minimal privacy, these brightly lit, anonymous chain

TOP 5 COFFEES

- **Bear Pond Espresso** Flower Child
- **Glitch Coffee & Roasters** Ethiopia Alaka Washed
- **Maruyama Coffee** Geisha Blend for Iced Coffee
- **Morihiko** No 1
- **Cafe de L'Ambre** House Blend

CAFE TALK – KIYOKASU SUZUKI

There's a new generation coming up who are interested in the potential of green beans. They're going out into the fields

cafes function as an important liminal space free from the pressures of home, work or school.

A few other points to note: iced coffee is popular in Japan and you'll often be asked if you want your drink hot or iced (the latter will be served with a packet of gum syrup for sweetening). And while most cafes also serve black tea and juice, one thing you won't likely find on the menu is green tea. That's drunk either at home, in a dedicated teahouse, or purchased, in a chilled bottle, from the convenience store.

Convenience stores and vending machines are also the places to try canned coffees (*kan kōhī*). While these don't win any awards for taste, the syrupy concoctions associated with middle-aged salarymen are another classic element of Japanese coffee culture and a must-try.

MARUYAMA COFFEE

Karuizawa, Nagano;
www.maruyamacoffee.com; +81 267 42 7655

◆ Food   ◆ Cafe
◆ Shop

Karuizawa is an old hill station in Nagano, 100 miles northwest of Tokyo, where the rich elite built their summer homes in the 19th century. It retains an unflappable cool, now with antique shops, craft boutiques, juice bars and Maruyama Coffee, a leader in the indie roaster movement since 1991 and, more recently, a source of excellent beans. Owner Maruyama Kentarō spends a good part of the year on the road and in the field.

At any given time, there are some 30 single-origin coffees on the menu. Maruyama prepares its coffee with a simple French press, to demonstrate that there's no sleight of hand involved; you too could make this at home. Visit in the summer – when most people do – and pick up some seasonal 'coffee jelly' sold at the attached shop.

THINGS TO DO NEARBY

Kyū-Karuizawa Ginza
The heart of old Karuizawa, this strip is the place to browse for locally made artisan goods and sample the bounty of area farms.
karuizawa-ginza.org

Harunire Terrace
A collection of boutiques and restaurants spread out over a riverside terrace in the woods of Karuizawa, part of the ultra-luxe Hoshino Resort. *www. hoshino-area.jp*

ROKUYŌSHA CHIKATEN

Kawaramachi-dōri, just south of the junction
with Sanjō-dōri, Kyoto; +81 75 241 3026

◆ Food ◆ Shop ◆ Transport
◆ Roastery ◆ Cafe

Rokuyōsha Chikaten, in business since 1950 and
arguably Kyoto's most famous coffee shop, is like
the platonic ideal of a *kissaten*. The long, narrow shop,
reminiscent of a railway car, is panelled in mahogany-
stained wood; the seats are low, quilted vinyl banquettes.
On each table there is a glass sugar jar and a ceramic
ashtray made in Kyoto.

Beans are ground to order. Water from a carafe is
poured, a little at a time, over a paper filter. Between
pours, the barista (though you wouldn't call them that

here) warms the carafe over the flame of a gas hob. Order
the house blend. Pair it with a doughnut made in-house by
the owner's wife – just don't come too late in the day, as
they often sell out.

THINGS TO DO NEARBY

Nishiki Market
Kyoto's centuries-old
covered food market
(see below) has dozens
of vendors selling local
specialities such as
pickles, cured fish and
rice crackers.

Pontochō
Don't miss an evening
stroll through one of
Kyoto's most atmospheric
streets. It's an old geisha
district, though the
wooden buildings now host
exclusive restaurants.

MORIHICO

26-2-18 Minami 2jo nishi, Chuo-ku, Sapporo, Hokkaidō;
morihiko-coffee.com; +81 11 622 8880

◆ Food ◆ Cafe
◆ Shop ◆ Transport

It started with a house, a charming wooden one secreted on an alley, built shortly after WWII. When 25-year-old designer Ichikawa Sōsuke happened upon it, he had recently finished work on a teahouse project. Perhaps, he thought, he could turn the house into a kind of salon for him and his friends. He bought it on spec, and spent the next three years labouring on the weekends to repair it.

Then he took a leap of faith and decided to indulge a long-held passion for coffee; the house became Morihico. More than two decades later, the cafe, shrouded in ivy, is a Sapporo institution – a symbol of the slow, simple life for which Japan's northernmost island, Hokkaidō, has become known. There are now several outlets around Sapporo, all different, and a roaster.

THINGS TO DO NEARBY

Sapporo Beer Museum
Learn about Japan's oldest beer brewer, aptly named Sapporo, inside the company's original brick factory (see left); follow it with cold pints in the attached beer garden. *www.sapporoholdings.jp*

Moiwa-yama Ropeway
Take the ropeway to the top of Moiwa-yama (531m) for views over Japan's fifth largest city. Best after dark. *www.sapporo-dc.co.jp*

Odori-kōen
The centre of life in Sapporo, this park is 13 blocks long, with art installations, fountains, lawns and excellent people-watching. Local festivals often take place here. *www.sapporo-park. or.jp/odori*

Ōkura-yama Ski Jump Stadium
Stare down the 133.6m slope created for the Sapporo Winter Olympics in 1972 and imagine yourself hurtling down it. Ski jump contests are still held here. *www.sapporowintersports museum.com*

Coffee here is hand-poured using what is called a 'nel drip' – a flannel filter shaped like a tea strainer, which the barista swivels with a well-practised turn of the wrist. Order a cup of Mori no Shizuku blend, only available at the original shop; the medium-dark roast mirrors perfectly the stain of the house-turned-cafe's beautifully restored exposed beams.

BEAR POND ESPRESSO

2-36-12 Kitazawa, Setagaya, Shimo-Kitazawa, Tokyo;
www.bear-pond.com; +81 3 5454 2486

◆ Shop   ◆ Transport
◆ Cafe

At Tokyo's famous Bear Pond, espresso is a matter of intense precision: owner Tanaka Katsuyuki (and only Tanaka) pulls a limited number of shots a day, and only until 1pm, on the La Marzocco FB80 machine he modified himself to extract exactly one half ounce of his signature 'angel stain' espresso, named after the streaks, thick like paint, that lash the sides of the white demitasse.

His tiny shop is in Shimo-Kitazawa, a neighbourhood known for its eccentric personalities. It's a good fit, as Tanaka definitely plays by his own rules – a characteristic which has earned him a reputation for surliness (his passion is coffee, not customer service). If you don't make the cut for the espresso, try Bear Pond's other signature drink, the Dirty – a delicately layered parfait of espresso and cold milk.

THINGS TO DO NEARBY

Haight & Ashbury
A Shimo-Kitazawa landmark and stylists' favourite, this vintage shop carries a century's worth of costume pieces and treasures.
haightandashbury.com

Nasu Oyagi
Local hangout 'Uncle Eggplant' serves Japanese-style curry with lots of spice (but not the hot kind), meat and veg.
+81 3 3411 7035

CAFÉ DE L'AMBRE

8 Chome-10-15 Ginza, Chuo, Tokyo;
www.h6.dion.ne.jp/~lambre; +81 3 3571 1551

◆ Roastery   ◆ Cafe
◆ Shop   ◆ Transport

THINGS TO DO NEARBY

Kabuki-za
Before or after coffee, catch a performance at Tokyo's only theatre dedicated to the centuries-old art of kabuki.
www.kabuki-za.co.jp

Akomeya
Hit up this food and kitchenware emporium for artisanal miso and soy sauce, and beautifully made cooking utensils.
www.akomeya.jp

Ginza Mitsukoshi
Trawl this classic Ginza department store for traditional ceramics and textiles, as well as tasty take-away in the basement food court.
mitsukoshi.mistore.jp

Shiseido Gallery
The cosmetic titan has long been a supporter of the arts; stop in to see exhibitions by contemporary artists, both local and international.
www.shiseidogroup.com/ gallery

Cafe de L'Ambre has a rare pedigree: Sekiguchi Ichirō first opened the shop in 1948, making it one of Tokyo's oldest remaining coffee shops. He's now more than 100, yet several days a week you can still see him, behind the window, roasting beans in small batches on an ancient Fuji roaster. Today, the shop is equal parts local gathering spot and pilgrimage destination.

Café de L'Ambre has a spectacular menu. First there are the aged beans – say a batch harvested from Bahia in 1973. Sekiguchi stumbled upon aged beans through the kind of accident that might not happen today: decades ago,

a shipment he ordered took five years to arrive. He roasted them anyway, and was pleased with the result; he's been experimenting ever since. A tireless tinkerer, Sekiguchi designed much of what is used in the shop, including the enamel kettles, copper pots and cups.

Then there are the speciality drinks, which reference a time before espresso machines became commonplace. L'Ambre's signature concoction is the No. 7 Blanc & Noir Queen Amber – house-blended coffee sweetened and chilled in a martini shaker before being served up in a champagne coupe with a river of cream floated on top.

GLITCH COFFEE & ROASTERS

1F 3-16 Kanda-Nishikicho, Jimbōchō, Tokyo;
glitchcoffee.com; +81 3 5244 5458

◆ Food   ◆ Shop   ◆ Transport
◆ Roastery   ◆ Cafe

Glitch stands apart from Tokyo's other third wave shops, by literally standing apart. Rather than picking an obvious location in one of the city's trendy indie coffee hubs, like Tomigaya or Kiyosumi, owner Suzuki Kiyokazu chose Jimbōchō, a neighbourhood more affiliated with coffee's first wave and a classic student haunt filled with universities, jazz bars and secondhand bookstores, in which to site his small shop. Glitch, opened in 2015, fits in nicely; Suzuki wants his shop to be a community hub and invites other shops to use his gleaming Probat roaster (which takes up nearly a quarter of the small premises). He personally favours a light roast; sample the hand-poured Ethiopia Alaka Washed, with notes of citrus and jasmine.

THINGS TO DO NEARBY

Imperial Palace East Garden
This Edo-era manicured garden (see below), with the ruins of a keep from an Edo castle, is the only part of the Imperial compound open freely to the public.
www.kunaicho.go.jp

Ohya Shobō
Don't miss this landmark, 135-year-old secondhand shop specialising in maps, guidebooks, comic and woodblock prints from Japan's Edo period (1603–1848).
www.ohya-shobo.com

LAOS

How to ask for a coffee in the local language?
Khony samadmi kafe dai dai kaluna
Signature coffee style? A strong black coffee served
with condensed milk
What to order with your coffee? Khao nom kok (sweet
coconut cakes)
Do: Remember to take your shoes off when entering
someone's home as a sign of respect – and never put
your feet up. It's considered the height of bad manners

Indonesia might be the best-known corner of
Southeast Asia when it comes to coffee (they don't
call it Java for nothing, you know), but it's not the only one.
The little land-locked nation of Laos has its own thriving
coffee industry too. Since being introduced during the French
colonial era, coffee has become an important source of
supplementary income for the country's farmers, and you'll
find coffee bushes growing everywhere – from large-scale
plantations down to a few trees growing in people's backyards.
The majority of Laotian coffee is Robusta, grown intensively to
supply the instant-coffee industry, but there's a growing move
towards higher-quality Arabica, with a focus on better beans and
more sustainable farming methods.

One of the country's most important coffee-growing areas is
the Bolaven Plateau, a large area of fertile volcanic highlands
which produces most of Laos' vegetables, including staples
such as rice and *manioc* (cassava), as well as the majority of its
coffee crop. Most people here still live a subsistence lifestyle,
with villages pooling crops as co-operatives in order to maximise
yield and secure the best prices. This is the way most of
Bolaven's coffee is produced, which means the emphasis tends
to be on quantity rather than quality, but with such an ideal
climate for coffee-growing, it surely won't be long before the
best Laotian coffee becomes more widely available overseas.

MYSTIC MOUNTAIN COFFEE

Bolaven Plateau;
+856 20 99 661 333

◆ Food   ◆ Shop
◆ Roastery   ◆ Transport

Just getting to Khamsone Souvannakhily's coffee farm is an adventure in itself. It's located high up on the Bolaven Plateau, several miles from the nearest village, so Khamsone himself will come down and pick you up in an antique Chinese-made jeep, rattling along the rough, rutted tracks all the way to his family-owned, organic coffee plantation.

Once you've arrived, Khamsone will take you through the coffee-making process, from growing and harvest to processing and roasting: he roasts every batch himself in an ancient cast-iron oven behind his house. You can join in with sorting the beans and watch the roaster in action, and then try the coffee over a traditional Laotian lunch inside his stilt house. Afterwards, you can hike local trails and visit nearby waterfalls before heading homewards – armed with a good supply of Khamsone's coffee, of course.

THINGS TO DO NEARBY

Tad Fane Waterfall
This impressive double waterfall drops 120m over a jungled slope, and looks like something out of *Jurassic Park*.

Paksong Market
This daily market is one of the biggest on the Bolaven Plateau, and is a great place to try local Laotian delicacies such as *khao poon* (noodle soup).

MALAYSIA

How to ask for a coffee in the local language?
Bagi saya satu kopi

Signature coffee style? Kopi ais – hot coffee poured into a big glass filled with ice cubes plus sugar and condensed milk; or Kopi Tarik, served at a Mamak (Indian) stall where milky coffee is aerated by pulling from one jug to another

What to order with your coffee? Toast with a runny boiled egg; 'roti canai', Indian flatbread with curry sauce; or 'nasi lemak', coconut-steamed rice with boiled egg, fried anchovies and sambal chilli paste

Do: Ask for 'kopi ais kurang manis' if you want your iced coffee to be less sweet

There are many issues that can divide Malaysia's multi-ethnic population of native Malays, Chinese and Indians, but they will all happily sit together 'chit-chatting' under a whirring fan in a *Kopi Tiam* over a cup of Malaysian coffee. These traditional cafes are the perfect introduction to the weird and wonderful world of coffee in Malaysia.

Only around 0.2% of the world's coffee is grown in the country, and the poor quality of local beans has long been disguised by adding all manner of ingredients during roasting – from sugar and margarine to ground wheat and burnt corn – to create a dark, heavy-bodied taste. And you can forget espresso machines or French pulls, the coffee is made by pouring boiling water through grounds held in a cloth sock filter. Then just for good measure, thick condensed milk and sugar are routinely added. As awful as this may sound, it becomes an acquired, almost addictive taste. If it doesn't, you can always order *kopi-O*, black coffee with sugar, or even unsweetened *kopi-O-kosong*, literally translated as 'coffee with nothing'.

Although these days every big Malaysian city is being converted to the craft coffee revolution, with exactly the same kind of hip barista bars and micro-roasteries opening up that you'd find in Sydney or San Francisco, only a tiny percentage of the population actually have the economic means to shell out for a flat white using expensive imported beans like Jamaica Blue Mountain. Fortunately, most Malaysians are more than happy with their very own *kopi*.

SIN YOON LOONG

15A Jalan Bandar Timah, Ipoh, Perak

◆ Food ◆ Cafe
◆ Roastery ◆ Transport

The phenomenon of Ipoh's white coffee took on a life of its own, spawning a Malaysia-wide cafe chain called OldTown White Coffee, with no link to the humble cafe that first brewed the recipe. However, Malaysian foodies continue to pile into ramshackle Sin Yoon Loong (as well as nearby coffee shops with suspiciously similar names).

After the trouble of fighting for a plastic chair, only the signature drink – white coffee – should grace your lips. And somehow, it tastes all the better when served in a traditional blue-and-white ceramic cup.

THINGS TO DO NEARBY

Street Art Trail
Renowned Lithuanian street artist Ernest Zacharevic created murals of coffee bags, pomelo fruit and a huge hummingbird; head to Jalan Panglima and follow the signs.

Kong Heng Block
Browse handmade souvenirs at the craft shops occupying this elegantly weathered block, and stick around for icy desserts; it's the ultimate hangout for Ipoh's art-loving crowd.

Lou Wong Chicken Beansprouts
This purveyor of Ipoh's signature dish – supple poached chicken served with plump beansprouts – is an even more popular epicurean pilgrimage site than Sin Yoon Loong.

Ipoh Train Station
Locals refer to the white-domed train station as Ipoh's Taj Mahal, and understandably so: this photogenic building is a masterpiece of early 20th-century Raj-style architecture.

Within a scruffy shophouse in Ipoh, a legendary Malaysian coffee has been perfected. Peer behind Sin Yoon Loong's green blinds and you'll see only a canteen, where plastic seats spill from a chipped-tile interior on to the pavement. But Sin Yoon Loong doesn't need style: it's in this humble *kopitiam* (coffee shop) that the famous 'Ipoh white coffee' was created, a double hit of sugar and caffeine that's slurped to this day. Coffee beans are roasted in margarine to give them a buttery taste. The resulting coffee is creamy, almost soup-like and best served with a sweetening splash of condensed milk.

BLACK BEAN COFFEE AND TEA

87 Ewe Hai St, Kuching, Sarawak;
+60 8242 0290

◆ Roastery   ◆ Cafe
◆ Shop   ◆ Transport

It can be quite a problem getting somewhere to sit in Kuching's most popular craft coffee shop, but that's hardly surprising as the minuscule Black Bean cafe only has three tables. In the heart of the old colonial city, its passionate owner and roaster, Jong Yian Chang, has converted a classic Chinese shophouse into a showcase for Borneo's homegrown coffee. The decidedly unhip decor consists of a few faded photos, a rickety wooden counter and tall tropical plants on the terrace.

What makes Black Bean so special is its use of a coffee grown in Sarawak plantations surrounded by Borneo's ancient rainforest. The bean is Sarawak Liberica, cultivated by sustainable smallholder farmers, primarily from the Bidayuh and Iban indigenous tribes, once better-known for their ferocious headhunting traditions. The beans are sun-dried, producing smooth, mellow coffee, low in acidity, with a marked exotic aroma. There are a lot of other choices on the menu, from Sarawak and Java Robusta to Tanzanian and Kenyan Arabica, but once you taste a double espresso of craft Sarawak Liberica you won't want to drink any other coffee while in Kuching. Or try a Condensed Milk Ice Blended, a Sarawak Liberica espresso shot and condensed milk, blended with ice.

If smitten, Chang offers a range of coffee-related activities, from tasting and cupping classes to longer workshops for aspiring cafe owners and day trips to the interior plantations.

THINGS TO DO NEARBY

Old Court House Building
The grand colonial courthouse has been transformed into Kuching's cultural hub, with hip cafes and bars, art exhibitions, theatre and live music.

Top Spot Food Court
Scores of stalls in this seething rooftop food court serve hundreds of hungry diners each night. Sit with the locals and feast off giant prawns, jungle vegetables and curried fish.

Sampan ferry
Walk down to the waterfront and take the sampan ferry which rows people back and forth across the wide Sarawak river. Perfect at sunset.

Sarawak Museum
Founded in 1891, the museum has barely changed, and contains tropical flora and fauna and insights into the culture of local indigenous tribes. *www.museum. sarawak.gov.my*

SINGAPORE

How to ask for a coffee in the local language?
One kopi please

Signature coffee style? Kopi (coffee with condensed
milk), kopi-o (black coffee with sugar) or kopi-c (coffee
with evaporated milk)

What to order with your coffee? Kaya toast. Rich coconut
jam is slathered with a thick chunk of butter between
two wafer-thin slices of toast

Do: What the locals do. If you're having coffee in
a hawker centre or food court, reserve your seat
(chope in Sing-lish) by placing a packet of tissue
paper on the chair or table. This way you can get
your coffee and food with a seat guaranteed

Coffee in Singapore has long been served in the
ubiquitous hawker centres and food courts that dot
the country. And it's cheap compared to the big chains and
speciality coffee shops – you can easily get a caffeine fix
here for US$1. Don't expect silky milk lattes or rich espressos
though; Singaporeans love their coffee dark, oily and sweet,
usually made from robusta beans roasted with margarine or
butter and sometimes sugar. If you want a taste of true local
coffee, order a *kopi* (coffee with condensed milk), *kopi-o*
(black coffee with sugar) or *kopi-c* (coffee with evaporated
milk). If you can't take sweet coffee, you can order the latter
two without sugar; just ask for it to be made *kosong* (which
literally translates as zero).

The brew method itself is worth watching. Ground
coffee is placed into a cloth 'sock'. Hot water is then
poured through the sock into a long-necked metal coffee
pot, with the coffee steeping inside. When you order a
coffee, it is poured into a cup and 'cut' with hot water. It's
an age-old method in the city. But Singapore, like many
affluent cities, is experiencing a speciality coffee boom.

With an international outlook and many bright young things
returning from universities in places such as Melbourne,
Sydney and London, you can now easily find great speciality
coffee in the city. And it's a trend that looks set to continue
despite soaring rents, with excellent roasteries and cool
cafes from hole-in-the-walls to uber hipster hangouts
popping out of the woodwork everywhere.

CHYE SENG HUAT HARDWARE

150 Tyrwhitt Rd, Jalan Besar, Singapore;
www.cshhcoffee.com; +65 6396 0609

◆ Food ◆ Classes ◆ Cafe
◆ Roastery ◆ Shop ◆ Transport

Run by the folks who started Papa Pahleta, one of Singapore's earliest speciality coffee roasteries and retailers, CSHH is now arguably Singapore's most successful cafe. The setting – a tasteful modern renovation – inside a former hardware and metal-working store is perfect for slugging back espressos and watching the world go by. Coffees here are made with beans roasted on-site and sourced from farms around the world. Choose an espresso, a pour-over or even a nitro cold-brew. If the coffee bug bites, sign up for a range of coffee classes – from cupping to latte art. CSHH applies its attention to detail to substantial meals too – such as a pan-roasted Iberico pork rack for lunch. Oh, and if you fancy something harder than coffee, the courtyard is home to the Beer Stall.

THINGS TO DO NEARBY

Tyrwhitt General Company
Just up the stairs from CSHH, this shop-workshop sells handcrafted goods such as wallets. Sign up for leather crafting, calligraphy or soap- and candle-making classes.
thegeneralco.sg

National Museum of Singapore
Learn about Singapore's history and food in this slick, modern museum (see below) before heading out the back for a walk through idyllic Fort Canning Park.
nationalmuseum.sg

© Kenny Teo Photography / Getty Images

COMMON MAN COFFEE ROASTERS

22 Martin Rd, #01-00, Singapore;
www.commonmancoffeeroasters.com; +65 6836 4695

◆ Food   ◆ Shop   ◆ Transport
◆ Classes   ◆ Cafe

Steps to opening a successful cafe-roastery in Singapore: combine popular Aussie barista Harry Grover with Australia's Five Senses Coffee, and get bankrolled by an entrepreneur with the Midas touch, Cynthia Chua (who made a mint opening a chain of successful spas, and started dabbling in food and beverage establishments).

Blazing like a shooting star on to the Singapore coffee scene in 2013, CMCR has enchanted locals with its buzzy contemporary vibe, extensive all-day brunch menu and, of course, its range of seasonal coffees, roasted in-house.

Its growth has continued unabated. In 2015, CMCR opened its first Academy, supported by the Australian Barista Academy, offering a plethora of coffee-related courses. It has been actively involved in industry events, organising cupping sessions and the Singapore AeroPress Championships. In 2016, soaring demand culminated in

THINGS TO DO NEARBY

STPI
The Singapore-Tyler Print Institute has been hosting residencies and attendant exhibitions for renowned artists since 2002. Alumni include David Hockney and Do Huh Suh.
www.stpi.com.sg

Asian Civilisations Museum
Housed in a gorgeous Colonial-era building, the ACM takes you on a journey through the art, culture and religions of the region.
acm.org.sg

The Quays
Robertson, Clarke and Boat Quays were once the lifeblood of the river trade in Singapore. Today they're a mix of posh apartments, eateries and bars.

Tiong Bahru
Singapore's 'it' neighbourhood draws hipsters from near and far with its art deco sensibilities and range of cool bars, restaurants and boutiques selling books, handicrafts and fashion.

CMCR moving its roastery off-site – and adding a 45kg roaster alongside the old 6kg faithful! Most recently, CMRC opened a slick outpost in Kuala Lumpur, Malaysia.

The cafe floor often mirrors CMCR's meteoric rise. If the bling and buzz get too much, we recommend you pop upstairs to Grounded, CMCR's cosy offshoot. You get the same great coffee with retro-oriented furnishing and views out to leafy surroundings.

NYLON COFFEE ROASTERS

4 Everton Park, #01-40, Singapore;
www.nyloncoffee.sg; +65 6220 2330

◆ Roastery ◆ Cafe
◆ Shop   ◆ Transport

Founded by life partners Dennis Tang and Jia Min Lee in 2012 after they returned from work in New York and London (hence NY-LON, geddit?), this cafe is a passion project from which great coffee is roasted and brewed for the increasingly sophisticated Singaporean palate.

Regulars and locals drop by for their coffee hits, a chat with the baristas and perhaps a bag of freshly roasted Ethiopian Mokanisa; all beans are roasted on-site on restored roasters and brewed by AeroPress, pour-overs or espresso machines. But a large part of what Nylon does happens behind the scenes. The owners take multiple trips to farms and cooperatives around the world to source their green coffee beans. So no, you won't find any food on offer here, for Nylon remains firmly about the bean.

THINGS TO DO NEARBY

Chinatown
Buzzy Chinatown is a 15-minute walk away. Check out the Chinatown Complex food centre for some local coffee and a slice of local life.

Hong Kong Soya Sauce Chicken Rice & Noodle
The queues are long, but the excellent chicken rice is why Michelin inspectors awarded this place a star. It's also cheap: US$3 per plate. *78 Smith Street*

THAILAND

How to ask for a coffee in the local language?
Kaw kafaa kaa ou nueng krap
Signature coffee style? Cloth 'sock' filtered coffee
What to order with your coffee? Thai sweets or savoury
Chinese snacks
Do: Chase your cup with a shot of weak Chinese tea

Think caffeinated beverages in Thailand, and most people picture Thai tea, the orange, milky, sweet beverage, generally drunk cold, that has travelled far beyond the country's borders. But few are aware that Thailand has a low-key but long-standing legacy of coffee drinking.

It was Chinese immigrants who introduced coffee culture to the southern and central parts of the country. The beans, which were grown abroad, were roasted until practically burnt, typically with sugar. The brewing method – still employed in old-school places today – was a cone-shaped

cloth bag that held the grounds and through which hot water was poured. The resulting coffee – bitter, fragrant and dark as night but lacking body – was typically poured into small glass tumblers pre-loaded with a few tablespoons of sweetened condensed milk and perhaps a teaspoon of sugar. To drink, the Thais swirl these elements together with a tiny aluminium spoon, sip, and follow with the tumbler of weak Chinese tea that's always provided as a chaser.

At least that's how it used to be. In recent years, Thailand's coffee scene has become just about as sophisticated as anywhere in the world – in the larger cities, anyway. These days, high-quality coffee beans are grown in the northern- and southernmost parts of the country, roasted domestically, and served in drinks. In small villages, you're likely to find an espresso machine, although it must be noted that these days the majority of Thais prefer their coffee sweetened and served over ice – just like that Thai tea.

ROCKET COFFEEBAR

Sathorn Soi 12, Bangkok;
www.rocketcoffeebar.com; +66 2 635 0404

◆ Food   ◆ Cafe
◆ Shop

THINGS TO DO NEARBY

Wat Pho
Bangkok's holiest – and
most visited – temple is
just a few blocks away.
Look out for the 46m-long
Reclining Buddha, swathed
in gold leaf.

Lumphini Park
An oasis of greenery among
the high-rises and office
blocks, with walkways,
ponds, trees and even
a monitor lizard or two.

Chao Praya river
Take a long-tail boat-trip
down Bangkok's great
river, a thrumming artery
of water that still carries
impressive amounts of
passenger traffic.

Wat Arun
The Temple of Dawn is
an unmissable landmark
on the Thonburi side of
the river.

There are no two ways about it – in terms of the
hipster coffee aesthetic, Rocket is the place in
Bangkok that has it all. Denim-aproned baristas pour from
Hario jugs into porcelain V60s set on the coffee station.
Beautiful Bangkokers sip flat whites at pavement tables,
or browse the counter for baked goods. Light streams in
through the windows, flooding an interior full of sleek wood,
dangling lightbulbs and Scandi-inspired furniture. And the
brunch menu of breakfast waffles, oat-rye porridge, Nordic
smørrebrod and acai bowls couldn't be more on-trend.

Rocket now has two locations across the city: this, the
original street cafe at Sathorn Soi 12, a few blocks from the
Chao Praya River, and a flashier new space at Sukhumvit
Soi 49, just off the city's main thoroughfare. We prefer the
original for its downtown location, but the coffee's good at
whichever address you choose: single-origin and sourced
from producers in Colombia, Ethiopia and Thailand. The
cafe bombón – a classic Thai coffee made with espresso and
sweetened condensed milk – is definitely an acquired taste,
but when Bangkok's infamously sticky weather gets too
much, don't sweat it: the Rocket boys and girls brew up
a killer iced latte, too. Rocket – we have lift-off.

ROOTS COFFEE

Thonglor 17, 55 Sukhumvit Rd, Bangkok;
www.rootsbkk.com; +66 97 059 4517

◆ Food　　◆ Shop
◆ Roastery　◆ Cafe

 Bangkok has an expanding line-up of espresso bars, but roasteries are still thin on the ground – largely because Roots has it covered. Supplying many of the city's cafes, hotels and restaurants, this micro-roastery was founded in 2011 and has made a name for itself across the city, and the rest of Thailand too.

There's an emphasis on Thai beans from areas such as Jaroon, Pa Hom Pok and Pangkhon, a rare chance to sample unusual coffees that are difficult to find outside Thailand; a good one to sample is the coffee from Huay Nam Khun, produced in Chiang Rai using the Freezer Honey method, which maximises sweetness and fruitiness.

The cafe itself is studiously uncluttered, heavy on concrete and wood, and its location couldn't be hipper, right in the middle of the Commons, a newly established collective of food stalls, delis, bakers, artisans and producers.

THINGS TO DO NEARBY

The Commons
With its tagline of 'building a wholesome community', this co-op enterprise offers a respite from Bangkok's relentless modern malls, with four spaces: market, village, play-yard and top yard. *thecommonsbkk.com*

Rot Fai Market Ratchada
Bangkok's newest Train Market is a super place to browse for clothes, crafts, collectables and kitschy knick-knacks, and has some fantastic food stalls. *www.bangkok.com*

AKHA AMA

Hussadhisewee Rd, Soi 3 Chang Phuak, Chiang Mai;
www.akhaama.com; +66 86 915 8600

◆ Roastery ◆ Cafe
◆ Shop

This cafe in temple-heavy Chiang Mai comes with a strong social angle. The Akha are one of many hill tribes found in northern Thailand, and for several decades have been producing coffee near the village of Maejantai, in Chiang Rai Province. The cafe was the brainchild of an Akha woman who wanted to provide a conduit for local farmers to sell, process and promote their coffee (*Ama* means mother in the Akha language, and her portrait now graces the cafe's logo). Using only Arabica beans and 100% organic farming methods, Akha's coffees are the definition of small-scale and sustainable. The cafe itself is simple (plain furniture, minimal frills) but it's a world away from the chains, and its coffee tastes good (try the *shakerato* – a double espresso made in an ice-filled cocktail shaker) – and does good, too.

THINGS TO DO NEARBY

Wat Phra Singh
Chiang Mai's most revered temple, which is arranged around a mosaic-covered inner sanctuary, is especially venerated for its 'Lion Buddha'.

Chiang Mai Night Bazaar
For bargain-basement souvenirs, this raucous, crowded and chaotic night market is just the ticket. Don't be afraid to haggle hard. *Thanon Chang Khlan*

YU CHIANG

112 Thanon Rama VI, Trang;
+66 75 218 106

◆ Food   ◆ Transport
◆ Cafe

THINGS TO DO NEARBY

Night Market
Trang's nightly convocation of commerce and regional cuisine is one of the best in southern Thailand.

Ko Ngai
This jungly island, ringed by coral and clear water, is an easy snorkelling destination from Trang.

Ko Muk
Sugar-white sands and limestone cliffs converge to make Ko Muk the ideal of the Thai island. Tham Morakot, a cave that ends in a cliff-walled beach, is a highlight.

Ko Libong
The most rural of the islands near Trang, Ko Libong is known for its Muslim fishing community and its native population of manatee-like dugongs.

The birthplace of contemporary Thai coffee culture is arguably the country's south. It was to this part of the country that Chinese immigrants introduced coffee shops, known locally as *rahn go þii*, that bring together dark, smoky coffee, Thai sweets and some noteworthy savoury snacks.

Trang, an otherwise sleepy town in the south of the country, is a virtual time capsule of southern Thai coffee culture. Today, the city remains home to several longstanding *rahn go þii*, many of which don't appear to have changed in decades. One of the best examples of the genre is Yu Chiang, a shop dating back at least 60 years, its age evident in its faded turquoise paint, marble-topped tables and antique wooden chairs. Indeed, probably the

only thing older than the furnishings are the clientele, who still prefer their coffee brewed the old way: with water from a charcoal-fired, pot-belly stove poured through a cloth strainer into a glass that's holding a generous dollop of sweetened condensed milk.

But it's not just about the coffee at Yu Chiang. Arrive early in the morning and each table will be topped with a tray holding an array of Thai-style sweets, many of which are artfully wrapped in banana leaves, as well as some savoury items such as steamed Chinese buns. But the thing that makes Yu Chiang the epitome of the Trang-style *rahn go þii* is the slightly sweet, tooth-shatteringly crispy roast pork, which, along with the coffee, has become emblematic of the city.

VIETNAM

Vietnam is fuelled on strong, sweet coffee. The French brought coffee to the country in 1857 and today it's the second largest bean producer in the world. As in France, old and young sit in cafes facing the street, but in Vietnam they perch on small chairs and stools. Unfancy coffee shops pepper nearly every street in Vietnam, but Hanoi is the caffeine capital. Vietnamese people like to linger over their coffee and socialise, not just get their hit and run.

Robusta is the dominant bean in Vietnam. It's cheaper and easier to grow than Arabica beans, and is the bean that goes into the iconic pour-over *phin* device that makes the most popular Vietnamese brew, *ca phe sua da*. The slow drip filter is filled with ground Robusta and hot water and, over five minutes, coffee drips directly into the cup. Then ice and condensed milk are thrown in, an echo of when fresh milk was hard to come by. Robusta is a dark, strong roast so the sweetness is also a good match. Extreme flavours maybe, but on a scorching, drowsy day, the sweet freezing rush is a welcome jolt. Even without the milk, the coffee hints at caramel flavours, as the roasting mixture includes a touch of sugar and cocoa – flavours that linger.

Hanoi is home to some surprisingly tasty concoctions where milk is substituted for whipped egg or yoghurt. In modern HCMC too, palates are changing; Vietnam's largest city flaunts designer air-conditioned cafes to be seen in. For those who want to sip on a smooth Arabica-bean brew, the emerging craft coffee scene offers stylish shrines to the drink – and great taste to match.

K'HO COFFEE

Bonneur' C Village, near Dalat;
www.khocoffee.com

◆ Roastery ◆ Cafe
◆ Shop

10km-ride from Dalat by mototaxi; visitors are welcome
to tour the farm, sample the different types of coffee and
buy the beans.

K'Ho Coffee is a co-operative of coffee farmers made up of K'Ho families, an ethnic minority living in the forests of Vietnam's Central Highlands. While Vietnam is the world's largest producer of Robusta, this co-operative nurtures heirloom Arabica trees, planted in Vietnam by French colonists in the 1860s.

The co-operative was launched as a fair-trade initiative by Rolan Co Lieng, a fourth-generation coffee farmer, and Josh Guikema. Their mission is to preserve both K'Ho minority culture and the ecology of the Central Highlands through sustainable coffee production. K'Ho Coffee is a

THINGS TO DO NEARBY

Hang Nga Crazy House
A surrealist masterpiece of colourful, lava-flow-like shapes, with slim bridges bursting out of a tangle of greenery and unique rooms, this house is Gaudi-meets-Tolkien.
3 Đ Huynh Thuc Khang

Elephant Falls
Named after a rock that resembles the head of a pachyderm, these powerful falls are reached via steep, uneven stairs, moistened by the bracing spray.

GIANG CAFE

39 Nguyen Huu Huan St, Hoan Kiem, Hanoi;
www.giangcafehanoi.com; +84 98 989 2298

◆ Food   ◆ Cafe
◆ Shop   ◆ Transport

THINGS TO DO NEARBY

Hoa Lo Prison
Understand the French legacy beyond coffee at the former prison where Vietnamese political revolutionaries were tortured, later nicknamed 'Hanoi Hilton' by more comfortable US prisoners. **+84 24 3934 2253**

Thang Long Water Puppet Theatre
The stage is a pool of water with pyrotechnics, smoke and family friendly Vietnamese folk tales told through lacquered wood puppets set to live music and sing-song acting. **thanglongwaterpuppet.org**

Hanoi Social Club
A beautifully converted Vietnamese house hosts a multilevel hub of live music, art and events such as meditation with music, while serving excellent fusion food and Italian-style coffee. **fb.me/ TheHanoiSocialClub**

Hoan Kiem Lake
All roads in the Old Quarter lead to the chaotic weekend festival of families, lovers and visitors on paths that ring the lake.

On a street overflowing with semi-outdoor cafes in the Old Quarter, brave the dark hallway of Giang Cafe and climb the stairs to an indoor patio. Once there, sit on a wooden stool for Hanoi's classic *ca phe trung* – egg coffee – which is part drink and part dessert, with a fluffy head of actual whipped egg along with condensed milk, cheese and butter. It even comes with a sprinkle of powdered coffee for a cheeky texture difference. Sounds disgusting? Think liquid tiramisu and the experience is likely to be less alarming to your tastebuds.

The cup is served in a bowl of hot water to keep the egg coffee smooth and warm. Dip your spoon in and pull the coffee through the layers to catch the fascinating balance of flavours – sweet and almost custardy, though light and not eggy. As you do, sit back and let the antiquated fans above you take you back to 1946, the year the proprietor's father said he invented egg coffee. Fresh milk was hard to come by and beating up yolks was his creative substitute while working as a barman at Hanoi's finest hotel, the Sofitel Metropole. If the hot egg foam is too offputting, try the cold version, with enough ice to make it more like a smoothie, while still capturing the Vietnamese spin on coffee.

THE WORKSHOP

27 Ngo Duc Ke St, District 1, Ho Chi Minh City;
+84 28 3824 6801

◆ Food   ◆ Classes   ◆ Transport
◆ Roastery   ◆ Shop

Climb up and up the winding staircase to this loft cafe and coffee hub and you'll discover a designer-industrial workspace with even loftier aspirations as HCMC's first speciality roaster. The bright space and fashionable locals make it seem like it's just for show, but the coffee is consistently the most delicious around, and it's often abuzz with courses going on in coffee roasting, brewing and appreciation.

The workshop brews and serves coffee in more than a dozen ways, including using mix-and-match, experimental pour-over devices alongside the more tried-and-tested Kalita wave and V60. If you can't decide how to go, we'd say stay local with a single-origin Dalat latte, and a cold-brew shot on the side.

THINGS TO DO NEARBY

Pasteur Street Brewing Co
Follow speciality coffee with Vietnam's craft-beer leader. Get educated with a tasting paddle of six beers that might include a jasmine IPA, green tea ale and a strong coffee porter.
www.pasteurstreet.com

Central Post Office
A vision of Vietnam's oh-so fusion ways with a French Gothic and Renaissance interior, ATMs in antique wooden booths, and a grand mosaic of Ho Chi Minh himself.

KAFFEOST (Finland & Sweden)

Swapping cubes of sugar for cubes of cheese in coffee isn't as strange as it sounds in these Scandinavian countries. Curdled milk and rennet is baked until golden, cut into cubes the size of croutons and then put in an empty cup topped with black coffee. Think of it as the lumpy alternative to adding milk.

SEA SALT COFFEE (Taiwan)

Served at Taiwanese coffee chain Café 85°C, this bestselling beverage consists of a thick layer of salty cream on top of sweetened cold brew coffee. The taste-bud enlivening sea salt is said to 'open' the complex flavours of the coffee, and results in something of a multi-layered creamy, sweet and salty taste extravaganza.

If you've mastered nitro brew and ristretto, it's time to up your coffee game with these oddballs from the global coffee menu. That could mean sipping something that's cheesy, oily and probably lumpy – all in the name of authenticity.

COFFEE

BULLETPROOF COFFEE (USA)

Taking inspiration from the salty, and some say wet-sock-like, delights of Tibetan yak-butter tea, an American health specialist formulated this recipe for coffee mixed with grass-fed butter and coconut oil. Fans say the resultant frothy, oily drink suppresses appetite and improves concentration.

MONSOON MALABAR (India)

In the 19th century, Indian coffee plantations exported raw green beans to Europe on wooden barges. Over the six-month journey, the beans became fat with moisture and discoloured, but they made a fine cup of coffee with a discernible lack of acidity. Today the 'monsoon' effect is mimicked by leaving coffee seeds in burlap sacks out in the open air to absorb moisture.

KOPI CHAM (Malaysia)

Coffee? Tea? Why not have both together. This ruthlessly democratic drink, popular in Malaysia, is comprised of a mix of coffee and milky tea. It is also known as *yuenyeung*, meaning mandarin ducks in Chinese, a symbol of lifelong love between a couple.

CÀ PHÊ TRUNG (Vietnam)

A bartender introduced egg yolk coffee to Vietnam in the 1940s during a milk shortage. He whisked the yolk and then poured black coffee over the top, leaving the egg to swirl and sink to the bottom. Other variations include condensed milk, sugar and creamy white cheese. The result is a thick, silky drink that tastes more like dessert than breakfast.

ODDITIES

KOPI JOSS (Indonesia)

In the 1960s a local Javanese fellow known as 'Mr Man' plopped a piece of glowing charcoal into his coffee to alleviate stomach problems. It worked, and today in Yogyakarta near the main train station you can try both the original *kopi joss* and its imitations at roadside stalls.

CAFÉ BOMBON (Spain)

Part coffee, part dessert, this sickly sweet drink originated in the city of Valencia, and is comprised of equal parts espresso and condensed milk. Served in a glass rather than a cup, the drink is a pleasing spectacle of black and cream bands, until stirred into its creamy blend.

EUR

TOP 5 Coffee TOWNS

OPE

LONDON

Britain's capital has embraced speciality coffee, and here you'll find a range of styles as multicultural as the population – from Antipodean-owned chapels to the flat white and Italian stalwarts, to Ethiopian cafes offering a traditional coffee ceremony and upscale workers' cafes. Fear not, tea is always on the menu.

ISTANBUL

Nothing will immerse you quicker in the story of coffee and Turkish culture than a sip of its namesake thick textured and sweetened coffee – now inscribed on Unesco's list of Intangible Cultural Heritage. Add to that a passionate crew of third wave roasters and baristas, and you have a multi-layered coffee experience.

TURIN

The country that invented the espresso machine and brought coffee to Europe does not want for fantastically caffeinated hot-spots, but Turin gets the vote for its young, progressive vibe and willingness to experiment with new techniques alongside traditional Italian dark-roasted espresso.

OSLO

Scandinavians roast their beans light, and there is no roast lighter and fruitier than in Oslo. Baristas here treat roasting and brewing with the messianic precision and zeal of a Michelin-starred chef. In fact, there are restaurants in the city that also have in-house roasters. Begin your education at Tim Wendelboe's cafe.

VIENNA

No other city in the world has been shaped by coffee like the Austrian capital, where opulent cafes stay open until midnight to serve you a fat slice of history and cake on a little silver tray. Today a new breed of cafe is challenging the grand palaces by focusing on excellence in bean sourcing and coffee-making over decor.

AUSTRIA

How to ask for a coffee in the local language?
Ein Kaffee, bitte

Signature coffee style? Melange: the Viennese take
on a cappuccino, served with milk and sometimes
whipped cream

What to order with your coffee? A decadent slice of
kuchen/torte (cake)

Do: Wait to be seated in formal places; take your pick
of the tables in casual coffee houses

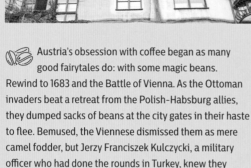 Austria's obsession with coffee began as many
good fairytales do: with some magic beans.
Rewind to 1683 and the Battle of Vienna. As the Ottoman
invaders beat a retreat from the Polish-Habsburg allies,
they dumped sacks of beans at the city gates in their haste
to flee. Bemused, the Viennese dismissed them as mere
camel fodder, but Jerzy Franciszek Kulczycki, a military
officer who had done the rounds in Turkey, knew they
had struck gold. The coffee beans were roasted and the
drink refined with milk and sugar. The Habsburgs and high
society went mad for it. And the rest, as they say, is history.

From those tiny beans grew an entire culture: coffee
houses began to pop up in Vienna and other Austrian
cities, and in poured the poets, philosophers, musicians
and artists. The *Kaffeehaus* became an extension
of society – a place to talk, read, write, dream, play
games and scoff fancy cakes. They were the apogee
of *gemütlichkeit*, the feeling of nostalgic warmth and
conviviality that belongs so utterly to Austria.

But as the country embraces the zeitgeist for single-
origin and small-batch roasts, things are changing. While
coffee is still served with a hefty slice of culture in coffee
houses that range from grungy to grand and boho to
rococo, the country has effectively come full circle, with
a new breed of micro-roasters and cafes once again
focusing on the magic of the beans...

220 GRAD

Chiemseegasse 5 (cafe), Maxglaner Hauptstrasse 29 (roaster), Salzburg;
www.220grad.com; +43 662 827 881

- ◆ Food
- ◆ Classes
- ◆ Cafe
- ◆ Roastery
- ◆ Shop
- ◆ Transport

The aroma of freshly ground and brewed coffee hits you like a crisp left hook as you step into 220 Grad, a little bubble of retro-cool style in a tucked-away corner of Salzburg's Old Town. Splashes of tangerine orange vamp up the cafe and decked terrace, where there is a mellow buzz any time of day except at breakfast, when it's as busy as a beehive.

220 Grad roasts its beans at a nearby roastery (yes, you can visit) and the name alludes to the ideal temperature for so doing. Skilled baristas whip up custom blends from South and Central America. The house blend, with notes of cocoa, hazelnut and caramel, is an excellent match for cakes like the avocado and chocolate torte. For the inside scoop, check out the regular three-hour coffee seminars.

THINGS TO DO NEARBY

Mozartplatz
Mozart, the city's most famous son, is literally and metaphorically put on a pedestal on this baroque square bang in the centre of the Old Town.

DomQuartier
The Residenz palace state rooms and gallery and the twin-spired Dom cathedral are the centrepieces of the DomQuartier in Salzburg's Unesco-listed baroque heart.

KAFFEE-ALCHEMIE

Rudolfskai 38, Salzburg;
www.kaffee-alchemie.at; +43 0681 20173143

- ◆ Food
- ◆ Cafe
- ◆ Shop
- ◆ Transport

Proof that there is always a pinch of alchemy involved in making great coffee, this nicely chilled cafe sits on the banks of the Salzach River, with a couple of sidewalk tables perfect for lingering over expertly crafted brews. The owner is none other than John Arild Stubberud, a Norwegian barista trainer and judge for the World Barista Championships and World Brewers Cup. It goes without saying that he knows his stuff, be it an AeroPress filter coffee or a light Scandinavian roast big on fruity, floral aromas.

John has scoured the globe from Ethiopia to El Salvador to rigorously source top-quality, Fairtrade beans from small-scale farms. Get him talking on his favourite subject and he might show you his coffee taster's flavour wheel. Sip a single-origin espresso brewed in a Marzocco GB5 or go off-piste with a subtle sweet coffee-leaf tea.

THINGS TO DO NEARBY

Residenzplatz
This stately baroque square is Salzburg's pride and joy, with its grand palace, street entertainers, horse-drawn carriages and enormous marble fountain, the Residenzbrunnen.

Salzburg Museum
Salzburg's flagship museum takes you on a fascinating romp through the city's past and present – from Roman ruins to glowering portraits of prince-archbishops.
www.salzburgmuseum.at

ALT WIEN KAFFEE

Schleifmühlgasse 23, Vienna;
www.altwien.at; +43 1 50 50 800

◆ Roastery ◆ Cafe
◆ Shop ◆ Transport

THINGS TO DO NEARBY

Naschmarkt

Vienna's Naschmarkt is a veritable feast of cafes, delis, kebab stands and food stalls selling everything from spices, cheeses and meats to exotic fruit and veg.

Secession

Topped by a lavish dome nicknamed 'the golden cabbage', this opened as the exhibition centre of Vienna's Secessionists in 1897. Its biggest draw is Klimt's exquisitely gilded Beethoven Frieze.
www.secession.at

Freihausviertel

This quaint, creative neighbourhood is at the heart of Vienna's hip and happening 4th district. Explore its cafes, workshops, galleries and delis on foot.

Otto Wagner

Viennese Jugendstil master Otto Wagner has left his indelible mark on the Wienzeile. Top billing on this sumptuous street goes to the Majolika-Haus at No 40, with its glazed ceramic tiles and flowing floral motifs.

Slip down a side street just back from the Naschmarkt and follow your nose to the tantalising aroma of Alt Wien. In 2014, the actual roastery was moved elsewhere in Vienna following complaints about the overpowering smell of coffee (to think it could cause offense!), but this remains one of the city's most outstanding places to drink a cup of joe. A coffee house in the truest sense, Alt Wien is the brainchild of Christian Schrödl, who since 2000 has invested time, energy and a whole lot of love into sourcing top-grade organic, Fairtrade beans. His mission? To make Vienna's very best coffee. Period.

Everything is angled towards the perfect cup. The shop at the front sells the good stuff in 250g and 500g bags, while the tiny bar at the back lets you sample a brilliant espresso for pocket-money prices. Christian is a purist, though: while he admits that taste in coffee is an individual matter and is not adverse to adding a splash of milk if you ask for it, he sees the 'latte scene' as watering down the true art of coffee-making. His baby is a Loring Kestrel roaster, which gives a smooth, golden, medium roast. Take-home varieties include the gourmet Jamaica Blue Mountain, with notes of cocoa, vanilla, almonds and tobacco, or the house blend Alt Wiener Gold, a full-bodied, nicely balanced Arabica.

KAFFEEFABRIK

Favoritenstrasse 4-6, Vienna;
www.kaffeefabrik.at; +43 660 178 9092

◆ Roastery ◆ Cafe
◆ Shop ◆ Transport

The small, whitewashed cafe-shop is emblematic of a place that likes to let the quality of the coffee speak for itself. Owner Tobias Radinger takes this responsibility personally – whether it's with a floral and acidic Guatemalan wet-processed roast, or a Sumatran Arabica that is full-bodied, spicy and chocolatey. Organic Austrian milk and non-dairy alternatives are available, while fruit juices from Burgenland bump up vitamin levels. Coffee heads might want to stock up on own-brand, attractively packaged coffees and the pro equipment for the job: ceramic slim mills, Hario V60 drip coffeemakers and the like.

THINGS TO DO NEARBY

Karlskirche
Standing proud on Karlsplatz, Vienna's most magnificent baroque church sports a huge elliptical copper dome and intricate frescoes by Johann Michael Rottmayr.
www.karlskirche.at

Musikverein
Every concert is an event at this resplendent concert hall, famed for having Austria's best acoustics and home to the Vienna Philharmonic.
www.musikverein.at

Wien Museum
Get a handle on Vienna's history from Neolithic times to the 20th century. Highlights include an Adolf Loos modernist living room and Secessionist works by Klimt and Schiele.
www.wienmuseum.at

Schloss Belvedere
Be floored by the extravagance of this baroque palace built for Prince Eugene of Savoy. Its frescoed halls are replete with artworks, while its landscape gardens command tremendous views of Vienna's skyline.
www.belvedere.at

If ever there was a sign that Vienna's coffee scene is winging its way into a freshly roasted future, Kaffeefabrik is it. The antithesis of the opulent, chandelier-lit coffee house more readily associated with the city, this cafe has a contemporary, stripped-back look with no *schnickschnack* (frills) and a loyal student following. Its reasonably priced speciality coffee is roasted in Burgenland in small batches to bring out the individual aromas of the Fairtrade beans sourced from Sumatra, India, Ethiopia, Ecuador, Brazil and Nicaragua. A Dalla Corte Evolution – the crème de la crème of espresso makers – and two Fiorenzato F64E grinders ensure that each cup is expertly made.

CROATIA

How to ask for a coffee in the local language?
Mogu li dobiti kavu, molim vas?
Signature coffee style? Strong espresso, served short
What to order with your coffee? A shot of rakija, the local firewater
Don't: Split the bill, ever; the person who did the inviting usually does the paying

For centuries, Croatia was fought over by three extremely well-caffeinated empires, with the Austro-Hungarians dominating inland, the Venetians along the coast and the Ottoman Turks periodically grabbing bits around its edges. With a brown tide washing over them from three directions, what choice did the locals have but to light a cigarette and reach for the sugar?

At home, Turkish-style coffee is the norm: finely ground, liberally infused with sugar and simmered on the hob in a metal pot until it's strong enough to wake the dead. Out and about, however, the espresso machine rules supreme.

While there are some fancy Viennese-style cafes in Zagreb where the Austrian influence was strongest, Croatian cafe culture is an egalitarian, all-ages affair. Croats treat their local cafe like Brits do their local pub. It's a place to

hang out, read newspapers, meet friends, play cards and watch sports on TV. It's perfectly fine to hold court and linger over a single espresso for hours – and many elderly men fill their days doing just that. It's less common to see elderly women doing the same; they're too busy at home doing all of the cooking and cleaning. However, Croatia's cafes are far from male-only preserves: teenage girls congregate in breathless clusters and young professional women descend after work to debrief on their days.

The minute the weather warms up, all the action spills outside – this is the Mediterranean after all. From Zagreb's legendary Saturday morning see-and-be-seen *špica* session to the languid Dalmatian seaside promenades, the image of locals chattering on sunny cafe terraces is an archetype of Croatian life.

COGITO COFFEE SHOP

Varšavska 11, Zagreb;
www.cogitocoffee.com

◆ Food   ◆ Shop   ◆ Transport
◆ Classes   ◆ Cafe

© Hannah Powlison Belkovic

THINGS TO DO NEARBY

Kino Europa
This arthouse cinema from the 1920s, Zagreb's oldest, comes with a boho cafe-bar alongside the stellar repertoire of screenings and events.
www.kinoeuropa.hr

Vinodol
Chow down on top-notch Central European fare at this landmark restaurant, known for its tender lamb or veal and potatoes cooked under *peka* (a domed baking lid).
www.vinodol-zg.hr

Trg Bana Jelačića
Zagreb's heart and soul, the main square is a prime spot for people-watching; grab a seat at a sidewalk cafe to watch the blue trams whizz past.

Dolac Market
Wander through the fruit and veg-laden stalls of Zagreb's main food market, just north of Trg Bana Jelačića, for colourful photo opps and tasty bites.

If there's one word you need to know about Zagreb, it's *kava* (coffee) and if there's one place to try it, it's Cogito Coffee. Coffee culture in Croatia has always had a strong social aspect; business deals and break-ups, gossip and flings, they all happen over *kava*. Drawing on this local love of coffee, the two men behind Cogito, both named Matija, decided to throw the coffee bean into the conversational mix, enlightening people on what is at stake in producing, roasting and preparing a great cup of coffee.

Matija Belković brought his zeal for speciality coffee to Croatia from his time studying in Boston; when he opened Cafe U Dvorištu, the artsy cafe was Zagreb's best spot for a serious cup of coffee. Soon after he teamed up with Matija Hrkać, one of the region's best baristas, and together they launched Cogito, quickly becoming Croatia's top boutique

roasters, and entirely devoted to quality from tree to cup. They source fresh green coffee beans seasonally and transparently from tropical growing regions around the world, and roast them at their roastery (next door to Cafe U Dvorištu); they also have four coffee shops, two in Zagreb, one in Zadar and another in Dubrovnik. At their first Zagreb outfit, don't miss the smooth Tesla Blend, featuring superlative in-season beans, or the moodier Blackout Blend, with notes of dark chocolate and roasted almonds. The affogato with Medenko, a local artisanal ice-cream, is also a favourite.

CYPRUS

How to ask for a coffee in the local language?
Kypriakos kafes ('Cyprus coffee') ena glyko (sweet),
ena metrio (medium) or ena sketo (without sugar)
Signature coffee style? Unfiltered, brewed using very
finely ground Arabica beans
What to order with your coffee? Cyprus coffee is always
served with a glass of ice-cold water
Don't: Ask for a Turkish coffee. In the south it will
irritate or offend, and north of the Green Line the
'Turkish' is unnecessary

Cyprus sits on the doorstep of the Middle East,
at the three-way intersection between Southern
Europe, Asia and Africa – all places with deep historical and
cultural connections to the coffee bean.

The Mediterranean island is a complex and multilayered
place with a fascinating past and an extraordinary present.
The country remains divided by the Green Line, separating
the Turkish north and the Greek south, but one common
denominator is the population's mutual love of the local
caffeinated elixir.

The island's popularity with sun-seeking package
holiday-makers means most coast-based cafes and
restaurants are accustomed to serving standard-fare filtered
coffees and cappuccinos. Ask specifically for a *kypriakos
kafes* (Cyprus coffee), or seek out a traditional *kafenio* in the
mountains or the city's back streets, however, and you'll get
something much more special.

Cyprus coffee is very distinctive, prepared with pride
and served with ceremony. Very finely ground coffee is
mixed with water (as well as sugar if desired) and heated
gently in a long-handled copper pot called a *mbrikia*
(or *briki/brike*, in Turkish a *cezve*) until a creamy froth
(*kaimaki*) forms on the top. Some Cypriots prefer to let

this foam rise several times before pouring the drink into
an espresso-sized cup.

The resulting brew is sensationally strong and
beautifully bitter – to be sipped, not supped. At the
bottom of the cup a thick layer of sediment collects,
which tradition claims contains future-divining
capabilities. One thing you can predict with confidence
is that you'll be back for another cup.

YFANTOURGEIO

67-71 Lefkonos St Phaneromeni, Nicosia (Lefkosia);
www.facebook.com/Yfantourgeio; +357 99 409900

◆ Food

◆ Cafe

There are cooler cafes and funkier roasteries in Cyprus – such as Beanhaus in Paphos and Limassol's Rich Coffee – but Yfantourgeio (the 'Weaving Mill'), offers something very different. Lined with bookcases (heaving with titles you can borrow) and populated with people sipping caffeinated brews over chess boards, this all-welcoming meeting place in the old heart of the world's last divided capital is a throwback to a time when coffee houses were truly places of contemplation and conversation, drop-in penny universities for people seeking cerebral stimulation.

Open until late, you can catch film screenings, art exhibits and impromptu musical sessions at Yfantourgeio, as well as ordering varietals of tea and freshly ground bean juice. The standout epicurean experience for discerning travellers is, of course, a Cyprus coffee.

THINGS TO DO NEARBY

Ledra Street
Hop into the hubbub of this shopping avenue between the two halves of the divided city, with Lokmaci Gate the portal to Northern Cyprus (bring your passport).

Walls of Nicosia
Explore the snowflake-shaped walls surrounding the old city, built in vain by Venetians in 1567 to protect the capital. The Ottomans mounted a successful invasion three years later.

ÖZERLAT CAFE

Arasta Sk, North Nicosia (Lefkoşa); www.ozerlat.com;
+90 392 227 2351 (cafe), +90 392 225 2238 (roastery)

◆ Food ◆ Shop
◆ Roastery ◆ Cafe

Just north of the Green Line that divides Nicosia, Özerlat is between Büyük Han and Selimiye Mosque, within walking distance of the Lokmaci Gate border crossing on Ledra Street. This family business, which now has a London presence, has been roasting, grinding, blending and brewing beautiful coffee since 1917. Sipping sessions and tours of the nearby roastery can be arranged from the cafe, where beans (Brazilian and Colombia Arabicas) are ground and blended to taste. Buy beans to take away, green or roasted, or take a seat outside the cafe and order from a menu that includes espresso, cappuccino and all the usual suspects. Here, however, amid the

THINGS TO DO NEARBY

Büyük Han
Built by the Ottomans in 1572, the 'Great Inn' (see opposite) is a caravanserai and marketplace with a mini mosque, fountain and fine restaurant, Sedirhan, serving cold Efes and magical meze.

Selimiye Mosque
Dating to 1209, the Cathedral of Saint Sophia was converted into a mosque and had twin minarets added when the Ottomans captured Cyprus from the Venetians in 1570.

Ottoman-era minarets and market stalls of Old Lefkoşa, a Turkish-style tipple is the best choice.

FRANCE

How to ask for a coffee in the local language?
Je voudrais un café s'il vous plaît
Signature coffee style? Espresso
What to order with your coffee? A croissant before noon,
otherwise simply a glass of water
Don't: Ever end your meal with a cappuccino, flat
white or other milky variation – un café (meaning an
espresso) is the only acceptable choice

In a country where espresso is the coffee de
rigueur, it's astonishing how long it's taken the
French to acquire a taste for serious coffee. Given their
innate passion for fine food and wine, you would imagine
them to be right there on the frontline revelling in the
heady highs – cocoa, caramel, almond, pepper, floral
nuances et al – of an aromatic, speciality-grade espresso
crafted from the finest artisan-roasted beans money
can buy. Not so. Coffee in France can be disappointing:
traditional cafes complacently serve the same café, aka
an espresso cup filled to the brim with dark bitter coffee
of low-grade Robusta beans, safe in the knowledge that
French cafe culture – the glorious pavement terraces, the
woven bistro chairs, the vintage zinc bars and glittering
literary heritage – is hallowed.

Those all-too-often wretched Robusta beans are a legacy
of the 17th and 18th centuries when France turned to its
Asian and West African colonies for coffee beans. Which
leaves the pursuit of speciality coffee in France down to
a handful of *nouvelle génération* coffee shops and craft
roasters, predominantly run by well-travelled baristas
with foreign-honed or -inspired savoir faire. Traditional
brewing methods, including the French Press or cafetière
patented by French designers Mayer and Delforge in 1852,
are still respected. But it is the careful sourcing – from

small independent coffee farmers around the globe – and
roasting of exceptional beans by craft roasters such as
Brittany's homespun Caffè Cataldi and Parisian pioneer
and boutique-roaster La Caféothèque that are ensuring
a serious cup of coffee can at last be found in France.

L'ALCHIMISTE

12 rue de la Vieille Tour, Bordeaux;
alchimiste-cafes.com; +33 9 86 48 37 93

◆ Food ◆ Roastery ◆ Cafe
◆ Shop ◆ Classes ◆ Transport

The Bordelais are accustomed to a quality tipple – some of the world's finest vineyards cocoon their graceful city on the banks of the River Garonne in France's hot southwest. Enter the Alchemist, the roaster who introduced speciality coffee to Bordeaux: Arthur Audibert – former management consultant, world traveller, devout Bordelais – learned the business from Antoine Nétien at Coutume Café in Paris in 2013 and now crafts his own artisan coffee like a fine wine, playing with different beans, blends and roasts to transform raw green beans into coffee gold with bags of notes and *nez*. He roasts at Magasin Général (87 quai des Queyries), a post-industrial space in converted army barracks with organic lounge-bar and grown-up play zone. Ultimate don't-miss at his cafe-boutique on cobbled Rue de la Vieille Tour in town? Espresso with a cream-stuffed Dune Blanche cake.

THINGS TO DO NEARBY

La Cité du Vin
Get tastebuds into gear with a guided visit around Bordeaux's ground-breaking wine museum – a dazzling decanter-shaped riverside building. Tours include tastings.
www.laciteduvin.com

Miroir d'Eau
Let your hair down in the world's largest reflecting water pool opposite the imposing, riverside Palais de la Bourse. Vapour jets add to the fun (and selfie ops).

LA BOÎTE À CAFÉ

3 rue l'Abbé Rozier, Lyon;
www.cafemokxa.com; +33 4 69 84 68 50

◆ Food ◆ Classes ◆ Transport
◆ Roastery ◆ Shop

Eminently beautiful, soft-green packets of Café Mokxa coffee stand sentry by the entrance, each labelled with the farm of origin, altitude, year of harvest, roasting date and tantalising tasting notes – marzipan, honey, Tonka bean, apricot, jasmine – clearly designed to throw coffee-lover tastebuds into instant 'I want!' mode.

This is La Boîte à Café in Lyon's edgy Croix-Paquet 'hood, vitrine for speciality coffee roasted each week by the country's most significant roaster outside Paris, Café Mokxa. The brand was ahead of the French curve when it opened in 2011, and its commitment to personally sourcing beans from farms in Brazil, Colombia and El Salvador, among others,

THINGS TO DO NEARBY

Musée des Beaux-Arts
Masterpieces by Picasso, Monet, Rubens, Rembrandt et al steal the limelight in Lyon's fine arts museum, overlooking one of the city's most beautiful squares.
www.mba-lyon.fr

Fresque des Lyonnais
Gen up on your Lyonnais history with this colourful riverside wall mural: spot superstar local chef Paul Bocuse, the yellow-haired Little Prince and his creator Antoine de Saint-Exupéry, among others.

Croix-Rousse Traboules
Explore the labyrinth of *traboules* (secret passages) in the hilltop district of Croix-Rousse, heart of Lyon's silk-weaving industry in the 1800s.

Vieux Lyon
Meander across the Saône river to Old Lyon and lose yourself in the cobbled lanes and cafe-thronged squares of this medieval World Heritage site.

and roasting them in its own roastery to create the finest pure-origin coffee is unfaltering.

Frenchman Sadry Abidi and New Zealander Rosamund Morris James are the bean nous behind Café Mokxa. The creative husband and wife team lived in Barcelona, trained as baristas in New Zealand, and then wisely plumped for the gastronomic capital of France in which to open their coffee shop, roastery and barista school. Their ongoing mission? To marry speciality coffee with quality food. It would seem to be working – while baristas deftly work the La Marzocco Linea PB espresso machine, hip flasks of cold-brew chill in the glass cabinet next to squat bottles of organic peach juice and generous plates of peanut cookies, blackberry cheesecake and cinnamon-spiced banana bread by sister bakery Konditori.

BELLEVILLE BRÛLERIE

10 Rue Pradier, 19e, Paris;
https://cafesbelleville.com; +33 9 83 75 60 80

◆ Shop ◆ Classes ◆ Transport
◆ Roastery ◆ Cafe

Powerhouse of Parisian roasters since 2013,
Belleville Brûlerie is a hub of coffee excitement.
Hidden behind an understated steel-grey façade in
staunchly working-class, multicultural Belleville in eastern
Paris, this artisan roastery requires dedication to track
down and only opens its doors to the public one day a week.
Professional Saturday-morning *dégustations* (cuppings)
– please don't wear perfume – allow groups of eight to
swirl, smell, slurp and spit the week's freshly roasted beans
around a large bespoke table hand-crafted in Serbia for
the occasion. Cuppings are led by celebrity *torréfacteurs*
(roasters) David Flynn and Thomas Lehoux, whose *nouveau*
French Roast turns the popular French Roast style – a dark
roast typically slammed as bitter and burnt – on its head.
Taste fruit, sugar, spice and prepare to be smitten.

THINGS TO DO NEARBY

Marché de Belleville
Few Parisian food
markets are as colourful
or raucous. In the biz since
1860, open-air stalls fill
Boulevard de Belleville
to bursting every Tuesday
and Friday morning.

Parc de Belleville
Climb to the top of this
hilly city park ensnaring 4.5
hectares of urban greenery
and swoon over Paris laid
out at your feet.

COUTUME CAFÉ

47 rue de Babylone, 7e, Paris;
www.coutumecafe.com; +33 1 45 51 50 47

◆ Food   ◆ Classes   ◆ Cafe
◆ Roastery   ◆ Shop   ◆ Transport

Coutume stands out from neighbouring chic Rive Gauche boutiques. Its innovative cafe-roastery is an airy industrial space, with retro furniture, tropical plants and a long coffee bar where baristas describe their coffee beans with the same enthusiasm as a wine sommelier. The cafe is a pioneer of digital detox, with laptops and tablets banned to encourage conversation over coffee.

The back of the space has a state-of-the-art roasting machine surrounded by sacks of coffee beans from plantations across the world, and Coutume supplies cafes and restaurants across Paris. Open through breakfast and lunch, the kitchen proposes healthy organic produce such as beetroot carpaccio with tabbuleh, while for your coffee, choose between a V60, latte, cortado or the espresso of the day, hand-pulled on a Synesso Cyncra. The choice of beans changes regularly, and includes Ethiopian Demisse Endema or Finca Deborah Gefha from Panama.

THINGS TO DO NEARBY

Musée Rodin
This stately mansion houses a vast collection of Rodin's works, including *The Thinker*, with many statues displayed in the extensive gardens.
www.musee-rodin.fr

Le Bon Marché
Built by Gustave Eiffel, the first modern department store has become a Parisian style icon. Chic shopping at its best; don't miss La Grande Epicerie, a foodie paradise.
www.24sevres.com

LOMI

3ter rue Marcadet, 18e, Paris;
www.cafelomi.com; +33 9 80 39 56 24

◆ Food ◆ Classes ◆ Cafe
◆ Roastery ◆ Shop ◆ Transport

Tourists rarely wander into this gritty corner of Montmartre, but Lomi is always packed with a mix of colourful neighbourhood locals and coffee enthusiasts drawn by its reputation as one of the most exciting craft roasters in Paris. The cafe section looks like an old abandoned factory, with rusty metal girders, peeling paint on the walls, simple wooden tables and old leather couches.

A glass wall at the back separates the roastery and lab area for testing the seasonal beans that are imported from more than 20 countries, as well as a space for cuppings, barista workshops and espresso classes. The food is simple, tasty and freshly cooked, and includes the challenging Cafe Fromage, a spoonful of tangy Bleu d'Auvergne cheese dipped into an espresso. The more traditional option would be a Gisuma, Chemex-filtered coffee from Rwanda; a lively, buttery, taste with hints of black tea.

THINGS TO DO NEARBY

Sacre-Coeur Basilica
The white domes and towers of this 19th-century basilica sit high above Montmartre like an ornate decoration atop a wedding cake. Spectacular views across Paris.
www.sacre-coeur-montmartre.com

Clignancourt Flea Market
This huge flea market attracts 3000 traders and 180,000 visitors each weekend. From high-priced antiques to cheap bric-a-brac, you're sure to find something here.
www.marcheauxpuces-saintouen.com

LOUSTIC

40 Rue Chapon, 3e, Paris;
www.cafeloustic.com; +33 9 80 31 07 06

◆ Food ◆ Cafe
◆ Shop ◆ Transport

With a sassy name ('Smart Alec' in old Breton) and sharp interior by hotshot Parisian designer Dorothée Meilichzon (think vintage-print Hermès wallpaper and exposed stone), Loustic is the good-looking espresso bar of London barista Channa Galhenage. When he opened on backstreet Rue Chapon in Paris' 3e arrondissement in 2013, Loustic was resolutely new wave: Paris had a dozen-odd specialist coffee shops at the time, compared to the 40 or so today. Beans arrive fresh from Antwerp roaster Caffènation and European guest roasters, and fans can sample a range of espresso and filter coffees (AeroPress, Chemex or V60). The fashion set's coffee of choice? A Loustic latte glacé, aka ice, maple syrup, cold full-cream milk and a double espresso mixed in a 250ml glass beaker.

THINGS TO DO NEARBY

Musée National Picasso
Admire masterpieces by Pablo Picasso inside the elegant 17th-century Hôtel Salé. The Spanish artist spent much of life living and working in Paris. *www.museepicassoparis.fr*

Marché des Enfants Rouges
Duck through green metal gates to lose yourself in a maze of food stalls cooking up delicious world cuisines at Paris' oldest covered market (1615).

GERMANY

How to ask for a coffee in the local language?
Einen Kaffee, bitte
Signature coffee style? Latte macchiato or black coffee
What to order with your coffee? Depends very much
on the region. In Berlin they serve some of the best
cheesecake you'll ever eat
Do: Tip. If paying with cash, just round up to the
nearest euro

Germany is undoubtedly Europe's biggest economy
and at the very centre of the continent, but despite
being a technological innovator and a global leader in the
manufacturing of outstanding products, its population has
some idiosyncrasies that set it apart from many leading
economies – people still love paying with cash, for example,
and while they might drive a Porsche they'll still happily buy
their groceries at the country's discount supermarket chains.
And when it comes to coffee, Germany is also less
developed than other European countries, such as the UK

or the Scandinavian countries; while there are some good
national coffee brands there are hardly any nationwide
coffee-shop chains, except Starbucks. But in recent years,
Berlin has led the charge in the demand for and appreciation
of speciality coffee, with the capital is now home to a vast
number of outstanding third wave coffee bars and roasters.
Other cities such as Hamburg, Cologne, Frankfurt and
Munich have taken longer to follow suit, but they're getting
there... slowly but surely.

One of the pleasures of exploring this booming coffee
scene and its independent shops is the sheer scale and
breadth of natural attractions in Germany; from the seas
in the north to the Alps in the south, and the wine-growing
regions in the west to the great lakes in the east, it's a
country with stunning scenery and great regional variation.

HAPPY BARISTAS

Neue Bahnhofstraße 32, Berlin;
happybaristas.com

◆ Food   ◆ Shop   ◆ Transport
◆ Classes ◆ Cafe

Widely considered one of the best coffee bars in the German capital, Happy Baristas is one of those places you never want to leave. Founders Roland Lodr and Marian Plajdicko have managed to create a welcoming place that isn't snooty about its fine coffees and can easily convert any coffee novice into a true aficionado in the blink of an eye.

They recently added Nitro coffee to their menu, something that's best enjoyed on the lovely terrace on a hot summer day. There are also home-brewing courses, and some of their coffee creations look so good they could easily grace the city's finest cocktail bars. Best come hungry too because the breakfast is to die for!

THINGS TO DO NEARBY

East Side Gallery
One of Berlin's most recognisable landmarks, the 101 paintings on the city's former wall between East and West is just a short walk from here.

Boxhagener Platz
This tiny square is a hub for locals, tourists and striders alike. At the weekends it has a great food market (Saturday) and flea market (Sunday).

THE BARN

Schönhauser Allee 8, Berlin;
thebarn.de; +49 1512 4105136

◆ Food   ◆ Classes ◆ Cafe
◆ Roastery ◆ Shop   ◆ Transport

Ralf Rüller, owner of one of Berlin's best-known coffee roasteries, is the enfant terrible of the local coffee scene, and might have made himself a handful of enemies by imposing strict bans on things one usually associates with coffee bars: buggies, laptops and dairy-free milk alternatives. But beyond this façade is a sensitive, kind and incredibly ambitious individual who successfully turned a small cake-baking business into a speciality heavyweight which can truthfully boast that its roasts are now served in some of the best coffee bars in the world. In Berlin, three sites bear the Barn name, but it's the Schönhauser Allee one, with roaster and coffee academy set in a space where rustic wood meets Nordic chic, that's the place to head.

THINGS TO DO NEARBY

Pfefferbräu
Elevated above street level and boasting a gorgeous square with pebbles and big trees, this local brewery and restaurant offers great beers and German food.

Kulturbrauerei
A stunning industrial space that's been converted into a multi-functional cultural centre hosting concerts, theatre shows, markets and much more.

ERNST KAFFEERÖSTER

Bonner Straße 56, Cologne;
www.ernst-kaffee.de; +49 221 1682 3207

◆ Food   ◆ Classes   ◆ Cafe
◆ Roastery   ◆ Shop   ◆ Transport

When Maren Ernst first opened her little coffee roastery in Cologne's Südstadt neighbourhood, she was something of a curiosity. Her coffees were so unknown to the local palate that it took locals a good while to warm to her and buy into what she was doing. Today, Ernst Kaffeeröster is an institution that has outgrown its humble beginnings, a bright and friendly affair where everything, including the sodas, is homemade and every coffee that goes over the counter is absolutely excellent. At the end of last year, the mini-empire expanded again with an impressive large-production roastery in another part of the city to accommodate growing demand for her delicious single-origins and espresso blends.

THINGS TO DO NEARBY

Cologne Cathedral
This masterpiece of gothic architecture is Germany's most visited landmark and one of the most magnificent churches in Europe.
www.koelner-dom.de

Museum Ludwig
This world-class modern art museum sits in the shadow of the city's cathedral and has one of the most impressive collections in the country.
www.museum-ludwig.de

BALZ & BALZ

Lehmweg 6, Hamburg;
www.balzundbalz.de; +49 40 6043 8833

◆ Food ◆ Shop ◆ Transport
◆ Classes ◆ Cafe

The speciality coffee scene in Germany's second biggest city is much less vibrant than Berlin's, but a few individuals – among them siblings Chris and Kathrin Balz – have created truly special homes for great speciality coffee and outstanding home-cooked food.

Chris actually lived in Berlin for many years, working the cocktail bar circuit in the capital before nailing his caffeine credentials at Röststätte Berlin. When he and his sister articulated plans to open their own coffee bar, they decided to do so in a city that still offered a lot of room for

THINGS TO DO NEARBY

Aussenalster
If there is one outdoor activity that brings all Hamburgers and visitors alike together, it's going for a walk around the city's massive lake. This is not to be missed.

Sternschanze
This happening neighbourhood is full of boutiques, bars and eateries and is always full of surprises.

Poletto Winebar
This is one of the best Italians in the city and deservedly always busy. Come here for fresh antipasti and delicious main dishes accompanied by outstanding wines.
poletto-winebar.de

Elbphilharmonie
Hamburg's answer to the Sydney Opera House is absolutely spectacular and is the jewel of one of Europe's largest inner-city developments.

growth, and chose Hamburg as their new home – clearly a good decision as the city's fast becoming Germany's hippest destination.

Their cosy coffee bar and kitchen is located just shy of the city's busy Hoheluftchaussee avenue and faces the lovely Isebeekkanal. Almost everything served at Balz & Balz is locally sourced, including the sausages that come from the Balz's own family farm. The soups, cakes and *stullen* (sandwiches) are divine, and with Chris performing some real magic behind the La Marzocco Strada, you're guaranteed an outstanding time at this lovely family-run coffee bar. They recently added some outdoor seating as well, a nice spot in which to soak up some sun while tucking into one of the many exquisite cakes.

COFFEE NERD

Rohrbacher Str 9, Heidelberg;
www.coffeenerd.de

◆ Food ◆ Cafe
◆ Shop ◆ Transport

THINGS TO DO NEARBY

Schloss Heidelberg

Don't miss this half-ruined castle with its sweeping views of the gorgeous natural surroundings and city centre. *www.schloss-heidelberg.de*

Alte Brücke

If heights aren't your thing or you like a romantic river stroll, then this old stone bridge over the Neckar offers gorgeous sunset views.

Mahmoud's

This no-frills Lebanese place offers incredible value for money and delicious mezze platters full of falafel, hummus, tabouleh and halloumi cheese. *www.mahmouds.de*

Weinloch

A local institution full of interesting characters and students sipping on proper draft beer and a great selection of local wines.

Most visitors to Germany will discover Heidelberg sooner or later. In summer, the city's Hauptstrasse is so crowded with tourists that it's hard to get from one end to another. They come to be charmed by the beautiful medieval city's architecture, its ancient castle and spectacular views of the Neckar river. But apart from being cute to look at, Heidelberg is also home to Germany's oldest and most renowned university, founded in 1386.

Coffee Nerd founder Thomas Mohr is a native to the city and returned home after spending a few years working in the corporate world in Berlin, where he first discovered the world of speciality coffee through Bonanza Coffee Roasters and God Shot. Indeed, he was so fascinated by it that he quit his job and returned to Heidelberg to open his own coffee bar.

While he struggled to get people to accept his fruity espressos and floral filter coffees at first, he also benefited from Heidelberg's huge student population and international visitors. Coffee Nerd attracts an eclectic mix of customers and serves one of the most delicious espresso tonics out there. If you happen to visit during summer when temperatures often rise into the mid-30s, this refreshing drink will properly cool you down.

MAN VERSUS MACHINE

Müllerstrasse 23, Munich;
mvsm.coffee; +49 89 8004 6681

◆ Food   ◆ Classes   ◆ Cafe
◆ Roastery   ◆ Shop   ◆ Transport

Given the fact that Munich is Germany's third-largest city, home of BMW, Oktoberfest and pretzels, it's hard to fathom that it still only has two proper speciality coffee roasteries. Luckily, one of them is Man versus Machine, the local pioneer that brought gorgeous, fruity coffees to the Bavarian capital. As its husband and wife team Marco and Cornelia Mehrwald like to point out, coffee is a fruit and should definitely not be bitter.

Set on a hip street just south of the city's old town, and courtesy of Marco's Probat roaster at the back of the snug and cosy space, it offers exquisite espressos, great filter coffees and even homemade coffee chocolate bars.

THINGS TO DO NEARBY

Deutsches Museum
Stroll along the Isar river to this temple of technology with interactive exhibits and engaging sections on cave paintings, geodesy, microelectronics and astronomy. ***www. deutsches-museum.de***

Ohel Jakob Synagogue
This modern monument to the local Jewish community is an architectural gem and a very important reminder of Germany's past.
www.ikg-m.de

HUNGARY

How to ask for a coffee in the local language?
Egy kávét szeretnék

Signature coffee style? Presszókávé, similar to an espresso

What to order with your coffee? A glass of soda water. However, if you're in a traditional Hungarian cafe with a confectionery (Cukrázda), try one of the cakes

Do: Go on a journey through Hungary's coffee eras; make sure you have a coffee in one classic cafe, one retro Eszpresszó and one new-wave coffee house

Hungary's relationship with coffee was forged with the arrival of the Turks in the 16th century. And when the 150-year-long Ottoman occupation ended, they left behind a knowledge of coffee and even a few Turkish words, such as *kávé*, the Hungarian word for coffee.

But Hungary's caffeinated legacy only really began to percolate in the 18th century, when the first coffee house opened in Pest close to the banks of the Danube. Soon, coffee became a core part of Hungarian culture, with writers, artists and intellectuals making the marble tables of the city's cafes their second home. By the turn of the 20th century, opulent coffee houses such as the New York Café and Gerbeaud had elevated the act of drinking coffee into a truly decadent experience under the glimmer of gold leaf and mirrored walls. It wasn't to last.

Communism brought Hungarian coffee culture down to earth, with proletariat-friendly coffee houses dubbed *Eszpresszós*, like Bambi Eszpresszó, drastically switching the grand backdrop to linoleum-lined floors, neon signs and shots of black *presszókávé* served in glasses. Coffee became a purely functional drink, appearing in intense dark shots, diluted milky concoctions or cappuccinos topped with squirted cream.

Fast-forward to the 21st century and it's a more mixed picture. While the speciality coffee scene has bloomed in Budapest, it's been slow to pick up outside the capital, but you'll still find new-wave cafes that take their brews and roasts seriously popping up in cities such as Pécs, Szeged, Debrecen and Eger. And while many coffee houses have been importing their roasts, a few local roasteries in Budapest give coffee lovers the chance to try some local brew.

KONTAKT

1052 Budapest, Károly körút 22;
kontaktcoffee.com

◆ Classes   ◆ Cafe
◆ Shop   ◆ Transport

Kontakt takes the quality of its coffee so seriously that all sugars and sweeteners are banned from the tiny coffee shop tucked away in a hidden courtyard in central Budapest. You won't find any Americanos offered on-site either. Dedicated purely to making excellent coffees, Kontakt offers a range of filter coffees and aromatic espressos, but if you want to try something different, go for the 'Roket'. Made from light-roasted, single-origin coffee, Roket is cold-brewed for 14 hours and undergoes multiple filtrations before it's put into kegs. It's served via a nitro tap, and comes out looking more like a craft beer than a coffee, with a thick, ale-coloured finish, a frothy, creamy head and a rounded, smooth feel.

THINGS TO DO NEARBY

Szimply
For some excellent food to go with your coffee, Szimply, located directly opposite the cafe, offers a range of breakfast dishes, from avocado toast to oatmeal.
www.szimply.com

Paloma Design
This courtyard full of design shops houses Hungarian wares from jewellery to bags and shoes, made by more than 50 up-and-coming local designers.
www.facebook.com/ PalomaBudapest

MADAL ESPRESSO & BREW BAR

1136 Budapest, Hollán Ernő utca 3;
madalcafe.hu; +36 20 281 9691

◆ Food ◆ Shop ◆ Transport
◆ Classes ◆ Cafe

While its name comes from the nickname of philosopher Sri Chinmoy, Madal embraces its own philosophy of 'Good Coffee Good Karma'.

Opening its first cafe in 2013, Madal now has three sites and its own off-site roastery, Beyond Within, which opened in 2014. Coffee comes served on elegant wooden platters embossed with the brand's motto, whether a shot of espresso made from a single-origin or blended coffee, or an AeroPress made by one of the championship-winning baristas.

This venue on the pedestrianised Hollán Ernő utca sits in a basement, but still sports a light, airy feel, with an outdoor terrace that's perfect for larger groups. Try an espresso or a creamy flat white made with one of the Beyond Within single-origin coffees.

THINGS TO DO NEARBY

Margaret Island
This lush car-free island in the middle of the Danube is a tranquil spot for a grassy picnic or wander round medieval monastic ruins.

Budapest Pinball Museum
A dedicated cult following come to this eccentric and interactive museum, home to Europe's largest display of vintage playable pinball machines. ***www.flipper muzeum.hu***

MY LITTLE MELBOURNE & BREW BAR

1075 Budapest, Madách Imre út 3;
mylittlemelbourne.hu; +36 70 394 7002

◆ Food   ◆ Shop   ◆ Transport
◆ Classes   ◆ Cafe

Around the trendy Madách tér area, populated with farm-to-table restaurants and bars plastered with stickers, My Little Melbourne is a pioneering bastion of Budapest's speciality coffee scene. Inspired by the coffee scene in Melbourne, its founders wanted to bring the taste of Australia's best brews back to Budapest, setting up shop in a tiny 35-sq-metre space in 2012.

This small cafe ignited the third wave coffee scene, being the first speciality shop in the country, and soon grew into a caffeinated emporium. After the success of its initial cafe, it expanded into the space next door with My Little Brew Bar, lined with wooden benches along a bar where you can watch the alchemy that goes in to the preparation of its caffeinated brews. Hungary's first brew bar offers coffee aficionados the chance to delve into the complex range of brewed and filter coffees made with Chemex, V60 and AeroPress through to Bunsen-like syphons and cold-brews. Since then, the My Little Melbourne group has launched a mini-empire of coffee shops, and has opened its own roastery, Racer Beans Coffee Co. They also train up aspiring baristas in the basement of My Little Brew Bar. Sample the numerous brews at one of the monthly cupping events.

THINGS TO DO NEARBY

Rumbach Sebestyén Utca Synagogue
Stop by this former 19th-century synagogue on the next street. The curious neo-Moorish building with its minaret-like towers now plays host to exhibitions and concerts.

Szimpla Kert
No trip to the Jewish Quarter is complete without a visit to Szimpla Kert, Budapest's first ruin bar, an offbeat watering hole in a dilapidated building.
www.szimpla.hu

Gozsdú Udvar
This passage connects a series of hidden courtyards in the former Jewish Quarter, now populated by bars and restaurants, and sometimes a quirky antiques market.
gozsduudvar.hu

Printa Design Shop
Upcycling and sustainable design are at the heart of this eco-friendly fashion label, which also offers Budapest-themed gifts and silkscreen prints.
printa.hu

ICELAND

How to ask for a coffee in the local language?
Ég ætla að fá kaffi
Signature coffee style? Black and strong pour-over
What to order with your coffee? A cinnamon bun
Don't: Panic if a baby is abandoned in a pram outside the cafe (in all weathers), it's totally normal!

Icelanders love coffee. They drink it strong. And they drink it a lot. Coffee first came to Iceland in 1703 and by 1760 almost every home had a grinder and a coffee-roasting pot to place over the fire, but the main purpose of the brew was to treat visitors – notably visiting clergy, though as dried chicory root was commonly added to the grounds to give it a bitter taste maybe it wasn't that much of a treat. Eventually coffee became a part of daily life and by 1850 it was a common part of the working day. Home-roasting ceased around the mid-1950s, with the advent of industrial

roasters, but today no social gathering, business meeting, wedding or birthday is complete without a pot of coffee.

Operating in sync with Iceland's recent food revolution, sharper attention is paid to ethically sourcing beans and respect for raw materials, along with a keen interest in processing and brewing techniques. And while it's true that the ratio of coffee shop to consumer is bordering on ridiculous in Reykjavik, a quality caffeine fix can be harder to source on a long road trip around the country. Village cafes and service station counters often have hot filter coffee on offer, and while your chances of finding a latte or cappuccino are increasing in remote areas, the quality can be hit or miss, and it's often likely to be from an instant coffee machine. Pallett Kaffikompaní in Hafnarfjörður and Akureyri in northern Iceland are your next best barista havens outside the capital.

REYKJAVIK ROASTERS

Kárastígur 1, Reykjavik;
www.reykjavikroasters.is/en; +354 517 5535

◆ Food   ◆ Shop   ◆ Transport
◆ Roastery   ◆ Cafe

Just the kind of cosy haven you might crave in Iceland: on a typical visit there'll be vinyl records playing, locals perched on vintage furniture knitting scarves, and the aroma of fresh beans from the bright blue 6kg Giesen roaster intermingling with the waft of cinnamon scones. Since opening in 2008 (though if you visited pre-2014, you may know it by its previous name of Kaffismiðjan), Reykjavik Roasters has prided itself on ethically sourcing beans from Guatemala, Costa Rica, Brazil, Kenya, Peru and Ethiopia. Antipodeans will be pleased to know that flat whites are made upon request. Otherwise there are various types of milk but no decaf, just serious coffee, and a quick glance at the trophy shelves will assure you of the depth of esteem in which this place is held in Iceland. Torfi Þór Torfason, one of the co-owners, won the Icelandic Barista Championships in 2013 and is chief roaster here.

The second site at Brautarholt 2 holds coffee workshops and has a slightly edgier vibe, but this original location draws queues of locals. You may want something warming most of the time in this country, but to really wake yourself up try the Shakerato: a double espresso shaken with ice.

THINGS TO DO NEARBY

Dill
Visit this Michelin-starred New Nordic restaurant that's credited with putting Icelandic cuisine on the map. Tap into the country's food traditions, interpreted with creative flair.
www.dillrestaurant.is

Brauð & co
Join the pre-dawn queues for the best cinnamon buns in town. The bakers are incredibly close to the customers, so you can watch all the action while you wait.
www.braudogco.is

Hallgrímskirkja
Reykjavik's most noticed landmark, this immense white-concrete church can be seen from all over town. Take an elevator up its 74.5m-high tower for panoramic views.
en.hallgrimskirkja.is

Tjörnin
Reykjavik's peaceful lake, surrounded by sculptures and home to 40 species of bird, makes for a pleasant place to stroll. Expect ice-skaters during the winter freeze.

© Kristinn Magnússon

ITALY

How to ask for a coffee in the local language?
Un caffè/macchiato/cappuccino/caffè latte per favore
Signature coffee style? Espresso
What to order with your coffee? A glass of water (during
the day) or a breakfast brioche (north) or cornetto (south),
which can be plain (vuota/vuoto) or filled with cream
(crema), jam (marmellata), honey (miele) or Nutella
Do: Tip – small change will do

Italians love coffee so much you might think
that they invented the drink. They didn't. But
their passion for the bean has inspired a coffee culture
unequalled anywhere else in the world. When coffee was
first shipped to Venice in the 16th century, it caused an
uproar and was almost banned. The so-called 'wine of
the Arabs' was considered a Satanic invention. However,
when Pope Clement VIII admitted a penchant for the drink,
the stigma receded rapidly and a coffee shop was opened
pronto on Venice's Piazza San Marco in 1683.

As coffee plantations became established in European
colonies, availability increased and price decreased,
popularising the drink and spreading the trend to cities
around the peninsula. In time, each city developed its own
style. In Trentino, ask for a cappuccino Viennese and you'll
be served a frothy coffee with chocolate and cinnamon. In
the Marche region, stop for a *caffè anisette* and you'll get
an aniseed-flavoured espresso, and in Sicily you'll find *caffè
d'u parrinu*, coffee flavoured with cloves, cinnamon and
cocoa powder. Rituals around coffee developed, too, such
as the Neapolitan practice of *caffè sospeso* (a suspended
coffee), whereby you pay for two coffees but leave one for
a stranger to enjoy for free.

It wasn't until 1906, however, that Italy's signature
espresso was first introduced. The brains behind it were

Luigi Bezzera and Desiderio Pavoni, two men whose
machine improved on the one invented in 1884 by Angelo
Moriondo, although it took another 40 years for Gaggia to
develop the lever machine with spring piston pressure that
we're familiar with today.

The technological marvel of the espresso machine has
powered the Italian workforce ever since. The shot-pulling
efficiency of the Italian barista offered busy factory workers
an invigorating pick-me-up during the mid-morning slump
when stomachs were empty. Mindful of the factory clock,
the drink had to be delivered fast, and the coffee was thick,
warm, bitter-sweet and stimulating.

Until the 1930s espresso was prepared with high-quality

TOP 5 COFFEES

Gardelli La Esperanza Gesha
Lavazza Espresso Super Crema
His Majesty the Coffee Modoetia
Ditta Artigianale Jump Blend
Nero Scuro Numerouno

CAFE TALK – BRENT JOPSON

It's an exciting time to be working in the coffee scene in Italy. Change is in the air and there's real momentum behind the speciality coffee movement

Brazilian Arabica beans, but when prices rose, Italian coffee houses went looking for lower-priced alternatives that had a similar profile. They found the solution with the Robusta variety, which delivered a similar flavour when blended but with a bigger caffeine hit and a more bittersweet finish. The addition of Robusta to blends also results in the signature amber froth on an Italian espresso, otherwise known as *crema*. More importantly, its lower price allowed Italian cafes to continue to serve a cup of coffee at the regulated price of €1.

But tradition has its downsides. Italy's multi-bean blends, dark roasts and short, sharp espresso shots are the antithesis of today's speciality coffee movement, and ingrained customs deter the very innovation that was the hallmark of Italy's 18th-century coffee scene. Things are slowly changing, however, thanks to a new breed of third wave coffee roasters such as Rubens Gardelli (four-times Italian roasting champion) and Davide Cobelli (head trainer at the Coffee Training Academy), who are championing single-origin speciality coffees while building on the values of quality and curiosity embedded in Italian coffee culture.

Seek out these pioneers at such places as Gardelli in Forli, Faro in Rome, Estratto in Brescia, Orsonero in Milan, Ditta Artigianale in Florence and ORSO Laboratorio Caffè in Turin, and you will discover a new Italian coffee scene that bodes well for the next century.

HODEIDAH

Via Piero della Francesca 8, Milan;
www.hodeidah.it; +39 02 342 472

◆ Food   ◆ Shop   ◆ Transport
◆ Roastery   ◆ Cafe

Enter this small, unassuming Milanese cafe and you enter a wonderland of coffee – the way it used to be. Dating back to 1946, waiters in white shirts and black bow ties man the bar in a room filled with jars of coffee beans, teas, candies and black-and-white photos of the coffee plantations of a bygone era. Little has changed in the 70 years that have passed since. Here, coffee is still a tradition and a passion, carried on by Fulvio Rossi, son of the former owner. At the heart of his humble shop is the art of roasting coffee. Peek into the back area and you'll see the original Victory roaster from 1946, which is still used today. Unlike modern methods it slow-roasts the beans over coal: a

THINGS TO DO NEARBY

Cimitero Monumentale
This striking marble-rich cemetery is home to some of the city's most beloved citizens, including literary figures, artists and, this being Milan, football players. *www.comune. milano.it*

La Fabbrica del Vapore
This former electric tram factory is now an artsy cultural site with an industrial vibe. Check out its changing programme of exhibitions, cinema, theatre and concerts. *www. fabbricadelvapore.org*

Arco della Pace
At the edge of Parco Sempione lies this impressive neoclassic arch. Built in 1807 to honour Napoleon's victories, after his defeat it became a monument to peace.

Chinatown
Visit the biggest and oldest Chinatown in Italy. Not only a great stop for dumplings, gaudy jewellery and cheap technology, it's also heaving with trendy bars.

practice that requires time and skill in varying the conditions according to the bean.

Choose from house blends (some of whose ingredients are a secret) or single-origin coffees, such as Jamaica Blue Mountain, and a wide range of 100% Arabicas from Brazil, India, Ethiopia and Guatemala. The beans can be taken home or enjoyed right there at the bar; follow the locals' lead and order *un cafe* (espresso), accompanying it with a *brioche* (croissant).

GRAN CAFFÉ GAMBRINUS

Via Chiaia 1-2, Naples;
grancaffegambrinus.com; +39 02 342 472

◆ Food ◆ Transport
◆ Cafe

This historic grand cafe, once frequented by the likes of Hemingway and Oscar Wilde, has a story to tell. Founded in 1860, it flourished as a meeting place for intellectuals and literary figures until 1938, when Mussolini shut it down for being an antifascist haunt. It might have ended like that save for the dream of one man – Michele Sergio who, with the help of his two sons and son-in-law, restored the space to its former glory. Now both tourists and locals come in droves to the ornate chandeliered, frescoed space to enjoy a classic Neapolitan espresso. For the uninitiated this means a short coffee that's dark, dense and piping hot. The pastries and ice-cream are excellent too, albeit a bit pricey.

THINGS TO DO NEARBY

Palazzo Reale di Napoli
Take a journey into the world of the Bourbon kings at this palace and museum brimming with baroque and neoclassic furniture, tapestries and paintings.

Galleria Borbonica
Who wouldn't want to explore an underground tunnel commissioned by a fearful king and used as an air-raid shelter in WWII? *www.galleriaborbonica. com*

LA CASA DEL CAFFÈ TAZZA D'ORO

Via degli Orfani, 84, Rome;
www.tazzadorocoffeeshop.com; +39 06 67 89 792

◆ Food ◆ Shop ◆ Transport
◆ Roastery ◆ Cafe

The venerable 'Golden Coffee Cup' opened in 1948, and it shows – in a good way. Just a few paces from Roman-temple-turned-church, the Pantheon, its long shop-front hides an interior that glimmers with polished brass and wood panels, populated by serious baristas in black and white. Walking in, you breathe in the sense of the past as well as freshly ground Central and South American blends. Offering a perfectly turned out espresso and cappuccino, the cafe is perhaps most famous for its hot-weather take on the bean. The *granita di caffè* is the perfect foil for the heat of the Roman summer: it's pure, sweet espresso, frozen and smashed into a crushed ice. Naturally it's layered with *panna* (cream) both *sopra* (on top) and *sotto* (underneath): why on earth not?

THINGS TO DO NEARBY

The Pantheon
A magnificent piece of architecture, its dome open to the skies, this temple-turned-church is even more miraculous when you consider it's some 2000 years old.

Trevi Fountain
This is fountain architecture as high drama, where foaming waters cascade, horses rollick and sea-god Oceanus glowers over tourists tossing coins to ensure their return to Rome.

SANT' EUSTACHIO IL CAFFÈ

Piazza di Sant' Eustachio, 82, Rome;
www.santeustachioilcaffe.com; +39 06 6880 2048

◆ Food ◆ Shop ◆ Transport
◆ Roastery ◆ Cafe

In a city that measures out its day in caffeine shots, Sant' Eustachio il Caffè is one of the Italian capital's most hallowed coffee bars despite being standing room only (with a couple of seats outside). Open since 1938 with a classic curved counter and glossy coffee machines, it feels as if not much has changed since then. The cafe makes use of a wood fire to roast its Arabica beans, and is also famous for its secret-recipe Gran Caffè – in making it, the baristas turn away and shield the magic formula from view. The resulting elixir has a dark froth (no milk), caffeine blast and sweetness (specify *senzo zucchero* if you don't want sugar) that will pick you up, pat you on the back and bounce you off along the cobbled street.

THINGS TO DO NEARBY

Piazza Navona
Built on an ancient Roman racetrack, this football pitch-sized public space is festooned by baroque fountains and is a perfect people-watching spot.

San Luigi dei Francesi
A church for the French built in the 16th century, this is most famous for its chapel decorated by baroque bad-boy Caravaggio, with three masterpieces depicting the life of St Matthew.
saintlouis-rome.net

ILLY COFFEE FACTORY

110 Via Flavia, Trieste;
unicaffe.illy.com; +39 80 0821021

◆ Roastery ◆ Shop ◆ Transport
◆ Classes ◆ Cafe

Trieste is a must-visit for coffee lovers. This historic Adriatic port has been importing coffee beans since the 18th century, and today some 2.5 million coffee bags pass through from plantations across the globe. So it's hardly surprising that Trieste is also home of probably the world's most well-known coffee brand, the family-run Illy, whose distinctive blend is sold in 140 countries. The factory sits at the edge of the city, with its own University of Coffee offering everything from barista classes to coffee economics, history and biology. But it is also possible to book, on regular dates, for a brief but fascinating one-hour factory tour past the selection laboratories, roastery and packing of Illy's iconic pressurised recyclable cans, which trap the coffee's seductive aroma for up to a year. At the end of the tour, try the Trieste Cappuccino, or Capo in B, an espresso in a small glass topped with a little steamed whole milk.

THINGS TO DO NEARBY

Piazza Unita d'Italia
The largest sea-facing square in Europe, Trieste's magnificent piazza is the unofficial town centre, lined with opulent palaces, churches and grand Art Nouveau cafes.

James Joyce Museum
An intimate museum dedicated to James Joyce, who wrote *The Dubliners* and *Portrait of the Artist as a Young Man* while living in his adopted home of Trieste.
www.museojoycetrieste.it

CAFFÈ AL BICERIN

Piazza della Consolata 5, Turin;
www.bicerin.it; +39 011 436 9325

◆ Cafe
◆ Transport

Coffee in Italy doesn't tolerate many variations, but Turin agrees to differ. The city that spawned Lavazza coffee and played a major role in popularising chocolate in the 18th century also came up with the *bicerin*, a beautiful collision of coffee and chocolate served in a small elegant glass and topped with a layer of creamy milk. The foggy roots of this bitter-sweet drink can be traced back to Caffè Al Bicerin, which first opened its doors in the heart of the city in 1763. Numerous luminaries have since graced the cafe's velvety interior to indulge in the rich beverage, including composer Giacomo Puccini, writer Alexandre Dumas, philosopher Friedrich Nietzsche and, more recently, actor Susan Sarandon.

THINGS TO DO NEARBY

Santuario della Consolata
Directly opposite the cafe sits this richly eclectic basilica, with architectural styles encompassing romanesque, Byzantine, baroque and neoclassical.
www.laconsolata.org

Museo della Sindone
Rarely has such an impressive study been made on an object of such dubious authenticity – the Holy Shroud. Enter intrigued. Leave no wiser.
www.sindone.it

NUVOLA LAVAZZA

Via Bologna 32, Turin;
nuvola.lavazza.it; +39 011 23 981

◆ Food   ◆ Cafe
◆ Shop   ◆ Transport

Founded in Turin in 1895, Lavazza is the sixth largest coffee roaster in the world. It's been owned by the same family for four generations and credits itself with inventing the concept of blending coffee varieties, which is a distinctive feature of all its products.

The company is heavily invested in ethical and economic sustainability – the Luigi Lavazza Center for Study and Research is an international network of more than 50 coffee schools around the world – and its latest project is the new LEED-certified headquarters. The Lavazza Cloud, as it is known, is an industrial-recovery project designed by architect Cino Zucchi in the Borgata Aurora district of Turin. Covering more than 30,000 sq metres, it incorporates offices, the company archive, a museum dedicated to the history of Lavazza, an exhibition space, a garden designed by botanist Camilla Zanarotti and an archaeological area displaying a 4th-century basilica, which was unearthed during construction.

Most exciting is the futurist, all-glass restaurant, due to open this year (2018), presided over by the world's most famous molecular gastronomist, Ferran Adrià, and run by Adrià acolyte chef Federico Zanasi. It is based on the philosophy of food democracy, so expect no tasting menus, just home-style dining informed by local ingredients. And this being Italy, there will, of course, be a space entirely dedicated to sweets and coffee; we recommend the Lavazza Club.

THINGS TO DO NEARBY

Museo Egizio
This houses the most important collection of Egyptian artefacts outside Cairo, including a statue of Ramses II (one of the world's most important pieces of Egyptian art). *www.museoegizio.it*

Mole Antonelliana
The symbol of Turin, this 167m-high tower was originally intended as a synagogue, but now houses the hugely enjoyable Museum of Cinema. *www.museocinema.it*

Cattedrale di San Giovanni Battista
Join the pilgrims visiting Turin's 14th-century cathedral to catch sight of the Shroud of Turin (a copy), the famous burial cloth in which Jesus' body is said to have been wrapped. *www.duomoditorino.it*

Grom
You can lick a Grom gelato cone in Paris and New York, but it's sweeter grabbing one in its home town. Look out for *gianduja* (hazelnut chocolate). *www.grom.it*

CAFFÈ FLORIAN

Piazza San Marco 57, Venice;
www.caffeflorian.com; +39 041 520 5641

◆ Food   ◆ Cafe
◆ Shop   ◆ Transport

Few cafes ooze history in the way that Florian does. Opened in 1720 under the colonnade of the grand Procuratie Nuove on St Mark's Square, Caffè Florian is the oldest continually operating cafe in Europe. It was also one of the very first to welcome women – which is partly why the world's most infamous lothario, Casanova, frequented it so enthusiastically. Inside its jewel-box interior, waiters in white jackets and bow ties still deliver cappuccinos on silver trays to awestruck tourists bedazzled by the frescoes, gilt-edged mirrors and general air of decadence. For an unmissable indulgence, sip an espresso at a table on the square as the house orchestra strikes up and the setting sun ignites the golden mosaics of St Mark's Basilica.

THINGS TO DO NEARBY

Basilica di San Marco
Venice's extraordinary cathedral is crowned by a profusion of Byzantine-style domes and blanketed in colourful mosaics and marble, inside and out.
www.basilicasanmarco.it

Museo Correr
Occupying the same palace complex as Caffè Florian, this extraordinary museum is packed with extravagant state rooms, ancient sculpture and religious art.
correr.visitmuve.it

TORREFAZIONE CANNAREGIO

Rio Terà San Leonardo 1337, Venice;
www.torrefazionecannaregio.it; +39 041 71 63 71

- ◆ Food   ◆ Shop   ◆ Transport
- ◆ Roastery ◆ Cafe

 The jute sacks of beans lining one wall of this *torrefazione* (roastery) are a fragrant reminder of the Venetian republic's pivotal role in introducing coffee to Europe. Venice may appear as if it's built on water, but it is also built on coffee – in addition to silk, spices and all the other goods that were lugged off ships and then traded here back in the days when the republic dominated the maritime routes between east and west.

Coffee was first traded in Venice in the 16th century and the city has numerous historic cafes, but Torrefazione Cannaregio is the only remaining roaster, providing tourist-swamped locals with a steady supply of expertly toasted beans for their stovetop espresso machines ever since 1930. Chipper staff sell bags of beans (ground to order), along with perfectly prepared espresso to the regulars and coffee-obsessed visitors lining the counter. Food is limited to a small selection of pastries, but you can stock up on chocolate-covered coffee beans and coffee-infused dry pasta to take home with you.

Be sure to try an espresso made from the signature Remér blend – a combination of eight varieties of quality Arabica beans, resulting in a chocolatey blend that's relatively low in caffeine.

THINGS TO DO NEARBY

Ca' Macana Atelier
The city's masquerade tradition is celebrated in all its creepy glory in this longstanding mask shop, hung with all kinds of weird and wonderful handmade creations. ***www. camacanaatelier.blogspot.it***

The Ghetto
The site of an old foundry (*getto*), this gated island was the first designated Jewish quarter in the world to bear that infamous name.

Museo Ebraico
Learn about the many significant achievements of Venice's historic Jewish community and then take a guided tour of the Ghetto's synagogues. ***www.museoebraico.it***

Panificio Volpe Giovanni
It doesn't serve coffee but this little kosher bakery sells delicious Jewish sweets and some of the best *cornetti* (Italian-style croissants) in town.
+39 041 715 178

© Marc De Tollenaere; © Matt Munro / Lonely Planet

CAFFÈ PIGAFETTA

Contrada Pescaria 12, Vicenza;
www.caffepigafetta.com; +39 044 432 3960

◆ Food ◆ Cafe
◆ Shop ◆ Transport

From its own smooth house concoction to renowned Italian and international roasts, this cafe has been serving quality blends since 1976. Wrinkly staff with encyclopedic coffee knowledge will guide you through the options with passionate hand gestures. Patrons are often greeted by their names as Caffè Pigafetta fills and empties, fills and empties again, and locals from all walks of life either dash in for their coffee fix, or, during quieter times of day, relax on the retro vinyl green chairs and Formica tables.

The menu lists 25 coffee and liquor combinations, including a chocolately Yemen Mocha Ismaili, Tiramisu al rum and a traditional Irish Coffee. But don't miss the Caffè del Doge, a thick and heady espresso, hot chocolate and whipped cream concoction; the prime spot to savour it is at the stand-up bar.

THINGS TO DO NEARBY

Piazza dei Signori
Vicenza's main square is a hub of activity filled with strolling families, buzzy cafes and grand limestone arches lining the Palladian Basilica (see opposite).

Teatro Olimpic
This elliptical Renaissance theatre was modelled after Roman amphitheatres and contains a trompe-l'œil stage, giving an illusion of city streets extending to the horizon. ***www. teatrolimpicovicenza.it***

NORWAY

How to ask for a coffee in the local language?
Kan jeg få en kaffe?
Signature coffee style? A classic light roast filter coffee, served black
What to order with your coffee? Norwegian waffles, served with cream and jam
Do: Discuss how beautiful Norway is; don't bring up whaling, it's a touchy subject

Like its Scandinavian neighbours, Norway is a country that has a coffee habit stretching back three centuries. The first coffee beans were imported to Norwegian shores in the late 17th century, and to begin with, coffee was solely the preserve of the country's aristocrats, merchants and gentry. By the late 18th century, however, Norway already had one of the highest coffee consumptions per capita in Europe, thanks in part to its rich tradition of global trading and seafaring. It's now an indelible part of the national character: in the Land of the Midnight Sun, where the boundaries between day and night are blurred for much of the year, it's perhaps hardly surprising that many

people resort to a good cup of coffee to keep them awake through the endless summer days.

One tradition that's particularly characteristic of Norway's coffee is the 'light roast', in which beans are roasted for a far shorter time to bring out the fruity notes, sweet aromas and more complex flavour profiles that are usually overpowered by longer roasts. It's a method that's catching on beyond Norway's shores, as roasteries look for ways to distinguish their product in an ever-more crowded marketplace. Norway's modern coffee culture properly kicked off in the late 1990s, and chains such as Stockfleths and Gødt Brod are now a ubiquitous sight. But it's the independent scene that continues to thrive.

KAFFEMISJONEN

Øvre Korskirkeallmenning 5, Bergen;
www.kaffemisjonen.no; +47 4505 0360

◆ Food   ◆ Cafe
◆ Classes   ◆ Transport

Oslo tends to steal the limelight away from Norway's other cities, in coffee as in all other things. But have no fear: venture away from the capital to Bergen and you'll find at least two excellent coffee shops at your disposal – Kaffeemisjonen (KM) and its sister joint, Blöm, across town. KM was the first to open, in 2007; it's a light-filled salon that's only a short walk away from the city's lovely Hanseatic harbour-front. 'Good coffee for the people!' is its stated credo, and it delivers in all areas: excellent espressos, fine filters, marvellous milk art, informative coffee courses and delicious pastries, supplied by Bergen's renowned Colonialen bakery. The setting is lovely, too: chequerboard floor-tiles, teal-blue walls, and windows onto the streets.

THINGS TO DO NEARBY

Bergen Fish Market
For centuries Bergen has survived on the fruits of the sea, and this brilliant fish market by the harbour is a must-see. The lobster rolls are off-the-chart good.
www.visitbergen.com

Bryggen
Take a guided walking tour of the rickety wooden buildings and wharfside warehouses in the Unesco-listed district of Bryggen, Bergen's historic heart.
www.bymuseet.no

SUPREME ROASTWORKS

Thorvald Meyers gate 18A, Oslo;
www.srw.no; +47 2271 4202

◆ Food   ◆ Shop   ◆ Transport
◆ Roastery ◆ Cafe

The tagline tells it like it is: 'no fuzz, just great coffee'. It's a simple mantra that sums up this cafe and micro-roastery in Oslo's boho Grünerløkka neighbourhood. Started in 2013, it's still relatively new on the block but has quickly become a firm favourite of Oslo's coffee lovers. True to their ethos it's a stripped-down affair: a few chairs, a stereo on the side and a roaster out back, plus a coffee counter and blackboards spelling out the day's coffees in retro, stick-on lettering.

Like many Scandi roasters, Supreme tends to favour a single roast, regardless of whether the beans are destined for espresso or filter. It gives its coffees a clarity of flavour, and allows more fruit-forward flavours to emerge in the cup; try one of the natural processed coffees, such as an Ethiopian or Brazilian pour-over.

THINGS TO DO NEARBY

Grünerløkka Bryghus
Sink a few choice craft beers at this trendy microbrewery, a favourite weekend haunt of the Grünerløkka crowd.
brygghus.no

St Hanshaugen
Order your coffee to go and stroll west to explore this peaceful city park, which was created in the 19th century and is renowned for its views over Oslo.

TIM WENDELBOE

Grünersgate 1, Oslo;
www.timwendelboe.no; +47 4000 4062

◆ Roastery   ◆ Cafe
◆ Shop   ◆ Transport

Though he wasn't the first Norwegian to take the top prize in the World Barista Championships (that would be Robert Thoresen, in 2000), Tim Wendelboe is arguably the man who's done more than anyone else to pioneer the evolution of Norwegian coffee. Having begun his career at Stockfleths in 1998, he's Norway's most decorated barista: Norwegian champion four times, a gold and two silvers at the World Barista Championships, and one-time World Cup Tasting Champion. Launched on the back of his success, he opened his own eponymous shop, and one of the capital city's first roasters, in Oslo's hip Grünerløkka district in 2007.

Unsurprisingly, Wendelboe's name is legendary in Norwegian coffee circles, and his eponymous cafe has

THINGS TO DO NEARBY

Markveien Mat & Vinhus
One of the top addresses in Grünerløkka for Norwegian food, with an antique atmosphere and a cosy cellar space.
markveien.no

Ny York
Pick up some retro collectables and vintage clothes at this second-hand store, one of several dotted around Grünerløkka.
www.facebook.com/nyyorkoslo

National Gallery
Edvard Munch's haunting *The Scream* is the centrepiece at Stockholm's main art museum, but there's heaps more besides.
www.nasjonalmuseet.no

Munchmuseet
Yet more Munch here; the museum has one of the world's largest collection of the artist's paintings and drawings.
munchmuseet.no

become a mecca for Oslo's coffee connoisseurs. He's a quietly spoken man, and the cafe itself is similarly understated; on a nondescript corner of Grünersgate, it's an unshowy blend of wood, brick and distressed stone. The coffees are known for their delicacy, precision and refinement, and the cupping is a treat to watch; try the Mexico Chiapas Light Roast, a fruity find from Wendelboe's Mexican adventures. Unfortunately, Tim's a rare sight behind the counter these days – he's been hard at work building a brand-new, purpose-built roastery, and providing coffee for super-chef René Redzepi of Noma fame, no less. Mr Wendelboe, sir, we salute you.

RISO MAT & KAFFEEBAR

Strandgata 32, Tromsø;
www.risoe-mk.no; +47 4166 4516

◆ Food ◆ Transport
◆ Cafe

You're 39°north, just a couple of hundred miles south of the Arctic Circle. Reindeer roam across the snowy wastes and the Northern Lights blaze overhead, as if Mother Nature has decided to put on a fireworks show just for you. You're in Tromsø – way, way, way north – and you're in need of a caffeine fix to keep you fuelled up for the night's auroral adventures. Take a tip from the townsfolk and head for Riso – a neighbourhood cafe renowned for its excellent espressos, delicious open-faced sandwiches and yummy homemade cakes. Nattily aproned baristas, the hum of conversation and tightly packed tables create a buzzy vibe here, and there's an element of theatricality to the pour-over procedure – not to mention the creative milk art (is that an alien in my cup?). For now, the aurora will have to wait – there's time for another coffee first. Probably a strong, black double espresso, dark as the polar night.

THINGS TO DO NEARBY

Arctic Guide Service
This aurora-spotting company runs a nightly tour in search of the lights. If you don't spot them, you get a discount on a second tour. ***www.arcticguideservice. com***

Tromsø Wilderness Centre
Learn how to pilot your own dogsled, pulled along by a team of fluffy huskies, for that full *White Fang* experience. ***www. villmarkssenter.no***

SPAIN

How to ask for a coffee in the local language?
Un café/cortado/con leche por favor
Signature coffee style? Solo (espresso; 'un café' will
be interpreted as a solo)
What to order with your coffee? An ensaimada –
a round spiral of pastry, dusted with icing sugar
Don't: Order a coffee with milk after about 11am
if you don't want to be marked out as a tourist

The Spanish were relatively late adopters of the coffee habit, which was introduced by Charles III (or more accurately, his Italian cooks, during his reign over Naples in the mid-18th century), but they were quick to catch on, and had a ready source of excellent quality beans from their colonies in the Americas. It was Italians too who opened Spain's first cafe, in Madrid, in 1764. Called the Fonda de San Sebastián, it became a cradle for the venerable Spanish tradition of the *tertulia*, a meeting of artists and thinkers who'd talk long into the night, fuelled by caffeine. Some of the grand old cafes favoured by the intelligentsia at the time, such as the Café Gijón in Madrid or Els Quatre Gats in Barcelona, still survive to this day.

Spanish coffee took a nosedive during the Civil War, when the concept of *torrefacto* – beans roasted with sugar in an attempt to both bulk out the grains and disguise excess bitterness – was introduced. The mix is on the wane, though many bars and hotels still serve it, but as the third wave makes quiet inroads into coffee-drinking culture on the peninsula it's easily avoided. Specialist coffee shops were once a rarity, and cafes roasting their own beans almost unheard of, but the last few years have seen a sea change in attitude. Outside the big cities you'll still struggle to find a freshly ground Jamaica Blue, but you can find a thoroughly decent morning hit almost anywhere.

CAFÉS EL MAGNIFICO

Carrer de l'Argenteria 64, Barcelona;
www.cafeselmagnifico.com; +34 933 19 39 75

◆ Shop   ◆ Transport
◆ Cafe

Inhale the coffee aroma wafting out of the door underneath the vintage stained-glass cafe sign as you enter this third-generation, family-run coffee roaster. It's been sourcing and grinding quality beans since 1919, and more than 300 blends are roasted across the street from the shop. The knowledgeable staff will happily explain the 40 or so blends on offer.

Milk is sourced locally, each cup is served with a chocolate square and while there are new trends such as cold-brew on the menu, embrace the history here and order a traditional Spanish cortado. You can perch on one of the few benches and ponder the antique coffee cup collection lining one entire wall as you do, but lingering is not the thing in this tiny space – sip, take in the action and go.

THINGS TO DO NEARBY

Picasso Museum
Spread over five medieval mansions, this museum (see above) focuses on Picasso's work from his formative years, many spent at a nearby art school. *www. museupicasso.bcn.cat*

El Born Cultural and Memorial Center
This grand iron-and-glass former market houses archaeological remains of the area once flattened to create a citadel. *elbornculturaimemoria. barcelona.cat*

NØMAD CØFFEE

Passatge de Sert 12, Barcelona;
nomadcoffee.es; +34 628 566 235

◆ Roastery ◆ Shop ◆ Transport
◆ Classes (at roastery) ◆ Cafe

Master barista Jordi Mestre is on a mission to see coffee treated with the same reverence as wine. 'The culture is changing, brunch is a thing here now, and people meet up during the day, not just at night,' he says. To this end, he set up Nømad to provide world-class coffee (roasted in his Poblenou space) to other cafes, and follows up sales with training and consultancy. The Nømad coffee lab and shop, located in one of the city's prettiest passageways, has all the friendly gravitas of a lab – feel free to fire questions, but don't even think about asking for sugar. If you're there during the long steamy months that constitute a Barcelona summer, you'll find the bottled cold brew something of a life-saver.

THINGS TO DO NEARBY

Palau de la Música Catalana
Gaudí's lesser-known contemporary, Puig i Cadafalch, was behind this wonderfully over-the-top concert hall, where floral motifs burst from every pillar and entire walls look good enough to eat. *www.palaumusica.cat*

Mercat de Santa Caterina
For all the clamour and smells of the famous Boqueria but without the selfie-sticks and queues, stock up on picnic fodder at the handsome Santa Caterina market. *www.mercatsantacaterina.com*

SATAN'S COFFEE CORNER

11 Carrer de l'Arc de Sant Ramon del Call, Barcelona; satanscoffee.com; +34 666 222 599

◆ Food   ◆ Shop   ◆ Transport
◆ Roastery ◆ Cafe

It would be natural to assume a Faustian pact was responsible for this cafe's cult following, but the devil has all the best brews because of good science and locally sourced beans. Caffeine flows through the veins of owner Marcos Bartolomé, who comes from a family of coffeemakers. Bartolomé sources beans in Castelldefels, barely half an hour from Barcelona, and he's as meticulous about the taste of his water as the grains steeped therein.

Entering the cafe puts you face to face with the baristas, while the minimalist interior ensures no distractions from your first sip (an inscription on the wall reads 'no wi-fi, no bullsh*t'). Order a cold brew to marvel at coffee so perfectly balanced that it needs neither milk nor sugar.

THINGS TO DO NEARBY

La Catedral
Stone gargoyles cling to this gothic cathedral (see below left) and stained-glass windows illuminate its vast interior. Climb the tower for panoramic views of the Barri Gòtic.
www.catedralbcn.org

Pont del Bisbe
Barcelona's Barri Gòtic is a melange of Roman walls, medieval buildings and 19th-century architecture, but its most photographed sight is this flamboyant-gothic-style bridge, built in 1928.

HOLA COFFEE

Calle del Dr. Fourquet 33, Madrid;
hola.coffee; +34 910 56 82 63

◆ Food   ◆ Shop   ◆ Transport
◆ Classes   ◆ Cafe

THINGS TO DO NEARBY

Museo Reina Sofia
This huge contemporary art museum is a must-visit for anyone with an interest in Spain's greatest artworks, including Pablo Picasso's *Guernica*.
www.museoreinasofia.es

Churros at Chocolatería San Ginés
Coffee rules, but not when it comes to churros, which have to be paired with hot chocolate. Enjoy them at their very best in this Madrid institution.
chocolateriasangines.com

Parque El Retiro
This stunning natural retreat is one of the city's biggest draws for locals and visitors alike, and there's nothing better than to come here for a relaxing sunset walk.

Evening drinks in Chueca
Chueca is Madrid's gay neighbourhood, and full of fun, with vibrant bars that spill out onto the street and plazas well into the early hours.

Hola Coffee founders Nolo Botana and Pablo Caballero are a great example of two young coffee entrepreneurs who are breathing life into Spain's most vibrant speciality coffee scene, and their wonderfully friendly coffee bar in pleasant Lavapies is a great place to visit if you're marathoning around the capital's two most impressive museums, El Prado and Reina Sofia.

Nolo and Pablo met while working for a commercial coffee roasting company following a few years working for Toma (see p190) and Federal Café, among others. After learning some of the most important elements of the trade, including how to roast fine coffees, the two friends decided it was time to go it alone and open their own cafe.

Located on a quiet street that's also home to various galleries, yoga studios and other small businesses, Hola is the kind of place you could see yourself visiting every day on your way to work. In a space featuring lots of seemingly obligatory wood and exposed brick, the cafe dishes up some simple food selections, but the real stars are the coffees. They serve all your favourite espresso and filter options alongside refreshing cold brew and various guest coffees from the batch brewer too.

If you need any more encouragement to visit, know that Pablo is Spain's 2016 Barista Champion, further testimony to the fact that these guys know their beans.

TOMA CAFÉ

Calle de la Palma 49, Madrid;
tomacafe.es; +34 917 02 56 20

◆ Food   ◆ Shop   ◆ Transport
◆ Classes   ◆ Cafe

Madrid was a relative latecomer to the speciality coffee scene, but the city has been making up lost grounds (ahem) fast, and Toma Café, which literally means 'drink coffee', was the first speciality coffee shop to offer Madrileños a taste of what was to come. And it seems they liked what they tasted.

Owners Santi Rigoni and Patricia Alda created a very casual space that wouldn't have felt out of place in Berlin, London or Melbourne... cue the obligatory racing bike hanging from the ceiling. Big floor-to-ceiling doors flood the place with light and offer guests a chance to dangle their legs onto the street while sipping on a refreshing glass of cold brew or a perfectly prepared cappuccino.

THINGS TO DO NEARBY

Lolo Polos
Grab yourself a refreshing and delicious ice pop and explore the lovely streets of vibrant Malasaña.
lolopolosartesanos.es

Ojalá
This friendly restaurant on lovely Plaza Juan Pujol serves affordable and delicious dishes, great brunch and has ice-cold Pimm's.
grupolamusa.com

LA MOLIENDA

Carrer del Bisbe Campins 11, Palma, Mallorca;
www.lamolienda.es; +34 634 52 48 21

◆ Food   ◆ Cafe
◆ Shop   ◆ Transport

Many visitors to Mallorca bypass Palma for the island's more rural charms: its beaches, rugged interior and beautiful mountains. But the capital is filled with hidden gems, and La Molienda is one of them. This coffee bar and food spot is run by cousins Miguel and Toni (at the espresso machine) and their friend Majo (in the kitchen). Their homely cafe, set on a shady plaza, is a great place to start the day. Tuck into a healthy serving of poached eggs or avocado on crunchy bread and wash it all down with a cup of filter coffee from the likes of Nømad, The Barn and Origin Coffee. Perfect.

THINGS TO DO NEARBY

Palma Cathedral
Overlooking the bay and towering over the city, the magnificent 13th-century La Seu is a sight to behold – as are the views from its bell tower. *catedraldemallorca. org*

Clandestí Taller Gastronòmic
This intimate restaurant only has space for 12 diners but dishes from its chefs Pau Navarro and Ariadna Salvadorare are incredibly inventive and based on local recipes. Book well in advance. *clandesti.es*

SWEDEN

How to ask for a coffee in the local language?
Kan jag få en kopp kaffe?
Signature coffee style? Black filter
What to order with your coffee? Kanelbullar, a sweet
cinnamon bun
Don't: Rush if you're invited to fika; it's a tradition
that's all about taking your time

It's a little-known fact but Sweden actually drinks
more coffee than practically any other country
on the planet – only the caffeine-crazy Finns drink more.
Drinking coffee is a national pastime in Sweden, and coffee
breaks are practically a mandatory part of everyone's day;
the Swedes even have their own word for it, *fika*, which
roughly translates as a cosy moment shared with friends,
ideally over a cup of coffee and something sweet such as
a cinnamon bun. The word itself is actually an inversion
of *kaffi*, Swedish for coffee; intriguingly, it was originally
used as a codeword by clandestine 18th-century coffee-
drinkers who were suspected of fomenting anti-monarchist
sentiment against King Gustav III, who had a paranoid terror
of the drink, and spent much of his life trying to ban it.

During the later 18th and early 19th centuries, coffee
became the preferred beverage for the aristocratic elite,
and *kaffeehus* (coffee houses) and *konditori* (pastry shops)
became a common sight on the streets of Stockholm,
Gothenburg and Malmö. Things have come on by leaps and
bounds since then: Sweden's baristas led the way during
coffee's third wave, and have become a regular feature
at events such as the World Barista Championships. The
country now boasts some of Scandinavia's top coffee
shops, in which cutting-edge brewing techniques are
blended with that stripped-back, effortless, eminently
enviable sense of Scandi style. Coffee isn't just a drink here:
it's an expression of self.

DROP COFFEE

Wollmar Yxkullsgatan 10, Stockholm;
dropcoffee.com; +46 8 410 233 63

◆ Food ◆ Classes ◆ Cafe
◆ Roastery ◆ Shop ◆ Transport

Ask any coffee aficionado for a Stockholm recommendation, and chances are they'll send you the way of this award-winning cafe and roastery in Mariatorget. Founded in 2009 by young roasters Joanna Alm and Erik Rosendahl (with the latter recently giving way to Englishman Stephen Leighton), it's become a

THINGS TO DO NEARBY

Gamla Stan
Have a wander around
Stockholm's quaint old
town, a maze of alleyways
and cobbled lanes on
a small island between
Sodermalm and Nordmalm.

Eriks Gondolen
This soaring glass-clad
restaurant by the harbour
offers the best seat in
the house for cocktails or
fine-dining, with birds' eye
views over the harbour.
www.eriks.se

staple fixture of the city's speciality coffee scene. Drop Coffee's trademark style is light, flavourful roasts; the same beans are used for both espresso and filter, which allows more rounded, delicate flavours to come through in their coffees, mostly sourced from Bolivia, Colombia, El Salvador, Ethiopia and Kenya.

The cafe itself is a small space, but it's a masterpiece of understated Scandi design: wooden tables and white walls contrast with day-glo chairs and industrial lamps. There's a big display of the company's coffees, all wrapped up in their trademark cardboard-brown or duck-egg blue packaging, alongside a huge arsenal of coffee-brewing equipment (you can pick up a bespoke coffee apron and accompanying tote bag). You'll find yourself among plenty of beautiful Swedish people; unsurprisingly, Drop is a hangout for students, creatives, models, photographers and shop-workers alike. Their courses are great, too: there's a roasting course, a coffee tasting lab and a manual brewing masterclass, along with a full-blown barista experience.

JOHAN & NYSTRÖM

Swedenborgsgatan 7, Stockholm;
johanochnystrom.se; +46 8 702 20 40

◆ Food ◆ Classes ◆ Cafe
◆ Roastery ◆ Shop

Johan & Nyström supplies coffee shops, restaurants and hotels all over Sweden from its well-respected roastery, which roasts only Fairtrade organic beans, but it also has its own flagship store in the centre of Stockholm's ever-trendy Södermal neighbourhood. In truth it's really more of a shop than a cafe: walls are lined with a bewildering array of the company's direct-trade, organic coffees, some stacked so high that they require a ladder to reach them.

Staff from the shop compete every year at the Swedish Barista championships, and invariably place highly, a clear sign of their expertise. AeroPress, siphon and pour-over are all on offer, as well as excellent espresso, and there are free afternoon cupping sessions. There's always a Roast of the Week, hand-picked from the roastery's own range.

THINGS TO DO NEARBY

Fotografiska
Brush up on your Instagramming skills at this excellent photography museum, with regular exhibitions of contemporary work in a former customs house.
fotografiska.eu

Pelikan
This lovely old beer hall offers a glimpse of old Stockholm, serving traditional dishes like meatballs and boiled pork under high ceilings, wood panels and chandeliers.
pelikan.se

THE NETHERLANDS

How to ask for a coffee in the local language?
Mag ik een kop koffie alsjeblieft?

Signature coffee style? Zwarte koffie (black coffee) or koffie verkeerd (a latte)

What to order with your coffee? Banana bread, cookies and apple pie are the most common sweet treats that almost everybody has on offer. Check the counter for interesting and often healthier alternatives

Don't: Light up a joint in a cafe unless you're sure you are in one where you can buy and smoke marijuana

If the spread of the exotic coffee bean around Europe can be attributed to one country above all others, that country is undoubtedly the Netherlands. Although some coffee houses already existed in places such as Venice, Istanbul and even Oxford, it wasn't until 1711, when the Dutch began importing commercially produced coffees from their former colonies in Java and Sumatra, that coffee became more widely accessible.

Today, almost every household in the country consumes some form of coffee, and while the Dutch no longer have their own Asian colonies or play any large-scale role in importing coffee into Europe, this small nation is still one of its biggest per capita consumers – depending on which list you trust, it appears in either 3rd or 5th place every year.

No surprise then that when speciality coffee began making its way across the European continent from around 2011 onwards, Amsterdam was at the forefront in developing its very own scene. This was largely fuelled by former employees of its very first speciality coffee roasters, Espressofabriek, and a few expats who were missing the kind of great coffee bars they have at home.

In the course of just one or two years, Amsterdam gained a huge amount of exciting new coffee spots, many of them also roasting in-house, and before too long this love for a better, tastier and more exciting coffee spread all over the country. Around the same time, Starbucks closed a deal with the national train company and quickly began opening coffee shops in all major stations as well as core locations in various city centres. And if that isn't enough, Dunkin' Donuts recently entered the Dutch market and plans to open up to 160 stores in the foreseeable future.

Compared with other European cities such as Berlin, Paris and London, one thing that is striking about the speciality coffee scene in Amsterdam is that it's almost entirely locally owned, while elsewhere Aussies, Kiwis and Americans are often running the show.

TOP 5 COFFEES

Stooker Roasting Co Ethiopia Idido
White Label Guatemala Triple
Friedhats Kenya Gaithini AB
Headfirst Coffee Roasters Ethiopia Aichesh
Blommers Coffee Roasters Ethiopia Kochere PB

CAFE TALK – LEX WENNEKER

Most people now use the right technology to make really good coffee, we're just waiting for the next big innovation to come along

And the Dutch are very smart entrepreneurs indeed. Many recognised the speciality coffee trend early and, often inspired by extensive worldwide travel, brought an international influence to their passion for coffee. The capital's scene proved such a success that an Amsterdam Coffee Festival was launched in 2014.

Although it's certainly true that there is still a great divide between those who think that Douwe Egberts is the best coffee and those who go the extra mile to source nothing but the freshest and most exquisite single-origin beans from their local roasters, the Netherlands is a certifiably great place to explore and enjoy really outstanding coffee. So grab your bike and get moving.

DE SCHOOL

Jan van Breemenstraat 3, Amsterdam;
www.deschoolamsterdam.nl; +31 20 737 3197

◆ Food ◆ Cafe
◆ Shop ◆ Transport

De School is a very special place. Part nightclub, part restaurant, part cafe, part gym and part small business centre, it is in some form the follow-up to legendary Amsterdam nightclub Trouw, which closed its doors in January 2015. Occupying a former state school's grounds, De School is widely regarded as the best techno club in the Netherlands and its restaurant has received rave reviews from a wide range of food critics who laud its easy-going character, inventive kitchen and incredibly good value. You can enjoy an outstanding seven-course dinner with excellent wine pairings before diving deep into the basement for a thumping nightlife experience.

However, if you just want to get a delicious cup of coffee, the cafe is open during the day and exclusively serves freshly roasted coffees from in-house coffee roaster White Label, which has its impressive production roastery along

THINGS TO DO NEARBY

Floor17
A short walk away, the Ramada Hotel's spectacular rooftop bar and restaurant Floor17 offers sweeping views across the city plus (slightly overpriced) glasses of wine. *www.floor17.nl*

De Clercqstraat
A great street for shopping, eating and drinking. Tuck into a roast chicken at Van 't Spit or the Rotisserie or enjoy delicious Italian cuisine at Cantinetta. *bysam.nl/de-leukste-spots-op-de-clercqstraat*

Rembrandtpark
This lovely park stretching along Amsterdam's western flank is one of the few places where you can still light a BBQ. *www.amsterdam.nl/projecten/rembrandtpark*

SportPlaza Mercator
A real hidden gem. This sports centre opposite De School has one of the nicest public outdoor pools in the city. *www.sportplazamercator.nl*

the corridor. White Label is run by local coffee legends Elmer Oomkens and Francesco Grassotti, who have their main cafe just down the road on Jan Evertsenstraat.

De School's cafe is a bit out of the way, meaning it's never overly crowded. It's a great place to come and work, enjoy a tasty sandwich for lunch and slurp an expertly prepared flat white while you do your best to meet that deadline.

LOT SIXTY ONE

Kinkerstraat 112, Amsterdam;
www.lotsixtyonecoffee.com; +31 6 1605 4227

- ◆ Food
- ◆ Classes
- ◆ Cafe
- ◆ Roastery
- ◆ Shop
- ◆ Transport

Located on a busy street corner in happening Oud West, Lot Sixty One was one of the earliest pioneers of the city's speciality coffee movement, and remains a force to be reckoned with. Founders Adam Craig and Paul Jenner brought a slice of casual Aussie hospitality to the city at a time when service was generally poor and no one really knew what a flat white was.

Today Lot Sixty One supplies many of the city's leading restaurants and hotels, including the chic Hoxton, with its Probast hand-roasted beans, and also maintains an outpost inside the Urban Outfitters store on Rokin. Its Oud West HQ is the perfect spot for people-watching while sipping on a tasty batch-brew filter coffee and enjoying a slice of cake or pastry.

THINGS TO DO NEARBY

Waterkant

Just a few minutes walk down the Kinkerstraat is Waterkant, the city's top waterside bar and restaurant; be prepared to queue – it's crowded year-round. *www.waterkantamsterdam.nl*

De Hallen

This spectacular former tram depot is now cinema, mini shopping mall, library and food court in one, and always worth a visit. *dehallen-amsterdam.nl*

NEWWERKTHEATER

Oostenburgergracht 75, Amsterdam;
www.newwerktheater.com; +31 20 57 213 80

- ◆ Food
- ◆ Cafe
- ◆ Shop
- ◆ Transport

The most exciting new arrival on Amsterdam's coffee scene is housed inside a disused theatre that now triples as HQ of a creative agency (...,staat), an events and co-working space and an outstanding coffee bar with food and drinks. Developed in collaboration with Berlin-based roaster Bonanza, NewWerktheater successfully localised a concept that is already commonplace in cities such as London, Melbourne and Copenhagen.

The founder of ...,staat, Jochem Leegstra, didn't necessarily plan on running a full-blown hospitality business in the foyer of his company's new home, but he reasons: 'If we can make this a place that nurtures creativity, is welcoming to everyone and serves a damn fine cup of coffee, who am I to complain?'

THINGS TO DO NEARBY

Artis + Micropia
The city's zoo is one of the oldest in Europe and one of the most charming. And right next to it is the world's first museum dedicated to micro-organisms. ***www.artis.nl***

Het Scheepvaartmuseum
The Dutch have a seafaring history unlike any other and this heritage is beautifully put on show at the city's national maritime museum. ***www. hetscheepvaartmuseum.nl***

SCANDINAVIAN EMBASSY

Sarphatipark 34, Amsterdam;
www.scandinavianembassy.nl; +31 6 8160 0140

◆ Food   ◆ Shop   ◆ Transport
◆ Classes   ◆ Cafe

When Rikard Andersson and Nicolas Castagno opened Scandinavian Embassy in 2014 it left many people scratching their heads. Here was a place, in hip De Pijp, that served lightly roasted coffees from Nordic roasters and paired them with cured meats from the likes of elk, moose and bear. And that was just the aperitif. Former lawyer turned chef, Rikard offers inventive Swedish-inspired dishes that use ingredients such as buckthorn jelly and ramson berries. He also makes his

© Mark Read / Lonely Planet

THINGS TO DO NEARBY

Sarphatipark
De Pijp's beautiful little island of calm is a great place to soak up some sun and the city's vibe. *www. amsterdam.info/parks/ sarphatipark*

Gerard Doustraat
This is the neighbourhood's loveliest little shopping street, full of independent boutiques and unusual pop-up stores.

Brouwerij Troost
If you need a break from all the coffee-drinking, head to this local brewery overlooking a quiet square. The IPA is delicious. *brouwerijtroost.nl*

Museumplein
A 10-minute walk from Scandy is Amsterdam's museum square, home to the Rijks- (see left), Van Gogh and Stedelijk Museums. *www.amsterdam.info/ museumquarter*

own fermented drinks and often infuses seafood with part of the coffee plant. Rikard's wife Domenika has joined the team and showcases her fashion line, SE Wardrobe, at the back of the shop. Scandy, as it's called by its fans, also makes Swedish cinnamon rolls, and is the only place in Amsterdam where you can sample coffees from the likes of La Cabra, Drop Coffee, The Coffee Collective and Per Nordby.

If you don't feel too adventurous with your food, or just want a simple and healthy breakfast, opt for the exquisite poached eggs with salted salmon or a nutritious porridge.

MAN MET BRIL

Vijverhofstraat 70, Rotterdam;
www.manmetbrilkoffie.nl; +31 6 4103 4864

◆ Food   ◆ Classes   ◆ Cafe
◆ Roastery ◆ Shop   ◆ Transport

THINGS TO DO NEARBY

Centraal Station
Don't miss the striking slanted roof of Rotterdam station's south entrance. It has really changed the way train stations can look.

Luchtsingel
This beautiful wooden bridge connecting Rotterdam Noord to the centre has been compared with New York's High Line. At the northern end you'll find tons of great bars.
www.luchtsingel.org

Aloha
Probably the coolest hangout in the city, Aloha used to be a water park and after many years in oblivion, it now offers the best terrace in town, fine food and great drinks.
www.alohabar.nl

Erasmus bridge
This iconic bridge connects Rotterdam with the southern suburbs. Walk across it to get a panoramic view of the city's skyline – it's the total opposite of what you would expect to see in the Netherlands.

Germany's second city may lack the beauty of Amsterdam and the beachside charm of The Hague, but Rotterdam locals are still very proud of their hometown's state-of-the-art infrastructure, including the spectacular new central station and the council's on-going redevelopment of formerly edgy areas like Katendrecht.

The founder of Man met Bril, Paul Sharo, roasted coffee in a variety of establishments before finding a new home in the arches below a disused train line. His Hoofdkantoor HQ is a bright and open space where espresso shots are pulled on a juiced-up Slayer espresso machine, filter coffees await in ready-made portioned containers and the lunch menu offers exquisite flatbreads with finger-lickin'-good toppings.

It is no exaggeration to say that Paul has always been and remains the closest that Rotterdam's small speciality coffee scene has to a celebrity, and his friendly demeanour and outstanding coffees are the reasons why so many people go out of their way to pay him a visit.

THE VILLAGE COFFEE & MUSIC

Voorstraat 46, Utrecht;
thevillagecoffee.nl; +31 3 0236 9400

◆ Food ◆ Cafe
◆ Shop ◆ Transport

Before most people in the Netherlands had even heard of speciality coffee, Angelo van de Weerd and Lennaert Meijboom had already reached cult status with their taxidermy-filled espresso bar on the happening Voorstraat in Utrecht. Since day one, the two friends ran this place like a mix between your best friend's living room and a tiny concert venue where you go to get caffeinated and make new friends.

Each shot from the espresso machine is carefully pulled, each filter coffee is expertly brewed, and if you swing by on the right kind of evening, you might catch some live music or a DJ set. There's another branch at the Science Museum.

THINGS TO DO NEARBY

Oudegracht
Utrecht's main canal is lined with many restaurants and bars that come to life in the evenings.

The Domtoren
Get a sweeping view of Utrecht by heading up the tallest church tower in the Netherlands. After climbing 465 steps you'll also come face to face with the cathedral's impressive bells. *www.domtoren.nl*

TURKEY

How to ask for a coffee in the local language?
Bir kahve lütfen
Signature coffee style? Türk kahve (Turkish coffee)
What to order with your coffee? Nargile (water pipe)
Do: Be specific when you're asked how sweet you
want your Turkish coffee: çok şekerli (very sweet),
orta şekerli (middling), az şekerli (slightly), or
şekersiz/sade (bitter)

True to its position on the edge of the Middle East, Turkey has a long-established coffeehouse culture, with cups glimpsed alongside backgammon boards in bazaar courtyards nationwide. Repairing to the *kahvehane* (coffeehouse) or *çay bahçesi* (tea garden) for a cuppa, accompanied by a gossip and a *nargile* packed with apple tobacco, is part of the Turkish philosophy of *keyif* – taking life easy. One puritanical 17th-century Ottoman Grand Vizier even banned coffeehouses, with transgressors beaten with a cudgel or thrown into the Bosphorus.

This long history has spawned numerous customs, dating back to the elaborate ceremonies of the Ottoman courts, in which 40 coffeemakers would prepare a brew for the sultan. Turkish men once selected a wife based on their coffee-making skills, and it was considered grounds for divorce if a husband could not provide daily coffee.

Tar-like Turkish coffee is normally downed in a few short sips and, afterwards, drinkers tip the sludgy residue into the saucer and read their friend's fortune in the patterns. This tradition of *kahve falı* is especially popular among Turkish women, having been introduced by the Arab nannies of the Ottoman elite. If your friend tells a favourable fortune (a tree pattern means you're going on holiday), you can remind them of the Turkish proverb about the camaraderie surrounding a shared cuppa: 'A cup of coffee commits one to 40 years of friendship.'

Roasters and baristas here are passionate, even if Turkish coffeehouses can be male-dominated. But rest assured, a good flat white is never far away in Istanbul.

COFFEE DEPARTMENT

Kurkcu Cesmesi Sokak No 5/A Balat Fatih, Istanbul;
coffeedepartment.co; +90 532 441 6663

◆ Roastery ◆ Cafe
◆ Shop ◆ Transport

Squirrelled away in hip Balat, a few streets inland from the Golden Horn waterway, Coffee Department takes its caffeine seriously, as evidenced by the filter-drip coffee-making kits for sale through to the cups they serve, using a global roster of beans roasted on site; while recommending the perfect bean for my flat white, the barista enthused in perfect English about plans to increase the Latin American selection. Indeed, the team's passion for coffee saw one barista represent Turkey at the World Brewers Cup 2017 in Budapest.

With its wood-and-metal aesthetic, the small cafe is a pleasant surprise in a country more readily associated with old-timers sipping Turkish coffee in the bazaar. For a silky smooth flat white with apple-pie and milk-chocolate notes, go for the Costa Rican beans.

THINGS TO DO NEARBY

Patriarchal Church of St George
One of Turkey's major pilgrimage destinations, this 19th-century Greek Orthodox church has an ornately carved wooden iconostasis, Byzantine mosaics, religious relics and a wood-and-inlay patriarchal throne. *www.ec-patr.org*

Kariye Museum
The home of the Chora Church is one of Istanbul's finest remaining Byzantine structures (see below), adorned with stunning 14th-century mosaics and frescoes, and is much more tranquil than the more famous Aya Sofya. *ayasofyamuzesi.gov.tr/en/kariye-museum*

FAZIL BEY

Kadıköy, Istanbul; +90 216 450 2870

◆ Roastery   ◆ Cafe
◆ Shop   ◆ Transport

THINGS TO DO NEARBY

Street art
Since the Mural Istanbul festival began in 2012, the Yeldeğirmeni area, between Fazıl Bey and the Haydarpaşa train tracks, has become a street gallery of epic murals.
muralistanbul.org

Ferry trip
Take the ferry across the Bosphorus, crossing between Europe and Asia with Istanbul's minaret-dotted skyline around you, for one of the city's best experiences.
www.sehirhatlari.istanbul

Kadife Sokak
For a glass of something stronger, hit Kadıköy's *barlar sokak* ('bar street'), where locals settle in with a game of backgammon.

Kadıköy Pazarı
Explore Kadıköy's fresh-produce market on a walking tour with the likes of Culinary Backstreets.
culinarybackstreets.com

Catch a ferry across the Bosphorus to experience what is arguably the city's very best cup of potent Turkish coffee. Opposed to mass production, Fazıl Bey actually roasts its favoured Brazilian beans on site, grinds them in a rather jolly red antique grinder, brews them in a traditional cezve – a small copper pan with a long handle – and serves up the thick black result with a glass of water and a cube of Turkish delight. This single-minded approach, which has been refined over a more than a century, inspired the UK's *Daily Telegraph* to rate the cafe as one of the world's finest in 2016.

There are a few branches, but the one on Serasker Caddesi is a longstanding favourite for its location on Kadıköy's busy *kahvehane* (coffeehouse) strip. Inside, black-and-white photos of old Istanbul reflect the heritage of this 1920s establishment, while the pavement seats offer a front-row view of locals hurrying to the nearby Kadıköy ferry terminal. The best drink here is the classic Turkish coffee, but seasonal drinks are worth trying too; such as the hot and milky *sahlep*, made from wild orchid bulbs, or *damla sakızlı*, Turkish coffee flavoured with mastic, a resin extracted from the Mediterranean tree of the same name.

UNITED KINGDOM

How to ask for a coffee in the local language?
I'd like a latte/cappuccino/black coffee, please
Signature coffee style? Probably a latte or, more
recently, a flat white
What to order with your coffee? A slice of cake: coffee
and walnut, perhaps
Don't: Jump the queue. Queuing is a sacred tradition in
Britain, and violators will be tut-tuttily disapproved of

We all know the clichés about how much the British love their tea, whether it's a builder's, a simple brew or a pot of char. In times of tragedy and triumph, every self-respecting Britisher reaches for a comforting cuppa to pull them through. But while the UK remains a nation of tea-drinkers, with 84% of people drinking at least one cup a day, it seems Britain is just as addicted to the bean as to the brew nowadays. Seventy million cups of coffee are consumed daily in the UK, and a third of people use at least one kind of coffee-making device on a regular basis – although it has to be said that instant coffee is still the norm, accounting for 7 out of 10 cups. But away from home, Brits have embraced espresso culture with enthusiasm and gusto: in a high-street cafe, people are in fact twice as likely to order a coffee-based drink as a cup of tea.

However, coffee culture has taken a long time to get going in the UK. Wind the clock back a few decades and Britain's coffee scene was about as frothy as a week-old cappuccino: freeze-dried instant was all that was on offer, and precious few people had ever heard of a latte, let alone a cold-brewed Chemex.

But by the early 1990s, things had begun to brew. Foreign travel and disposable income led people to seek out more diverse forms of coffee. Cafetieres appeared alongside teapots on the nation's shelves. Coffee shops started to spring up in the cities. Fresh coffee became more widely available in supermarkets. And slowly, British people began to get more educated about the complex and intoxicating world of coffee.

Spin forward to the 21st century, and well, the game's changed. Coffee's everywhere these days. In the cities, you can get your fix on practically every street corner, and even in the humblest of village cafes and back-of-beyond pubs, espresso machines are a staple appliance. Big chains dominate the high street, but there's a thriving specialist scene too. Small, indie cafes are commonplace, and while in-house roasting tends to be a rarity, the UK has an ever-growing list of top-notch, small-batch microroasters to handle the supply side, including names such as Square

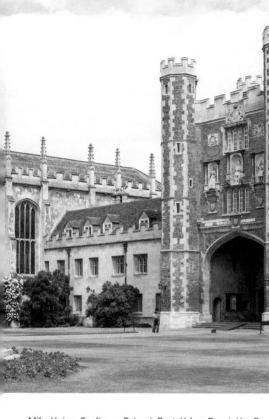

TOP 5 COFFEES

Square Mile Red Brick Seasonal Espresso
Union Revelation
Coaltown Black Gold No 3
Extract Original Espresso
Has Bean Costa Rican Finca Licho Yellow Honey

CAFE TALK – GEMMA SCREEN

Now you can find good coffee available in a huge variety of places – from the garden centre, to the local bike shop – even the laundrette

Mile, Union, Coaltown, Extract, Pact, Urban Roast, Has Bean and Origin. Coffee-themed events sprinkle the calendar: Edinburgh, Manchester and London all host major coffee festivals, while the UK Coffee Week in April and the UK Barista Championships in May attract coffee geeks from across the globe.

In short, coffee has well and truly percolated into the nation's consciousness. Most Brits are addicted to their morning coffee – whether that means a latte, flat white or even (shudder) a morning instant. But while coffee's on the up, let's not get too carried away here: it'll be a black day in Blighty indeed before the British are finally convinced to give up their daily cuppa for good.

Come to think of it – anyone for a brew?

COALTOWN COFFEE

The Roastery, Ty Nant y Celyn, Glynhir Rd, Llandybie, Ammanford, Carmarthenshire; www.coaltowncoffee.co.uk; +44 1269 400105

◆ Roastery ◆ Shop
◆ Classes ◆ Cafe

The rolling hills above a neglected South Wales mining town do not seem an obvious location for a burgeoning business… or do they? For decades Ammanford proudly produced high-quality coal, or 'black gold', but the colliery closed in 2003. Now Coaltown Coffee is rejuvenating the town with a different sort of black gold. Headquartered up a hard-to-find lane in now-picturesque former mining country, this rural roastery is no storm in an espresso cup, but South Wales' only speciality coffee roaste. Each bean is sourced from specific farms guaranteeing an 80 + point international coffee grading score.

Now sporting a wondrous 1958 coffee-roasting machine, the company is expanding from being the region's gourmet coffee supplier to opening a suave roastery, cafe and barista training school in central Ammanford. Its aim: to bring jobs to town and make it famous for black gold again.

THINGS TO DO NEARBY

Wright's Food Emporium
Staying with the theme of phenomenal middle-of-nowhere culinary ventures, this delicious cafe-deli 16km northwest of Ammanford showcases local foodie delicacies and is particularly renowned for its wines. *www. wrightsfood.co.uk*

Carreg Cennen Castle
Towering above a westerly flank of the Brecon Beacons 11km northeast of Ammanford is this strikingly located 13th-century fortress. *carregcennencastle.com*

COLONNA & SMALL'S

6 Chapel Row, Bath;
www.colonnaandsmalls.co.uk; +44 7766 808 067

◆ Classes   ◆ Cafe
◆ Shop   ◆ Transport

THINGS TO DO NEARBY

**Royal Crescent
& the Circus**
Designed in the late 18th
century by architects
John Wood the Elder and
Younger, these street are
where you'll find Bath's
most beautiful houses.

The Roman Baths
Bath's geothermal waters
led the Romans to build
a magnificent bathhouse
in around 70AD, and it's
amazingly well-preserved.
www.romanbaths.org.uk

Holburne Museum
Enjoy a treasure trove of
17th- and 18th-century
English art collected by
aristocrat Sir William
Holburne, including works
by Thomas Gainsborough.
www.holburne.org

Bathwick Boating
What could be more
English than steering
a punt or a rowboat along
the tranquil waters of
the River Avon? *www.
bathboating.org.uk*

The stately Georgian city of Bath has been at the forefront of English fashion for nigh-on three centuries, so it's no surprise to find that its well-to-do streets are also home to one of the nation's foremost speciality coffee shops. Founded in 2009, it's owned by Maxwell Colonna-Dashwood, one of the leading lights of the UK coffee scene, not to mention UK Barista Champion in 2012 and 2014. The cafe itself is located in a converted Georgian townhouse: fireplaces and glass-fronted cupboards greet you as you walk through the door, with the main cafe beyond occupying a high, narrow A-framed room, with shiny white walls, blond wood floors and skylights. It's a small space: the coffee bar takes up one side, tables and stools line the other, and murals outline processing methods.

Maxwell takes a purist's approach: there's a daily choice of three espressos and three filters (served in your choice of AeroPress, clever dripper or syphon), and to appreciate the coffee's flavour, customers are discouraged from adding milk, unless you've ordered a flat white, of course. It's an enlightening, rather than elitist, approach: let yourself be guided, and learn. A bag of Colonna's top-grade rare beans is a top-end takeaway treat (£15 for 150g).

© Finn Beales

QUARTER HORSE

88-90 Bristol Street, Birmingham;
www.quarterhorsecoffee.com; +44 121 448 9660

◆ Food   ◆ Shop   ◆ Transport
◆ Roastery   ◆ Cafe

Walking into Quarter Horse almost feels like stepping into the pages of an interior design magazine. It's a beautiful, airy space, all clean, minimal lines, whitewashed walls, Edison lightbulbs, potted plants and pale wooden furniture. Light streams in through big windows; on one side there's a smart white-tiled bar, and on the other stands an impressive roaster, the only one in Birmingham, which prepares all beans in-house. It's a treat to sit, chill, and watch the coffee-making process from roaster to cup. With such control over its product, the coffee is unsurprisingly superb (the trademark house blend Dark Horse Espresso is especially good with milk), and co-owner Nathan Retzer is a stickler for quality. Originally from Normal, Illinois, he opened his first shop in Oxford before adding this Midlands outpost. We hope there are more horses yet to come.

THINGS TO DO NEARBY

The Diskery
Allegedly the oldest record store in Britain, with a heritage dating back to the 1950s, this is the place in Birmingham to pick up rare and collectable vinyl. *thediskery.com*

Birmingham Back to Backs
Take a time-travel tour around this terrace of 19th-century 'back-to-back' houses, restored by the National Trust. Don't forget to stock up at the 1930s sweet shop. *www. nationaltrust.org.uk/ birmingham-back-to-backs*

SMALL BATCH COFFEE COMPANY

111 Western Road, Hove, Brighton:
www.smallbatchcoffee.co.uk; +44 1273 731077

◆ Food   ◆ Classes   ◆ Cafe
◆ Roastery   ◆ Shop   ◆ Transport

THINGS TO DO NEARBY

Brighton Pier

You can't go to Brighton and *not* take a stroll along its seafront pier (see below), a classic of the British seaside. It's about a mile's walk east from Hove.
www.brightonpier.co.uk

The Lanes

A few blocks north of the pier, this warren of streets is where you'll find Brighton's quirkiest shops: jewellers, record stores, vintage clothes and bric-a-brac galore.
www.visitbrighton.com/ shopping/the-lanes

Small by name, but this Brighton specialist has moved on to big things since roasting its first beans in 2007. Despite launching in the teeth of the financial crisis, its roasting and mail-order business has gone from strength to strength, and fuelled rapid expansion – it now has eight locations spanning Brighton, Hove and Worthing. The original cafe is in Hove at Goldstone Villas, but this Norfolk Square branch is the loveliest of the bunch: a high-ceilinged, tall-windowed affair with a handsome wooden bar, plenty of space to sit and views over the greenery of the square. They're not fans of coffee snobbery, so you can feel as comfortable ordering a straight flat white here as a single-origin pour-over. Most admirable is its 'farm-to-cup' sourcing ethos: Small Batch's coffee has a strong ethical dimension. A rich, chocolatey Goldstone espresso, named after the first shop, is the thing to go for here.

FULL COURT PRESS

59 Broad St, Bristol;
www.fcpcoffee.com; +44 7794 808 552

◆ Food   ◆ Shop   ◆ Transport
◆ Classes   ◆ Cafe

The home town of Banksy and Massive Attack is known for its quirky, alternative character, as well as a thriving media scene, so it's not surprising to find the city swimming with coffee shops. FCP is the cream of the crop. It's in the old city, not far from the lively harbour, in a period building overhauled with minimalist style: neutral walls, modern furniture, an original stained glass window. There's an uncompromising focus to the coffee here – just two filter and espresso blends per day, and milk and sugar are limited to encourage customers to experience the proper flavour profile. There's a nice pastry selection sourced daily from local bakeries, and courses cover barista skills and better filter brewing. These guys know their beans. A nice touch is the takeaway service; the baristas will package up any of the day's coffees in a bespoke 250g take-away bag.

THINGS TO DO NEARBY

St Nicholas Market
Sheltered within a beautiful Georgian arcade, this fantastic indoor market offers vintage stalls galore, as well as a fantastic food court: look out for pies by local legend Pieminister. *www.stnicholas marketbristol.co.uk*

M-Shed
Centuries of Bristol history are explored in imaginative ways at this museum, in a huge warehouse alongside the city's docks and disused cranes. *www. bristolmuseums.org.uk*

© Tom Sparey

HOT NUMBERS

Unit 5/6 Dales Brewery, Gwydir St, Cambridge;
hotnumberscoffee.co.uk; +44 1223 359966

◆ Food   ◆ Classes   ◆ Cafe
◆ Roastery   ◆ Shop   ◆ Transport

THINGS TO DO NEARBY

Fitzwilliam Museum
One of the first public art museums in Britain, 'the Fitz' is full of quirky collections including ancient Egyptian relics, master paintings, watches and armour. ***www. fitzmuseum.cam.ac.uk***

The Backs
This beautifully manicured stretch of reclaimed land runs right along the back of the riverside colleges on the banks of the River Cam, offering unparalleled views of academia.

Hot Numbers is passionate about single-origin coffee (ethically sourced and directly traded), locally made food and great music, a recipe that has earned it a reputation as Cambridge's best roastery and coffee shop. But this is no temple to artisan pretension. Rather, you'll find a large, laid-back space in a decommissioned brewery with stripped wooden tables, comfy sofas and bare brick walls which turns into a jazz den and event space come the evening.

Using a Giesen roaster which feeds into Cropster data-logging software, owner Simon Fraser is able to carefully control each roast to retain the character of the beans over four daily choices; Swiss water-processed decaf, a lighter filter roast and two espresso roasts – one to drink black, the other best paired with a textured milk option. Order the creamy new 90 + Nitro, which is brewed hot and crash-chilled. There's a smaller branch of Hot Numbers on Trumpington Street.

BREW LAB COFFEE

6-8 South College St, Edinburgh;
www.brewlabcoffee.co.uk; +44 131 662 8963

◆ Food   ◆ Shop
◆ Classes   ◆ Cafe

THINGS TO DO NEARBY

National Museum of Scotland
Caffeine up before you head into this repository of historical treasures, the nation's foremost museum, encompassing everything from 12th-century chessmen to the stuffed remains of Dolly the Sheep. *www.nms.ac.uk*

Holyrood House
Take a tour around the Queen's official Scottish residence, located at the bottom end of the famous Royal Mile overlooking the green sweep of Holyrood Park. *www.royalcollection.org.uk*

Arthur's Seat
This extinct volcanic plug on the edge of the city is an irresistible target for hikers. Some good coffee will help you on the way, but it's best not attempted on a hangover.

The Elephant House
Stop in for a pot of tea and a cake in the cafe where JK Rowling famously penned the first words of the Harry Potter books. *www.elephanthouse.biz*

There's an almost scientific attention to detail at Edinburgh's leading coffee emporium. In business since 2012, this central cafe on South College St has earned a reputation for its painstakingly precise approach to its coffee, from the sourcing process right through to the point of brewing. Just two espressos and two pour-over filters are on offer every day, selected to complement each other; one fruity and light, perhaps, the other dark, malty and roasted. Espressos all come from renowned roaster Has Bean, and brewing gear is equally top-class: espressos are processed through a Victoria Arduino VA388 Black Eagle, while filters pass through premium Kalita Wave pour-overs. They're always innovating here, too: the gas-conditioned Nitro Cold Brew will change your mind forever on what iced coffee can be, with its rich, creamy texture close to Irish stout.

The setting itself feels urban – bare brick, wood floor, a stonking great metal slab for a counter – but the cafe's popularity means that it can be tricky to find a free table, something that's exacerbated by the great lunch and brunch menu. But good as the food is, the coffee is the heart of things here – and there's a super academy if you want to delve deeper, offering latte art, espresso training and even sensory coffee courses.

© Jordan Anderson

ESPRESSINI

39 Killigrew St, Falmouth;
www.espressini.co.uk; +44 1326 236582

◆ Food   ◆ Cafe
◆ Shop   ◆ Transport

THINGS TO DO NEARBY

National Maritime Museum Cornwall
Explore Falmouth's nautical history at this impressive museum. Expect historic boats and sea-themed exhibitions: recent subjects explored the history of tattoos and Captain Bligh. *nmmc.co.uk*

WeSUP Gylly
Pilot a stand-up paddleboard along the seafront of Gyllyngvase Beach, with fine views along the coast to the Tudor castle of Pendennis. *wesup.co.uk*

Once an illustrious seafaring town, now a creative hub thanks to the proximity of the university nearby, the Cornish town of Falmouth has its own premium coffee house in the excellent Espressini. Owner Rupert Ellis worked for some of the big coffee chains before setting up his own shop, and his experience shows: beans are hand-picked from local outfits Olfactory and Yallah Coffee, plus a select band of other European roasters.

In a converted shop that has been filled with a mix-and-match selection of furniture, coffee fans will find a great brunch menu and a wall-sized blackboard of coffee selections to choose from; but it's the bespoke copper-fronted espresso machine, a thing of genuine beauty, that they will really appreciate. Sample a pour-over brewed with Yallah Coffee beans, hand-roasted nearby at Argal Farm on a reconditioned 1950s roaster. There's also a second outpost, Espressini Dulce, across town in a former sweetshop on Arwenack St.

BOLD ST COFFEE

89 Bold St, Liverpool;
www.boldstreetcoffee.co.uk; +44 151 707 0760

◆ Food   ◆ Transport
◆ Cafe

Liverpool's first (and still finest) espresso bar was opened in 2007 by a group of like-minded baristas who were tired of toiling in service of someone else's caffeine-driven corporate dream. So they pooled resources and set up their own shop, and have never looked back. It's in the middle of the Ropewalks, a hip neighbourhood favoured by the city's musicians, artists, designers and creatives – and Bold St is very much a place to hang, with big blackboards, wooden tables, work by local illustrators on the walls and a punky, street-art aesthetic. Coffee mainly comes from four roasters: Has Bean, Square Mile, Workshop and the Berlin-based Barn. It's all refreshingly easy-going, a place to forget about the snooty terminology and just appreciate the quality of coffee.

THINGS TO DO NEARBY

FACT
Catch a double feature at this excellent cinema and art gallery, which screens a mix of mainstream and arthouse, and also hosts regular exhibitions.
www.fact.co.uk

Forbidden Planet Liverpool
Browse for rare Marvel comic books or pick up some movie collectables at this temple of geekery.
forbiddenplanet.com

BAR ITALIA

21 Frith Street, Soho, London;
www.baritaliasoho.co.uk; +44 20 7734 4737

◆ Food   ◆ Transport
◆ Cafe

Opened in 1949, this Soho stalwart is so legendary that it's had at least two songs written about it. On Pulp's classic Britpop album, *Different Class*, it was the place to go after a seedy night's clubbing when you're 'fading fast and it's nearly dawn'. To its credit, Bar Italia still looks and feels like an authentic 1950s Italian cafe-bar, not a London approximation of one, and despite various refurbs still retains formica from 1949.

Until recently, this was one of the only places in the West End where you could be guaranteed a decent coffee. While there are now far trendier (and, arguably, better) cafes in Soho, Bar Italia has held strong. You can still rely on its trusty Gaggia machine to produce the perfect, no-nonsense espresso.

THINGS TO DO NEARBY

Chinatown
This compact enclave of restaurants, supermarkets and shops is the place to be during the lunar New Year celebrations.

Soho Square
Landscaped back in 1684, this pretty little square springs to life whenever the sun is shining.

© Samuel Kaye; © Alex May

CLIMPSON & SONS

67 Broadway Market, London;
www.climpsonandsons.com; +44 20 7254 7199

- ◆ Food
- ◆ Classes
- ◆ Cafe
- ◆ Roastery
- ◆ Shop
- ◆ Transport

Speciality coffee shops and artisan roasters are ten-a-penny in the capital these days, but Climpson & Sons offers something a little different. Based on Broadway Market in Hackney, one of the East End's trendiest neighbourhoods, this renowned coffee shop blends the best of old and new. Founder Ian Burgess started the business around a decade ago with a coffee cart on Broadway Market, but soon moved up to occupy the cafe's current premises, a shabbily stylish shop that brings to mind the East End of yesteryear, with its old-school panelled windows, peeling wooden frames and stark black-and-red lettering, looking rather like a butcher's shop from the 1940s (which, appropriately enough, the premises once was).

Inside, there are no tables, just benches and chairs, to encourage customers to mingle – all part of the aim to serve as a hub and meeting-point for the market community. Coffee comes fresh every day from its own roastery-bistro, a characterful space squeezed under railway arches near London Fields. The company also runs a coffee training academy, and for purists, you can still buy an espresso from the original coffee cart that started it all. If you're stuck for choice, try the signature Climpson Estate Espresso Blend.

THINGS TO DO NEARBY

Hackney Empire
This venue hosted such luminaries as Charlie Chaplin and Stan Laurel in its days as a music hall, and still hosts gigs, comedy, theatre and an annual panto. *www.hackneyempire.co.uk*

Broadway Market
One of London's top food markets runs right outside the door, with stalls serving everything from Egyptian street food to Balkan bites, scotch eggs and classic British pies. *broadwaymarket.co.uk*

Victoria Park
This 86-hectare public park – London's oldest – is well off the regular tourist track, and great for a weekend wander, with lakes, lawns and an Oriental-style pavilion.

The Viktor Wynd Museum of Curiosities, Fine Art & Natural History
An oddball museum that houses a cornucopia of curiosities, from dodo bones to occult artwork, taxidermy and excruciating medical instruments, alongside a tiny cocktail bar and cafe. *www.thelasttuesdaysociety.org*

KAFFA COFFEE

Gillett Square, Hackney, London;
www.kaffacoffee.co.uk; +44 7506 513267

◆ Food   ◆ Cafe
◆ Roastery   ◆ Transport

Kaffa Coffee brings rural Ethiopia to the unlikely setting of Gillett Square in the heart of happening Hackney via this small stall serving punchy brews made from beans grown on owner Markos's wild coffee plantation in Ethiopia. Markos roasts the beans daily, and the morning scent entices a mixed bag of skateboarders, office workers, artists and parents, who sip coffee while watching their kids enjoy the square's pop-up playground.

Twice a week fabulous *injera* (pancakes) and Ethiopian stews are served here, but to experience a real taste of Ethiopia, come on Saturday, when a traditional Ethiopian coffee ceremony is held outside the stall, with aromatic and super-strong coffee traditionally prepared in a shapely clay *jebena* (kettle), heated on a smoking charcoal stove.

THINGS TO DO NEARBY

The Vortex

The volunteer-run Vortex on Gillett Square (see below) is home to one of Hackney's best venues, with a packed roster of jazz and experimental music.
www.vortexjazz.co.uk

Abney Park Cemetery

Head north from Gillett Square to the picturesque and leafy tangle of Abney Park Cemetery, where Hackney's non-conformists lie buried among the trees and shrubs.
www.abneypark.org

© Jeffrey Blackler / Alamy Stock Photo. © londonstills.com / Alamy Stock Photo

MONMOUTH COFFEE

27 Monmouth St, Covent Garden, London;
www.monmouthcoffee.co.uk; +44 20 7232 3010

◆ Food   ◆ Cafe
◆ Shop   ◆ Transport

The queue spilling out of Monmouth Coffee in Covent Garden is a testament to the longevity of good coffee. Cafes come and go in London but Monmouth has been roasting and brewing for more than 35 years.

A pioneer of quality coffee, Monmouth remains as contemporary and relevant as ever, and a visit to its original store is in order for caffeine heads. Don't bother grabbing one of the few booth seats inside (it's too hot!). Instead, get a takeaway coffee and pastry and snag a spot on the bench outside. While the milk-based coffees here are always well

THINGS TO DO NEARBY

Covent Garden Market
The touristy stalls might be a touch commercial, but walking the cobblestoned streets of this 19th-century market is a quintessential London experience.

Dishoom
Dishoom combines its deft, modern take on Indian cuisine in a fun, playful environment inspired by Mumbai. The queues don't seem to deter anyone!
www.dishoom.com

Forbidden Planet
Geeks and pop-culture aficionados rejoice! Forbidden Planet is a shrine to comic books, graphic novels, trading cards, manga, board games, toys and more.
forbiddenplanet.com

Ronnie Scott's
Ronnie Scott's in Soho has been hosting top-notch jazz artists since 1959, and alumni include Wynton Marsalis and Chick Corea.
www.ronniescotts.co.uk

done, we much prefer to pick from the range of beans on offer. These are then weighed, ground and brewed with a pour-over. Knowledgeable staff are on hand to describe the flavour profiles of the beans – the Ethiopian Aroresa's 'black tea and citrus with fresh acidity and zesty body' and El Salvadoran Finca Malacara's 'mandarins and caramel with yellow cherry acidity and medium body', for example. There are also Monmouth outposts in Borough Market and Bermondsey.

OZONE COFFEE ROASTERS

11 Leonard St, Shoreditch, London;
www.ozonecoffee.co.uk; +44 20 7490 1039

◆ Food   ◆ Classes   ◆ Cafe
◆ Roastery ◆ Shop   ◆ Transport

THINGS TO DO NEARBY

St John
Where London's 'nose-to-tail' eating movement began, thanks to acclaimed chef Fergus Henderson, this Michelin-starred restaurant consistently makes 'best of' lists. Serious carnivores will be in heaven.
stjohnrestaurant.com

Barbican
Love or hate the Brutalist architecture, but you'll enjoy many a concert, play or exhibition in this labyrinthine arts space, the largest multi-arts venue in Europe.
www.barbican.org.uk

Colombia Rd Flower Market
Time your visit for a Sunday to see blooming beauties at this sprawling flower market, packed with more than 60 independent stalls and barrow-boy East London charm (see left).
www.columbiaroad.info

Old Spitalfields Market
Trading as a covered market in this location since 1638, there's plenty of atmosphere here; browse the many stalls offering food, antiques, clothing and vinyl.
www.spitalfields.co.uk

You may be momentarily thrown by the predominantly Australian- and Kiwi-accented service at Ozone but there's no denying that you're in London's Shoreditch, in this industrial dual-level warehouse down a side street just off the 'Silicon Roundabout' near Old St station. The best seat in the house is definitely a bar stool at the huge island on the first floor that circles both an open kitchen and the barista action; watch eggs being poached, flipped and fried on one side or check out the AeroPress action on the other.

Ozone opened a branch in London in 2012 but has its origins in New Zealand, where it started life in 1998. The healthy all-day brunch menu is a highlight, with vegetarians and vegans well catered for (new potato, spiced onion and sprouting broccoli tortilla with lime pickle, spring greens, halloumi and a poached egg is just one of many temptations). Coffee purists will delight in the tasting notes that accompany the filter coffee, roasted in-house in the huge Probat roaster downstairs, where it's almost film-set-like in atmosphere, with high ceilings and quite possibly the largest designer toilet cubicles ever encountered. Roasting demonstrations, cupping and home-brewing classes here are extremely popular. Meet both your cocktail and coffee needs with the Cold Drip Negroni.

PRUFROCK COFFEE

23-25 Leather Ln, Clerkenwell, London;
www.prufrockcoffee.com; +44 20 7242 0467

◆ Food   ◆ Shop   ◆ Transport
◆ Classes ◆ Cafe

After winning the 2009 World Barista Championship, Gwilym Davies graduated from a coffee cart to opening Prufrock Coffee in 2011, bringing his winning ways with him – the cafe has garnered its own accolades aplenty in the years since, including Best European Independent Coffee Shop at the European Coffee Awards.

The chilled-out space is a stripped-back affair with wooden floors and simple furnishing, suggesting the focus here is clearly on the coffee. Expect a range of roasted beans from British and international roasters, including the UK's Square Mile, Five Elephant (Berlin), La Cabra (Aarhus), Drop Coffee (Stockholm) and Belleville (Paris). Drink these as an espresso or let the barista hand-brew one of the week's top-scoring coffees for you. Whichever you go for, we suggest pulling up a seat by the brew bar and picking the barista's brains for brewing tips, gear recommendations and

THINGS TO DO NEARBY

British Museum
One of London's best museums is also home to the fabled Rosetta Stone, sculptures from the Parthenon and an array of Egyptian mummies.
www.britishmuseum.org

Somerset House
The stately Somerset House is a neoclassical beauty overlooking the Thames. Come by for a revolving door of contemporary arts exhibitions and live events. **www. somersethouse.org.uk**

Theatreland
You can't come to the West End and not go to the theatre... From *Harry Potter and the Cursed Child* to *Les Miserables*, be dazzled.

Sir John Soane's Museum
This historic 19th-century house belonged to famed architect Sir John Soane. Virtually untouched since his passing, it's a fascinating step back in time. **www.soane.org**

for help identifying coffee flavour profiles. If you get hungry, reasonably priced home-cooked dishes such as sandwiches, salads, tarts, cakes and pastries will sate you.

Davies' commitment to coffee and his craft extend to Speciality Coffee Association of Europe-certified courses held in the basement of the cafe. Come to pick up some new skills – perhaps perfecting your latte art, cup coffees, and learning new brewing gadgets, and leave with shiny new coffee gear.

THE GENTLEMEN BARISTAS

63 Union St, Borough, London;
www.thegentlemenbaristas.com

◆ Food ◆ Shop ◆ Transport
◆ Classes (at Store St location) ◆ Cafe

THINGS TO DO NEARBY

Borough Market
Stronger in community spirit than ever, Borough Market has operated for more than 1000 years, recently inspiring London's food renaissance. Chat with friendly traders, taste and buy the freshest produce. **www.boroughmarket.org.uk**

Tate Modern
Enjoy international modern art exhibitions alongside Thames views from the top of the 10-storey Switch House extension. 'Tate Late' after-hours events are held on the last Friday of the month. **www.tate.org.uk**

Shakespeare's Globe
Heard of a playwright called Shakespeare? Step back in time and take in a performance at this historical venue designed as a replica of the 17th-century original. **www.shakespearesglobe.com**

Flatiron Square
London's newest foodie hub, Flatiron Square is an indoor/outdoor feast for the senses, sprawling under seven railway arches and within Grade II-listed Devonshire House. **www.flatironsquare.co.uk**

'We wanted to get away from this emergence of "baristocracy",' says Henry Ayers. 'Coffee should be for everyone, it should bring people together.' He and Edward Parkes founded the Gentlemen Baristas in 2014, since which time their well-mannered coffee and their spirit of inclusivity have successfully attracted a diverse clientele to their Borough location. A second site (Store St near Holborn) swiftly followed, but it's here that Old London's coffee history permeates the stripped floorboards, exposed-brick walls and original fireplace.

The address was actually registered in the 17th century as The Coffee House, and this nod to the past can be seen in original dusty almanacs lining the bookshelves (*Minute Book No 2 Coffee Trade Federation*) beside decorative vintage hats. The beans follow this quirky hat theme: Top Hat, Deerstalker, Trilby, Gatsby, Bowler, Pith, Panama, Troubador, Boater, and the seasonal Fez or Stovepipe. And

in keeping with the 'all-welcome' ethos, decaf drinkers will appreciate 'The Pretender', a Swiss water-decaffeinated organic Brazilian roast. The upstairs space and garden terrace are dedicated to weekend brunches, as well as supper clubs on Thursday to Saturday evenings. Coffee, sir/madam? Try the Top Hat espresso, a single-origin from Nicaragua: citrusy with botanic overtones.

COFFEE'S NE

As demand for speciality coffee grows, pioneers are identifying new – and revitalising old – regions of the world to plant with the precious bean. Here are four new growing regions coming soon to a coffee shop near you.

SOUTHERN CALIFORNIA

In the last five or six years around 30 individial farms in southern California have turned plots over to coffee. This new interest has largely been prompted by the success of Good Land Organics located near Santa Barbara. Good Land grows only top-quality varieties, and at over US$50 for a pound of green beans, it is unlikely to become your next go-to brew. Nevertheless the excitement surrounding the USA's first coffee-growing region outside of Hawaii is infectious.

DEMOCRATIC REPUBLIC OF CONGO

After decades of conflict all but decimated Congolese coffee production, the country is slowly getting back to its beans. Millions of dollars of foreign and domestic investment is pumping into the industry in the hope of unleashing the potential of the country's rich, volcanic soil and tropical climate – thought to be some of the best growing conditions in the world. While many challenges remain, production of speciality coffee is on the up, and sources confirm it is very, very good. The country even has a fledgling coffee festival – the Saveur de Kivu – held annually in Bukavu.

SOUTH SUDAN

Bordering Ethiopia and Kenya, war-torn South Sudan has what it takes to produce top-notch coffee and is one of the few countries in the world where plants thrive in the wild. Despite these assets, violence and displacement have made it almost impossible for the coffee industry to get a toe-hold. However, in late 2015, after years of hard work and investment, not to mention some celebrity endorsement from George Clooney, South Sudan exported coffee for the first time in the young country's history.

V FRONTIERS

MYANMAR

Myanmar's emergence from military rule in 2011 and its subsequent gradual opening up to the outside world had a dramatic effect on the state of its coffee. Investment in farming practices and farmers' education has seen quality improve year on year, and with better access to markets, produce is becoming more widely available. Early adopters of Myanmarese coffee praise its bright and fruity flavour and easy-drinking finish. Look out for Bourbon and Geisha varieties grown in the Shan state.

OCEANIA

WELLINGTON

Windy Welly may be a long way to go for some but the quality of the coffee here is unsurpassed. One of the disputed homes of the flat white, Wellington is rightly proud of its perfectionist baristas and quirky coffee shops found on every street corner. Clear your caffeine buzz with a stroll on the waterfront or up to Mt Victoria.

MELBOURNE

Smashed avocado, communal tables and the best coffee of your life – the Melbourne cafe is becoming the global archetype of an excellent coffee purveyor. Australia's capital of culture is also a wonderful coffee touring city: head off on a pilgrimage down graffiti scrawled laneways to legendary cafes such as St Ali and Proud Mary.

AUCKLAND

Thanks to Auckland-based roasters such as Allpress and Atomic (and their knowledge-sharing ways) it's now hard to find a bad cup of coffee in New Zealand. Pop in for some barista training, or there are plenty of other spots to enjoy NZ roasts. When you've had your fill, hop on a ferry to Waiheke Island for beaches and wineries.

AUSTRALIA

How to ask for a coffee in the local language?
Can I please have a (insert coffee preference here)?
Signature coffee style? A long black for the purists or an
Australian-invented (if you believe Australians) flat white
What to order with your coffee? Smashed avocado on toast
Do: Your research. Ordering a 'black' or 'white' coffee in
Australia won't get you very far – specify the kind of black or
white coffee you want

You can't have a conversation about coffee without mentioning Australia. Aussies didn't invent coffee, nor were they first to serve it, but the country – in particular Melbourne – has helped make coffee what it is today across the world.

Until the late 1800s Melbourne's CBD was scattered with coffee stalls that stayed open into the early hours of the morning. The first establishments where people could gather and sip coffee were 'coffee palaces', which provided all the amenities of a hotel without any grog during the temperance movement. They were popular for about a decade before the banking system collapsed in 1890, taking many of the city's coffee palaces with it.

During WWII American troops introduced Melburnians to the latest roasting and grinding techniques and by the 1930s, Australia's first espresso machine was installed at Cafe Florentino on Bourke Street (now Grossi Florentino). But it wasn't until the 1950s, and the arrival of post-war immigrants, that today's coffee culture took root and Australia's first wave broke.

The second wave was spurred by demand for better quality espresso both at cafes and to make at home. Today third wave coffee has taken over, with beans considered an artisanal product as opposed to a commodity. Australia is leading the charge here, with dedicated baristas educated in every step of the coffee-making process, from farming beans through to brewing. More than ever before there's a trickle-down effect where consumers are concerned with the sourcing and sustainability of their beans. We don't just want a pick-me-up; we want to feel part of something more.

It's a country where coffee isn't a practicality but part of a lifestyle where drinkers also care about where their food comes from and which designers they support. And the fact that Starbucks failed here doesn't make Australians coffee snobs – we're more likely to write down our five favourite cafes for you to try than to judge your order.

And while for some the scene can seem faddish – with its bright blue algae lattes and huge menus of piccolos,

CAFE TALK – SALVATORE MALATESTA

I remember a time when we used to look overseas for coffee inspiration. Then in about 2009 I realised Australia was ahead of the curve

TOP 5 COFFEES

- **Proud Mary** Ghost Rider
- **St Ali** Orthodox Blend
- **Everyday Coffee** All Day Blend
- **Seven Seeds** Golden Gate Espresso Blend
- **Market Lane** Seasonal Espresso

short macchiatos, batch brew, cold-drip and so many more – really, at the heart of Australia's coffee scene is a group of passionate pioneers. It is thanks to these pioneers that Australian cafes with names like Little Collins are so successful in big cities like New York.

Looking forward, as pioneers do, Salvatore Malatesta of the St Ali coffee empire predicts that cafes will shift away from industrial-chic interiors to Japanese minimalism. But more importantly he's already defined what could become fourth wave coffee: 'The next generation of baristas is more akin to tech-nerds or scientists with an emphasis on precision,' he says. 'I think the ultimate evolution of the barista is that he or she will be more like a wine sommelier.'

© pisaphotography / Shutterstock; © Javen / Shutterstock

EXCHANGE COFFEE

Shops 1&2, 12-18 Vardon Ave, Adelaide;
www.exchangecoffee.com.au; +61 415 966 225

◆ Food   ◆ Shop
◆ Cafe   ◆ Transport

Having trained at Workshop in London, owner Tom Roden opened the doors of Exchange Coffee in mid-2013 with a view to offering the best coffee experience for Adelaidians. Little did he know that the South Australian capital was about to undergo a massive coffee revitalisation, and Exchange Coffee would become the benchmark for the others to follow.

Tucked away off Adelaide's East End dining strip Rundle St, Exchange Coffee is the best place to experience AeroPress in the state – so much so that it's hosted its own AeroPress championships, partnering with the crew from Dawn Patrol Coffee (see p237). Roasts have been exclusively sourced from boutique blenders Monday in South Australia and Market Lane in Melbourne. Hands-down the best place in the Adelaide CBD for a hearty brekkie and a curated brew.

THINGS TO DO NEARBY

National Wine Centre of Australia
Housed in a building that looks like a huge deconstructed wine barrel in the picturesque Botanic Gardens, this absorbing space offers an interactive walk through Australia's wine history. *www. wineaustralia.com.au*

Adelaide Oval
One of Australia's premier sporting grounds offers an unforgettable and dizzying roof climb. Inside, the Bradman Collection is a free exhibition dedicated to, arguably, the world's best cricketer. *www.adelaideoval.com.au*

BLYNZZ COFFEE ROASTERS

43 Ford St, Beechworth, Victoria;
www.blynzzcoffee.com.au; +61 423 589 962

◆ Food   ◆ Shop   ◆ Transport
◆ Roastery ◆ Cafe

THINGS TO DO NEARBY

Bridge Road Brewers
Beer and pizza are on
the menu at Ben Kraus's
Ford St brewery and both
are outstanding. The
family-friendly venue is
a favourite for lunch and
weekend evenings. ***www.
bridgeroadbrewers.com.au***

**Beechworth Historic
Precinct** Beechworth's gold
era buildings include the
Court House, the town's
Telegraph Station and the
Burke Museum, dedicated
to Robert O'Hara Burke,
an explorer with a poor
sense of direction.
www.beechworth.com

There's a lot to do in Australia's best-preserved
19th-century gold rush town, which looks much the
same as it did in the notorious bushranger Ned Kelly's day.
However, he would not have had the delicious distractions
of the Bridge Road Brewery, Provenance restaurant,
Beechworth Honey – where you can taste dozens of honeys
– or a caffeinated pick-me-up at Blynzz.

The shop, on Ford St, which runs through the centre of
Beechworth, sells about 20 varieties of Arabica bean, mostly
from Africa and South America, all freshly roasted on-site
and sold ground or whole as required. The cafe is open from
Thursday to Sunday: four different coffees are available
daily as espresso but on a hot day sit at the bar and try
a cold-drip brew.

SIXPENCE COFFEE

15 Wills St, Bright, Victoria;
www.sixpencecoffee.com.au

◆ Food ◆ Shop ◆ Transport
◆ Roastery ◆ Cafe

Any self-respecting adventure town must have a great coffee shop and in Bright, the gateway to the Australian Alps, that's Sixpence, where there's always a row of bikes stashed outside. Sixpence was started in 2014 by Luke and Tabatha Dudley, who wanted to bring a bit of Melbourne's coffee scene to northeast Victoria. 'We were drawn to Bright's amazing community and the great location,' says Luke.

In late 2017, Sixpence moved into a new town-centre space with roaster, cafe, shop and distillery under one roof.

The team consists of three friendly baristas and two bakers, who supply the cafe with fresh sourdough and snacks. Sixpence's signature blend is the 3741, a full-bodied cup with mild citrus acidity and notes of chocolate, nuts and spice.

THINGS TO DO NEARBY

Bright MTB Park
Bicycles are big in Bright, with the Murray to the Mountains Rail Trail ending here, a mountainside laced with trails for off-road riders, plus bike rental.
www.visitbright.com.au

Bright Brewery
After a ride, sink some ales at the renowned local brewery, where the beer is made with water from the Ovens river that flows just outside.
www.brightbrewery.com

THE CUPPING ROOM

1 University Ave, Civic, Canberra;
www.thecuppingroom.com.au; +61 262 576 412

◆ Food ◆ Shop ◆ Transport
◆ Classes ◆ Cafe

Be prepared to queue for a table at Canberra's best cafe as it's well worth the wait. Local speciality roaster Ona Coffee set up the Cupping Room as a concept cafe with an educational component, but customers pour in for the exceptional food, laidback vibe and excellent coffee. It's not as simple as ordering a short black or a flat white here. If you order a black coffee you'll be presented with a choice of single-origin beans and if you order a white, a choice of blends – all of which are revised daily. Otherwise you can simply ask what hot filter or cold-brew

they're currently pouring. We're particularly fond of the dark fruit and chocolate notes of flat whites made using the Founder blend.

THINGS TO DO NEARBY

Drill Hall Gallery
The Australian National University's main art gallery hosts exhibitions, but the main draws are Sidney Nolan's magnificent Riverbend panels.
dhg.anu.edu.au

Australian National Botanic Gardens
Don't miss this showcase of native flora, sprawling over 85 hectares at the foot of the Black Mountain.
www.nationalbotanic gardens.gov.au

VILLINO COFFEE ROASTERS

30 Criterion St, Hobart, Tasmania;
www.villino.com.au; +61 362 310 890

◆ Food   ◆ Shop
◆ Cafe   ◆ Transport

Keeping many of Hobart's finest businesses in beans, this Italian-style cafe (Villino means 'small home with a yard') has an extremely loyal clientele, thanks to its excellent coffee and friendly service (if you're buying beans, they'll want to know all about your taste preferences and your equipment at home). It has three Probast roasters offsite at Huntingfield (15km south of Hobart's CBD), with beans sourced from Guatemala, Ethiopia, Kenya, Panama, Brazil and Colombia. Owner Richard Schramm also runs cafe Ecru further down Criterion St and is proud to have his baristas representing Tasmania in national competitions. The cold drip served over ice is ideal on a summer day at an outdoor table but the Synergy blend flat white with the perfect swan artwork is what everyone talks about.

THINGS TO DO NEARBY

MONA

The brilliant and irreverent Museum of Old and New Art brought Hobart world attention. Arrive via ferry from Brooke St pier for maximum viewing pleasure.
www.mona.net.au

Salamanca Market

Go souvenir hunting at this lively outdoor Saturday market; more than 300 stallholders sell gourmet produce, street food, arts, crafts and vintage clothing beside Hobart's waterfront.
www.salamanca.com.au

DAWN PATROL COFFEE

65 Days Rd, Kangarilla, South Australia;
www.dawnpatrolcoffee.com.au; +61 412 397 536

◆ Food   ◆ Shop
◆ Roastery ◆ Cafe

Picturesquely set on the corner of a vineyard on the outskirts of McLaren Vale, one of South Australia's premier wine regions, sits the southern state's best boutique coffee roaster, Dawn Patrol Coffee. Cleverly adopting the wine industry's cellar-door approach to tasting coffee, owners Dom and Nick fling open the doors of their roasting shed on a Sunday, inviting the general public in to smell, touch and taste their premier blends.

As the record player spins relaxed tunes and chickens graze in the yard, the Dawn Patrol boys take you through a pour-over sampling of their roasts with the aim of demystifying the coffee experience for the taster. Adopting a philosophy of 100% traceability back to the point of origin, their roasts are created from beans sourced primarily from Africa and Central America, dense with lime, berry and apple notes. It's worth the trip into wine country to check out this creative outfit, one that is determined to make coffee more approachable for the average punter.

THINGS TO DO NEARBY

Yangarra Estate Vineyard
Multi-award-winning organic and biodynamic winery Yangarra, Aboriginal for 'from the earth', offers the best southern French varietals to be found in this wine-rich state.

The Kitchen Door at Penny's Hill
One of McLaren Vale's most picturesque dining spots, offering an ever-changing seasonal menu comprised of South Australia's best produce.
www.pennyshill.com.au

AXIL COFFEE ROASTERS

322 Burwood Road, Melbourne, Victoria;
www.axilcoffee.com.au; +61 3 9819 0091

◆ Food ◆ Classes ◆ Cafe
◆ Roastery ◆ Shop ◆ Transport

Axil Coffee Roasters has a simple motto: to source, roast and produce the best cup of coffee. Easy words to say but they carry weight when backed by founder David Makin, 2008 World Barista Champion runner-up. He founded Axil together with his wife (who is also the head roaster), Zoe Delany.

They stay true to their philosophy by establishing relationships with farmers, offering them 25% above standard fair-trade prices. This translates to quality beans, roasted on-site, and served in an expansive, contemporary setting. Great food (the house-made taleggio crumpet with seasonal mushrooms, poached egg, sage, truffle oil and savoury granola is a winner) and a variety of coffee classes – latte art to the basics of espresso making – seal the deal on a genuinely great cafe run by genuine folks.

THINGS TO DO NEARBY

Walk the Yarra River
A couple of kilometres southwest of the cafe is the Yarra River. Stroll along part of its 242km, which stretches from the Yarra Ranges to Hobsons Bay. *walkingmaps.com.au/walk/1717*

Glenferrie Road
High streets are still the focal point of neighbourhoods in Melbourne. Glenferrie Road is a slice of suburban Melbourne, and home to the fantastic Readings independent bookstore.

© Tim Grey

INDUSTRY BEANS

3/62 Rose St, Fitzroy, Melbourne, Victoria;
www.industrybeans.com; +61 3 9417 1034

◆ Food   ◆ Shop   ◆ Transport
◆ Roastery   ◆ Cafe

THINGS TO DO NEARBY

The Everleigh
Service is so attentive
at this intimate cocktail
bar that your drink will
be refrigerated while
you're using the facilities.
Let bartenders surprise
you with a customised
concoction.
www.theeverleigh.com

Cutler & Co
Fine dining in an
architecturally designed
former metal works factory.
Book in advance for chef
Andrew McConnell's
degustation delights or
just pop into the bar for
seafood classics. *www.*
cutlerandco.com.au

Rose St Artists' Market
Up to 70 stalls sell local
arts and crafts by talented
designers on weekends.
Compare purchases
afterwards at the rooftop
bar (Young Blood's Diner).
www.rosestmarket.com.au

Lune Croissanterie
Queues formed even
before *The New York Times*
announced its croissants
the best in the world.
Book ahead for the
Lune Lab's three-course
pastry flight. *www.*
lunecroissanterie.com

This is where coffee and food dreams are made:
lovers of both could weep for joy at Industry Beans,
although the establishment may seem a little overwhelming
at first. Prepare to see Instagrammers standing on seats to
get the best flat-lay pictures of artfully presented brunches.
Prepare for the awe of the award-winning designer
warehouse space, featuring a roastery and open kitchen.
Prepare to repeatedly read the detailed coffee menu, with
its compositional bean graphs and colour coding, paralysed
with indecision. Then prepare for a sensational seasonal
meal, with your coffee matched, if you so desire.

The Simmons brothers (Steve and Trevor) founded this
ode to the palate in 2010, but rest assured that all the
style is backed up with substance. Attention to detail and
quality of ingredients are important here. Warmed coconut
chocolate cake with cherry ganache and rum-infused
butterscotch? Paired with the winter espresso blend, which

carries notes of Cherry Ripe (an Australian chocolate bar),
blood orange and spiced rum? Yes, oh yes. There's a single-
origin or blended coffee and method (espresso, filter, cold-
brew, cold-press) for everyone here, so try a few varieties.
But there is only one coffee-rubbed wagyu burger with chilli
jam, cheddar, pickled zucchini (courgette) on a brioche bun.

MAKER FINE COFFEE

47 North St, Richmond, Melbourne, Victoria;
www.makerfinecoffee.com; +61 3 9037 4065

◆ Food ◆ Classes ◆ Cafe
◆ Roastery ◆ Shop ◆ Transport

THINGS TO DO NEARBY

Abbotsford Club
Another cup? Check out
the back-street roastery,
brew bar and shop of New
Zealand speciality coffee
pioneer Coffee Supreme
(see p265).
www.coffeesupreme.com

Main Yarra Trail
Wander east along North
Street and find your way
down to the Yarra Trail –
a bike and walking path
that stretches 38km along
Melbourne's main river.

Carlton Brewhouse
Wondering where all the
beer at an Australian pub
comes from? Take the River
of Beer tour at Carlton
and United Breweries'
Abbotsford HQ to find out.
*www.carltonbrewhouse.
com.au*

**Victoria Street, North
Richmond**
Hop off the 109 tram
heading back towards the
city along the Little Saigon
strip between Church
Street and Nicholson Street
for great pho – Vietnamese
rice-noodle soup.

You could easily miss Maker when walking by – it's
tucked behind a roller door among a bunch of
warehouses down a residential back street – but you don't
want to. Owners John Vroom and Stephanie Manolis once
ran tiny Ora in neighbouring Kew, which served some of
Melbourne's best cafe food – seasonal ingredients sourced
and cooked with loving attention to flavour, texture and
presentation. At Maker, they have focused that passion on
roasting and brewing some of Melbourne's best speciality
coffee. The clean, white space hosts a tiled bar with a big La
Marzocco Strada and a range of filter gear. Out back, behind
a huge sliding glass door, Vroom and his roaster Rafael Sans
roast seasonal single-origin beans to produce memorable

cups. A short black – maybe a Maven from Huila, Colombia,
served in a hand-made ceramic cup – is a masterclass in
speciality espresso extraction: subtle and complex, bright
but not acidic. V60 brews of a weekly roster of single-origins
are equally complex. On summer days the roller door goes
up and a glass of Maker's coffee soda – spiked with orange
oil and coconut blossom sugar – is the go, maybe with a
pastry or toastie from the minimal food selection.

MARKET LANE COFFEE

Shop 13, Prahran Market, 163 Commercial Rd, Melbourne, Victoria;
www.marketlane.com.au; +61 3 9804 7434

◆ Food ◆ Classes ◆ Cafe
◆ Roastery ◆ Shop ◆ Transport

Market Lane has five stores around Melbourne, but this Prahran Market locale is where it all began in 2009 and where all its coffee is roasted. It's also where you're most likely to bump into Melbourne's coffee royalty, co-founder Fleur Studd (daughter of Australia's cheese guru Will Studd). Fleur previously worked at London's Monmouth Coffee Company (see p223) before returning to Australia in 2008 to establish Melbourne Coffee Merchants, the first importer of ethical quality green coffee beans into the country. There's a lot to learn from Fleur but you can also take coffee-roasting classes here (some even in Japanese). As for what to drink, indecision needn't be paralysing; the Pour Over Flight gives you the chance to try three of the current filters.

THINGS TO DO NEARBY

Prahran Market
Beyond the stately 1891 façade, Australia's oldest continuously run food market (see below) has an atmosphere that's vibrantly modern. Some stallholders are descendants of the original traders. *www. prahranmarket.com.au*

Royal Botanic Gardens
On the banks of the Yarra River, Melbourne's Botanic Gardens (see below left) are 36 hectares of picnic paradise, hosting native and world plants alongside concerts and events. *www.rbg.vic.gov.au*

PATRICIA COFFEE BREWERS

Cnr Little Bourke & Little William St, Melbourne, Victoria;
www.patriciacoffee.com.au; +61 3 9642 2237

- ◆ Food
- ◆ Cafe
- ◆ Shop
- ◆ Transport

Like all good things in Melbourne, Patricia can be hard to find. But rest assured that once you're here, choices are refreshingly simple: standing-room only; black, white or filter. The space is tiny, but look up and you'll see 'sunshine' (written in fluorescent lighting on the roof). Look behind the counter and you'll see nothing but a blue-steel-like focus on quality, whether it's the sourcing of canelés from artisan bakeries (try one bobbing in an affogato: a 'cloud mountain') or beans on rotation from Melbourne's best roasters, such as Market Lane (see p242) and Proud Mary (see p244). It has a loyal, discerning clientele, but you'll still feel at home thanks to impeccable service. The Colombian long black is worth queuing for.

THINGS TO DO NEARBY

French Saloon
Accessed via an unmarked door, this *trés chic* space features a zinc-topped bar all the way from France. Beneath red ceilings customers pair cocktails with oysters and caviar, while others dive straight into the dry-aged steak.
www.frenchsaloon.com

Ian Potter Centre: NGV Australia
Set in Melbourne's Federation Square, this striking three-storey building showcases a comprehensive collection of indigenous and non-indigenous Australian art, from past to present.
www.ngv.vic.gov.au

© Barbara Di Castro / Lonely Planet

PROUD MARY

172 Oxford St, Collingwood, Melbourne, Victoria;
www.proudmarycoffee.com.au; +61 3 9417 5930

◆ Food ◆ Cafe
◆ Shop ◆ Transport

THINGS TO DO NEARBY

Abbotsford Convent

A former convent (1861) turned hub of food, art and culture. It has an excellent Slow Food Market on the fourth Saturday of each month. ***www. abbotsfordconvent.com.au***

Son in Law

The place for creative Thai food (even the cocktails feature Thai spirits). Choose from traditional curries or fusion twists; the Son-in-Law Eggs are a winner. ***www.soninlaw.com.au***

Above Board

This tiny, minimalist speakeasy is the place to go for 'cocktails and bad banter', masterfully shaken up with hand-cut ice. ***www.aboveboardbar.com***

Collingwood Children's Farm

Not just for children. Get to know cows, donkeys, horses and pigs by name at this charming urban farm. ***www.farm.org.au***

You might find it tricky to get a table here at weekends and hard to hear your companions in this buzzing raw-brick space once you do, but Proud Mary is deservedly popular nonetheless. The beans are freshly roasted at Aunty Peg's (essentially its cellar door), just steps away on Wellington St, where you can taste-test, take cupping classes or even book in for a 'barista boot camp' at the education hub known as the Collingwood Coffee College. It may have dreams of expansion (a Proud Mary outlet opened in Portland, Oregon in June 2017), but here at home base, on Oxford St, it's simply all about the coffee,

along with an impressive breakfast/brunch offering from a small, seasonal menu.

Proud Mary has been the go-to for caffeine connoisseurs since Nolan Hirte opened the business in 2009. His attention to sourcing and purity is evident, from his annual trips to bean producers' farms to the way he customised two of his three-group Synesso machines to create Australia's only six-grouper; each single-origin has its own extractor so there is no cross-contamination of flavour. The nitrogen-infused cold-press is excellent, but go for a single-origin espresso for potentially the purest coffee of your life.

SEVEN SEEDS

114 Berkeley Street, Carlton, Melbourne, Victoria;
sevenseeds.com.au; +61 3 9347 8664

◆ Food   ◆ Classes   ◆ Cafe
◆ Roastery   ◆ Shop   ◆ Transport

Mark Dundon is something of a legend in the Melbourne coffee scene. He actually founded (and sold) St Ali, another top cafe listed in this book (see p246), and used the proceeds of the sale to open a more laidback cafe-roastery: Seven Seeds.

The name takes inspiration from Baba Budan who, legend has it, smuggled seven seeds of fertile coffee out of Yemen into India in the 16th century. Until then, coffee was highly regulated and protected within by the Yemenis and only sold baked or roasted. The rest is history.

Today, the cool warehouse vibe of Seven Seeds is the scene for tasty brews. On any given day, you might find one of several Kenyan single-origins sitting alongside

THINGS TO DO NEARBY

Queen Victoria Market
Venerable Queen Victoria Market (see below left) is great for snagging fresh produce, a piping hot bratwurst roll, and souvenirs for friends back home. *www.qvm.com.au*

Royal Exhibition Building, Carlton Gardens
This World Heritage building has been hosting exhibitions since the 1880s. From design markets to Lego, Oktoberfest to art fairs, you'll have fun here. *museumsvictoria.com.au*

Lygon Street
The heart of Melbourne's Italian community is home to a selection of great Italian restaurants and, of course, *gelati*. DOC Pizza and Pidapipo Gelateria are our picks.

University of Melbourne
Australia's best university is a sprawl of buildings dating back to the 1850s, making the grounds of this sandstone institution well worth strolling through.

Brazilian and El Salvadorian varietals as filter coffee or cold-brews. Well-rounded espresso-based coffees are also offered. Public cupping sessions, where you learn to taste and identify beans, are held every Tuesday at 9am for a $4 donation which goes to charity. Dundon has since put on several new hats: he's a coffee importer, co-owns a farm in Honduras and is currently in LA bringing his Antipodean style of coffee to fussy Angelenos.

ST ALI COFFEE ROASTERS

12-18 Yarra Pl, Melbourne, Victoria;
www.stali.com.au; +61 3 9686 2990

◆ Food   ◆ Classes   ◆ Cafe
◆ Roastery   ◆ Shop   ◆ Transport

Destination cafe is the term that probably best defines St Ali. In 2005, Mark Dundon opened one of Melbourne's first cafe-roasteries in a warehouse on a quiet street in South Melbourne. It didn't take long for word to get out, and queues became commonplace. While ownership of St Ali has since transferred to Salvatore Malatesta, the spirit of the original remains. Today, Matt Perger, runner-up in the 2013 World Barista Championships, heads the coffee section. When we checked, you could buy 13 different types of beans to take home, and an extensive range of classes includes lessons by 2016 World Latte Art Champion, Shin Fukuyama.

St Ali is also popular for its seasonal food, so much so that local paper *The Age* awarded it Best Food Cafe in 2013. During its themed food nights. St Ali teams up with an eatery such as Madame Truffle, for example, for dinner with wine pairings. It's another indicator of a well-oiled operation that runs at a million miles per minute.

THINGS TO DO NEARBY

National Gallery of Victoria
Australia's largest, most-visited art museum (see below, right) walks visitors through the gamut of Australian and global art, textiles, photography and more. **www.ngv.vic.gov.au**

South Melbourne Market
Stroll over to this market to pick up super-fresh produce, tasty chocolates or take a cooking class at the Neff Market Kitchen. *southmelbournemarket. com.au*

St Kilda Beach
Hop on the tram down to the beach at St Kilda. Stroll down the promenade and enjoy some classic amusement rides at historic Luna Park.

Avenue Books
Everyone needs a neighbourhood bookstore like this one, full of nooks and crannies to perch with literary fiction, cooking, gardening, art and children's books.

BAREFOOT BARISTA

Shop 5/10, Palm Beach Ave, Palm Beach, Queensland;
www.barefootbarista.com.au; +61 7 5598 2774

◆ Food   ◆ Shop   ◆ Transport
◆ Classes   ◆ Cafe

Don't be fooled by the laid-back name; the two owners here take the business of coffee very seriously, and are responsible not only for training baristas and developing the region's industry, but for serving up some of the country's best flat whites (plus cappuccinos, espressos etc) to board-bearing surfers, local businessfolk and walkers. You'll get as much buzz from reading the cafe's accompanying tasting notes as from its Sumatran highland single-origin coffee, one of many from around the world supplied by roaster Gabriel Coffee in Sydney. Pair your choice with one of the muffins or cakes made by ace chef and co-owner Liz Ennis for an even better experience.

Next door to the smart and airy cafe, the training facility and shop displays every coffee gadget and gizmo in coffeeworld: think AeroPress to Ottos and a wealth of other coffee-making 'toys'.

THINGS TO DO NEARBY

Palm Beach
Head east for 150m and you hit the sands where you can multi-task: sipping on your take-away brew while watching the waves.

Currumbin Boardwalk
Wander along the Currumbin Boardwalk, a little piece of mangrove paradise wedged between the Gold Coast Highway at Palm Beach and Currumbin Creek.

LA VEEN

90 King St, Perth, Western Australia;
+61 8 9321 1188; laveencoffee.com.au

◆ Food   ◆ Transport
◆ Cafe

At almost 2m long, La Veen's custom-made, six-group head machine is one of the largest in Australia. It drills, hums and screams as each cup is expertly made to a temperature between 58°C and 62°C. Owner and coffeemaker Benjamin Sed is as measured as one of his precision grinders. One-part coffee nerd and two-parts coffee educator, he teaches customers that warm, steamed milk unlocks a sublime creamy sweetness, whereas the hot stuff burns and spoils.

Within La Veen's heritage red brick walls and picture windows are nine different types of coffee on the go at any one time. All are direct trade and changed seasonally, some suited to the espresso machine, others filter, or 15 hours of cold-drip brewing. For something boundary stretching, Sed recommends his signature tonicpresso; it sounds bitter but the blend is remarkably sweet.

THINGS TO DO NEARBY

Varnish on King
Hidden below the
pavement, this New
York speakeasy-inspired
whiskey den is loved for
its quirky bacon and liquor
flights, its black-only
coffee policy and its sharp
eats. *varnishonking.com*

Uncle Joe's
Enter this lane-like space
and clock a new-wave
barber to your left and
a cafe ahead, spilling into
an industrial-feel enclosed
terrace with no roof.
unclejoes.com.au

PIXEL COFFEE BREWERS

2/226 Oxford St, Leederville, Western Australia;
+61 448 085 889

◆ Food ◆ Cafe
◆ Shop ◆ Transport

Pixel Coffee Brewers squeezes just four tables into a narrow space decorated with native flowers. But its diminutive size bears no relationship to its prodigious output. The bright tiled cafe is run by two female state-champ baristas who were formerly in the employ of local roaster Five Senses, yet they're not slaves to the brand; Pixel runs its own speciality Five Senses custom blend through its white Synesso, but rotates various single-origin roasts by others, including Perth's Mano e Mano and boutique outfit Coffeefusion. The house espresso blend cuts through locally produced milk with well-balanced chocolate and salted caramel tones, its *crema* crafted into the image of a swan.

THINGS TO DO NEARBY

The Re Store
Enter this old-school Italian delicatessen and winestore and you'll soon be ordering shavings of mortadella or mozzarella from the matronly, white-uniformed staff. The crusty rolls are legendary.
www.facebook.com/ReStoreOxford

Luna Leederville cinema
For anything off-the-wall, Australian-made or with subtitles, the Luna is your go-to. In summer, the popular hub opens an outdoor cinema for under-the-stars viewing pleasure.
lunapalace.com.au

© Catherine Sutherland / Lonely Planet

TELEGRAM

Inside the State Buildings, Cnr St Georges Tce
and Barrack St, Perth, Western Australia;
telegramcoffee.com.au; +61 8 9328 2952

◆ Food ◆ Shop ◆ Transport
◆ Classes ◆ Cafe

TELEGRAM COFFEE

When you're housed in the heritage bones of
your capital city's first General Post Office, history
deserves a nod. Telegram bows, both with its name and its
artisanal construction. A polished eucalyptus-wood box
envelopes the cafe, and each day, like a letter being opened,
its moving panels reveal the contents inside. They're
wound back using an iron pulley system salvaged from the
building's 140-year-old dumb waiter which, in its former
life, transported postal files between floors. With this much
attention to sculptural architecture, you can imagine the
care bestowed on the coffee.

Telegram's bossman and chief barista Luke Arnold has
a reputation for perfection. So much so that fans have

followed him as he's ground, frothed and poured at different
locations around Perth, before opening his eucalyptus
capsule in 2015. His coffee beans, like the telegrams of
old, connect to all corners of the globe. Arnold spent three
months testing countless bean combos with local roaster
Leftfield to create the Telegram blend. The result tastes
of chocolate, hazelnuts and fudge, and marries perfectly
with milk. For batch-brew filter coffees and single-origin
espressos, he carries beans by Perth roasters Twin Peaks
and Blacklist.

Queues are long at this inner-city must-visit, so there's no
time for pour-overs, but chilled filter coffee is there for those
who are on the go.

THINGS TO DO NEARBY

Petition Kitchen
Some of the city's classiest
fare – rare 'roo with
smoked labneh, say, or
pickled mussels dressed
with fennel pollen and
Pernod – is found within
these stripped-paint walls.
petitionperth.com

Kangaroo sculptures
This family of kangaroos
mount the pavement and
drink from the fountain
on the edge of the Stirling
Gardens, the inner city's
oldest public gardens.
The sculptures are
astonishingly lifelike.

Council House light show
By night, Perth's
unmissable 1960s pile of
Brutalist architecture turns
disco, care of 22,000 LED
lights warping the shell
into a vision of dancing
technicolour. *perth.wa.gov.
au/council-house*

Long Chim
Steamy, fiercely authentic
Thai street food finds
its home in Long Chim's
vaulted basement space.
The walls of street art
alone are worth a visit.
longchimperth.com

CAMPOS COFFEE

193 Missenden Rd, Newtown, Sydney, New South Wales;
www.camposcoffee.com; +61 2 9516 3361

- ◆ Food
- ◆ Cafe
- ◆ Shop
- ◆ Transport

The aroma of freshly ground beans tantalises as you fall in behind the doctors, nurses and students lined up at the counter. It's a tight fit, with only a few tables at the back and some seats along the window, but most customers scurry to the nearby hospital or university with takeaway cups anyway. The emphasis here is firmly on the coffee, although there are always tasty pastries stacked alluringly near the till. If you're bored with espresso, try one of the speciality filter or cold-drip brews. Campos prides itself on buying directly from producers and funding development projects in each of the countries it sources beans from. Single-origin coffee is available but make sure you try the excellent Campos Superior Blend.

THINGS TO DO NEARBY

King St
Newtown's boho-chic shopping strip has some wonderfully idiosyncratic bars, restaurants and stores. It's good for books, kooky boutiques and vintage clothes.

Camperdown Cemetery
Join the local goths and amateur photographers within the picturesque confines of this pleasantly ramshackle Victorian graveyard.
www.neac.com.au

EDITION COFFEE ROASTERS

265 Liverpool St, Darlinghurst, Sydney,
New South Wales; editioncoffeeroasters.com

- ◆ Food
- ◆ Cafe
- ◆ Shop
- ◆ Transport

Coffee is one commodity that is not in short supply in Darlinghurst. Even so, owner Daniel Jackson of Edition Coffee Roasters has made the city's cafe landscape a more interesting place. Step into this modern light-filled Scandi-inspired space and the hours can seriously slip away. Here, only single-origin coffee is served, black coffee is king, and the cuisine and coffee share the same philosophy: to celebrate great ingredients. Chef Jack New's menu is inspired by Japanese gastropub-style *izakayas*, with seasonal dishes such as the *chirashizushi* tacos and courgette flower salad eliciting double-takes as they make their journey from the kitchen. This Darlo darling is now open for dinner, so you can start and end the day with a batch-brew filter coffee.

THINGS TO DO NEARBY

Brett Whiteley Studio
The hard-to-find studio belonging to late artist Brett Whiteley has been preserved as a gallery that shows off some of his best works. ***www.artgallery.nsw.gov.au/brett-whiteley-studio***

Darlinghurst Theatre Company
Darlinghurst is the home of the arts in Sydney, and this theatre company is where you will find everything from old plays to fringe shows in the works. ***www.darlinghursttheatre.com***

MECCA

26 Bourke Rd, Alexandria, Sydney, New South Wales;
meccacoffee.com.au; +61 2 9698 8448

◆ Food　　◆ Classes　　◆ Cafe
◆ Roastery　◆ Shop　　◆ Transport

THINGS TO DO NEARBY

The Brewery Bar
Keep your beer miles in
check by nursing a Convict
Lager brewed in the
gleaming vats just metres
away from the Brewery Bar.
rocksbrewing.com

Urban Winery Sydney
Don't have time for a tour
of NSW cellars? Visit
Australia's first large-scale
urban winery, set up by
experimental winemaker
Alex Retief. *urban
winerysydney.com.au*

Sydney Park
Look for the towering
brick kilns that stand
like sentinels over this
sprawling 40-hectare park,
which includes wetlands
and a playground.
*www.cityofsydney.nsw.
gov.au*

Culture Scouts
Discover a different side
to Sydney on a private or
public walking tour that
offers insider knowledge
of the city's cultural hubs.
*www.culturescouts.
com.au*

A mecca is a place that attracts a particular group
of people with a particular interest. The group
attracted to Mecca Coffee have been worshipping the
Darkhorse blend for more than a decade. Outlets can
be found in Circular Quay, the CBD, Ultimo and at this
Alexandria hub, which has the added benefit of great
food thanks to Mecca CEO Paul Geshos' association with
Brickfields, the Chippendale corner bakery much-loved for
its European breads, tarts and pastries.

The cafe is housed in an old industrial warehouse where
a steel and windowed wall divides a former paint factory
from the cafe space... which was once a brothel. Hunker
down in the cafe for the signature 'Gesh spesh' – a tasting
plate of pickled and fermented vegetables – while keeping
an eye through the glass partition on head roaster Daniel
May at work because really, it's all about the coffee here.

Geshos is one of Australia's coffee pioneers and travels
the world to build great relationships with producers and
source the best product for his cafes. Beans are then roasted
to maximise complexity of flavour in the cup.

Don't just take our word for it though; try the Kalita filter
coffee and feel the love.

SINGLE O

60-64 Reservoir St, Surry Hills, Sydney, New South Wales;
singleo.com.au; +61 2 9211 0665

◆ Food   ◆ Cafe
◆ Shop   ◆ Transport

This Luchetti Krelle designed space – inspired by coffee, paper and filtration – is where the Single O story began in 2003, and although the roasting plant has since relocated to Botany, the aroma of fresh-roasted coffee beans still fills the air at this kerbside hang where the cool kids converge. To this day, the staff at Single O are forever sourcing, sampling, cupping, roasting, measuring, calibrating, tweaking, blending and tasting.

Years ago the cafe, which features wall art by Brett Chan, felt a bit like an underground club. Now there's almost a national movement dedicated to serving ethically sourced food with single-origin coffee. The Surry Hills stalwart also does a lot of good in its 'hood – including raising money for homelessness and supporting the Bread & Butter project (which provides stable employment for refugees). And staff

THINGS TO DO NEARBY

Chicken Institute
Be it fried, sticky, garlicky or peri peri, this Surry Hills gem is completely devoted to the bird. Order a craft brew to chase down that chicken. *www. chickeninstitute.com.au*

Prince Alfred Park
This pretty 7.5-hectare park is a top spot for a picnic. It includes children's play areas, tennis courts and a 50m outdoor heated lap pool.

Surry Hills Market
Comb the racks to find fabulous vintage fashion at the Surry Hills Markets, held on the first Saturday of the month. *shnc.org/events/ surry-hills-markets*

The Cricketers Arms
The Crix is a beloved local. Quaff a fancy pint and check the specials board at the bistro for deals on pub grub such as steak and chips for AU$10. *www.cricketersarmshotel. com.au*

have also declared a war on waste, encouraging customers to purchase Single O-branded Keep Cups and co-creating a milk-on-tap system called The Juggler, which is designed to reduce single-use plastics. Order a Mothership Bowl of black rice and seasonal vegetables, followed by a filter of the week, before filling your bag with Reservoir blend beans.

THE GROUNDS OF ALEXANDRIA

7A/2 Huntley St, Alexandria, Sydney, New South Wales;
thegrounds.com.au; +61 2 9699 2225

◆ Food   ◆ Classes   ◆ Cafe
◆ Roastery ◆ Shop   ◆ Transport

If you want to see just how much Sydney's cafe culture has changed, rewind to a time before The Grounds of Alexandria existed. This well-established cafe roasts its own beans on site and reaches for the highest rung when it comes to quality. The sleek space can get crowded during prime times because it's so easy to sit and linger in the sleek space over one of the pastries baked here daily. On Saturday mornings, the beautifully landscaped grounds morph into a market where, in addition to the superior coffee made using the latest filter and espresso technologies, you can choose from a selection of stalls and pat farmyard favourite Kevin Bacon (the pig). Get your coffee geek game face on for the coffee tasting board for two.

THINGS TO DO NEARBY

Mitchell Road Antique & Design Centre
Embrace the vintage vibe at this inner-urban antique jungle, where painstaking fossicking will unearth great finds. *mitchellroad. wordpress.com*

The Potting Shed
Those who miss out on getting into The Grounds of Alexandria can enjoy comfort food and cocktails at this pretty oasis next door. *thegrounds.com.au/ Spaces/potting-shed*

TOBY'S ESTATE

32-36 City Rd, Chippendale, Sydney, New South Wales;
www.tobysestate.com.au; +61 2 9221 1459

◆ Food   ◆ Classes   ◆ Cafe
◆ Roastery   ◆ Shop   ◆ Transport

Toby's Estate has come a long way from its origins in the courtyard of Toby Smith's mother's house in the central Sydney suburb of Woolloomooloo. Now it supplies beans to more than 600 independent cafes and has its own signature cafes in Sydney, Melbourne and Brisbane – not to mention Singapore, Manila and New York. It also runs a coffee school in Sydney, instructing both baristas and home enthusiasts in the black arts. And Toby now has an actual estate – the Finca Santa Teresa coffee plantation in Panama. The flagship Chippendale cafe occupies an old warehouse opposite Victoria Park, with a menu influenced by the countries from which its beans are sourced. Sip on a siphon brew, while watching the roasters through the rear windows.

THINGS TO DO NEARBY

Victoria Park
University students drape themselves languidly around this 9-hectare expanse of lawns centred on an ornamental lake and outdoor swimming pool.

Nicholson Museum
Hidden within the rarefied confines of the University of Sydney, this often-overlooked museum houses the southern hemisphere's largest collection of antiquities. *www.sydney.edu.au/museums*

WOLFPACK COFFEE ROASTERS

10 Edwin Street, Mortlake, Sydney, New South Wales;
www.wolfpackcoffee.com.au;

◆ Food ◆ Classes ◆ Cafe
◆ Roastery ◆ Shop ◆ Transport

Urban Dictionary defines the word wolfpack as 'a group of friends bounded together by loyalty, love and respect'. Wolfpack owners Daniel Plesko and his wife Irene design their blends with their 'wolfpack' in mind, and have put Mortlake on the map with blends such as the Alpha, a dark, chocolatey union that references an obsession with the Cherry Ripe bar.

Their newly relocated corner cafe and roastery is situated in a light-industrial area of Mortlake opposite a small park. Here the pack mentality is in evidence with everyone from MAMILs (middle-aged men in Lycra) to tradesmen and mums with their bubs refueling on caffeine and ham-and-cheese toasties. Enjoy a perfect piccolo in a puddle of sunshine and take a bite of a cronut or lemon, pistachio and almond teacake. Aaaarooooo!

THINGS TO DO NEARBY

CNR58 Café
Part cafe, part gift shop, this little corner eatery is making its mark in Concord with great lunch options such as miso salmon with eggplant.

The Kokoda Track Memorial Walkway
This 800m walk was created to pay tribute to the Australian troops who fought during WWII. Follow the track as it hugs the curves of Brays Bay. *www.kokodawalkway.com.au*

NEW ZEALAND

How to ask for a coffee in the local language?
I'll have a flat white, thanks mate
Signature coffee style? Flat white
What to order with your coffee? Louise cake – a slice with
a biscuit base topped with jam and coconut meringue
Don't: Say 'Let's meet at Starbucks'; Kiwi coffee-lovers will
presume you're joking

There's no denying it: little New Zealand, sitting
in splendid isolation at the bottom of the South
Pacific, has had a disproportionate impact on contemporary
global coffee culture. New Zealand's transformation from
the 'Land of the Long White Cloud' to the land of the flat
white coffee is as surprising as it was sudden.

The country was colonised by tea-supping Brits in the
19th century, and coffee was for a long time the preserve
of Mediterranean immigrants. It was in the 1980s that the
seeds of the coming revolution were planted. While the
jangly indie music of Flying Nun Records was percolating
up from the southern city of Dunedin, bohemian cafes
such as Auckland's Cafe DKD and Wellington's Midnight
Espresso became the favoured haunts of indie musos,
undergraduates and alternative-minded teens too young to
hang out in pubs.

It was around this time that the term 'flat white' was
coined, referring to an espresso served in a small cup and
topped with milk that's been gently heated to a silky smooth
consistency. Cafe owners on both sides of the Tasman Sea
claim the credit for its invention with those in the NZ camp
arguing that its very name sounds Kiwi – right up there in
terms of no-nonsense pragmatism with North Island and
South Island. In any case, the main difference between the
Kiwi and Aussie versions is that NZ's flat whites are stronger;
a double shot of espresso is standard.

By the early 1990s, some of the architects of this new
breed of cafe added roasteries to their operations and
started supplying their competitors with beans. These
speciality roasters quickly realised that their reputation
rested not just on the quality of their product but on the
ability of their client cafes to know what to do with it. They
started offering training in the dark arts to their customers,
teaching them how to extract the perfect espresso and
'stretch' milk to a flawless flat-white consistency. By the
mid-1990s, there were quality cafes in all the main centres,
followed rapidly by all the major towns and then pretty
much every corner of the country.

Cafe culture is now mainstream in NZ and a certain
quality is taken for granted. By the time the big American
chains tried to make inroads with their coffee-esque

259

CAFE TALK – SAM CROFSKY

In places with a bigger population, mediocrity is OK. But here, if you aren't any good, you will fail

TOP 5 COFFEES

- **Coffee Supreme** Supreme Blend
- **Havana Coffee Works** Cuban Real Trade
- **Atomic Coffee Roasters** Veloce Blend
- **Allpress Espresso** Rangitoto Blend
- **Hummingbird Coffee** Re:START Blend

confections, Kiwis were already used to a far superior brew at their neighbourhood cafe. However, it's not a pretentious scene: phrases such as 'third wave' have little currency here, and while some cafes cater to connoisseurs with single-origin cold-brews and siphons, most people would far prefer a high-quality espresso blend.

New Zealanders are inveterate travellers and the 'Big OE (Overseas Experience)' is a rite of passage for many. Aside from the weather, the biggest complaint from young Kiwis and Aussies visiting the UK (the most common OE destination) was the paucity of decent cafes. Some took up the opportunity to open their own, transforming London's cafe scene in the process. From Heathrow to Houston, Antipodean-trained baristas are now hot property and NZ-style cafes are bubbling up all over the place. Find one, and you'll find a guaranteed damn fine cup of coffee.

ALLPRESS ESPRESSO

8 Drake St, Freemans Bay, Auckland;
www.allpressespresso.com; +64 9 369 5842

◆ Food   ◆ Classes   ◆ Cafe
◆ Roastery   ◆ Shop   ◆ Transport

One of the trailblazers of the New Zealand coffee scene, Allpress grew from a coffee cart operated by a young Michael Allpress in 1986, just around the corner in Victoria Park, to one of only a handful of independent roasters worldwide operating in multiple countries. Although it has its own showcase roastery cafes in Auckland, Christchurch, Dunedin, Melbourne, Sydney, Byron Bay, Tokyo and London, the focus is on supplying independent cafe owners with a consistent quality of beans (roasted according to its own hot-air method) and barista training. Allpress now supplies more than a thousand cafes in five countries, and even publishes a magazine, *Press*, which shines a spotlight on some of the interesting artistic types working in Allpress-affiliated cafes worldwide.

THINGS TO DO NEARBY

Victoria Park Market
Dominated by a tall brick chimney, this surprisingly elegant complex of Victorian-era, industrial buildings contains a smattering of shops, bars and restaurants. *www.victoriaparkmarket.co.nz*

Wynyard Quarter
The redevelopment of this section of Auckland's waterfront is a work in progress but the restaurant-lined promenade is an appealing place for a stroll. *www.wynyard-quarter.co.nz*

Sky Tower
The southern hemisphere's tallest structure provides spectacular views over the city and gulf. If that's not thrilling enough, you can jump off it attached to a wire. *www.skycityauckland.co.nz*

Ponsonby Road
A byword throughout New Zealand for fashionable shops, bars, cafes and restaurants, Ponsonby Road offers myriad options for upmarket grazing and supping. *www.iloveponsonby.co.nz*

This Auckland roastery occupies an old warehouse tucked into a back lane on the city fringe, with its own small cafe and art gallery on the ground floor. Food is limited to simple stuff such as breakfast bowls, sandwiches, cakes and a delicious range of biscotti. Coffee is the hero here and, while you can order a cold-brew, Allpress considers itself an espresso expert. Various blends are available, but Rangitoto (named after Auckland's iconic volcanic island) is the one to try.

ATOMIC COFFEE ROASTERS

420c New North Rd, Kingsland, Auckland;
www.atomiccoffee.co.nz; +64 9 846 5883

◆ Food   ◆ Classes   ◆ Cafe
◆ Roastery   ◆ Shop   ◆ Transport

A pivotal player in the explosion of Auckland coffee culture in the early 1990s, Atomic is now something of an institution. However, it still manages to successfully compete with the young bucks: one of its baristas took the 2017 national latte art championship. The Kingsland branch is the archetypal Auckland cafe, with a vintage caravan parked out the front, an industrial-chic warehouse interior, a counter groaning with food and a window showcasing the shiny roasting machines at the back. There are four blends and two single-origins on offer, along with a variety of different milks (regular, low-fat, soy, coconut, almond). Give the cold-brew with soda a swerve and opt for a Veloce-blend short black instead.

THINGS TO DO NEARBY

Eden Park
Don't pass up an opportunity to see the All Blacks play at home in one of the world's most famous rugby stadiums.
www.edenpark.co.nz

Mt Eden
At 196m, this is the tallest of the dozens of volcanoes on the Auckland isthmus. Climb to the top to see the crater and the views.

C1 ESPRESSO

185 High St, Christchurch;
www.c1espresso.co.nz; +64 3 379 1917

◆ Food   ◆ Shop   ◆ Transport
◆ Roastery ◆ Cafe

When the earthquakes of 2011 wiped out their original cafe, the determined young C1 crew stoically dusted themselves off and started again. By the following year they had secured the ground floor of an art-deco post office, one of a handful of buildings in Christchurch's city centre that had survived the cataclysm, and re-opened while most of the surrounding streets were still flattened.

Materials recycled from earthquake-wrecked buildings fill the interior, including Victorian oak panelling rescued from a convent and bulbous 1970s light fixtures from the Arts Centre. Other nifty features include a water fountain fashioned from a Singer sewing machine, a sliding bookcase that conceals the door to the toilets and pneumatic tubes that deliver burgers and beer directly to your table.

Sustainability is a big focus as well, with solar panels, a 5000L rainwater tank, an extensive kitchen garden out the front (tended by homeless people), and a development programme which works with families in Samoa to produce single-origin Kofe Samoa beans, Koko Samoa (a canned cold-brewed cocoa drink), fruit nectars and speciality teas, including cascara made from coffee cherries.

For something a little bit different, try a Fat Black: the signature house-roasted C1000 blend poured over a mixture of coconut butter, vanilla and cinnamon.

THINGS TO DO NEARBY

Quake City
The 2010 and 2011 earthquakes destroyed large chunks of Christchurch and killed 186 people. This small museum recounts those events through artefacts and video testimonies. *www. canterburymuseum.com*

Cathedral Square
Check out the progress of restoring the civic heart of the city and its namesake cathedral, left partly in ruins by the February 2011 earthquake.

Transitional Cathedral
Designed by Japanese architect Shigeru Ban as a temporary replacement for badly damaged Christchurch Cathedral, the 'Cardboard Cathedral' (see left) has at its core 98 cardboard tubes. *www. cardboardcathedral.org.nz*

Christchurch Art Gallery
Displayed behind the wave-like glass facade is the city's premier collection of New Zealand and international art, alongside interesting temporary exhibitions. *www.christchurchartgallery. org.nz*

HUMMINGBIRD COFFEE

438 Selwyn St, Addington, Christchurch;
www.hummingbirdcoffee.com; +64 3 379 0826

◆ Food   ◆ Classes   ◆ Cafe
◆ Roastery ◆ Shop   ◆ Transport

Hummingbird has notched up various firsts over the years: the first New Zealand roastery to import Fairtrade, organic beans; the first to be certified 100% organic. However, the people of Christchurch remember it most fondly as the first business to sign up for the Re:START Mall. The opening of this open-air mall constructed from shipping containers gave the city a much-needed fillip when it sprung up among the ruins, eight months after the devastating 2011 earthquake. Hummingbird also launched the Re:START blend, donating 30c from each bag sold to reconstruction projects. Its flagship cafe and roastery occupies the Oddfellows Hall, a Victorian-era structure that once held Suffragette meetings and hence played a part in another first: NZ becoming the first country to give women the vote in 1893.

THINGS TO DO NEARBY

Court Theatre
Hummingbird donated NZ$130,000 raised from sales of its Re:START blend towards rehousing this esteemed theatre company in 'The Shed', its new Addington home. *www.courttheatre.org.nz*

Hagley Park
This vast park stretches for 165 hectares, with lawns, cherry trees and the Avon River looping through it. At its centre is Christchurch's beautiful Botanic Gardens. *www.ccc.govt.nz*

DEVIL'S CUP

44 Bedford St, Patea, South Taranaki;
www.devilscup.co.nz; +64 21 176 9177

◆ Roastery   ◆ Shop
◆ Classes   ◆ Cafe

Located on an isolated stretch of the North Island's west coast, Patea is best known in New Zealand for 'Poi E', a chart-topping track by the local Māori club which became 1984's highest selling single. That this town of 1140 people has its own organic fair-trade roastery speaks volumes about the all-pervasive, non-pretentious nature of New Zealand's coffee scene. Operating out of an 1874 bank building which doubles as his home, Kevin Murrow roasts beans sourced through respected local fair-trade organisation, Trade Aid. He mainly sells his blends online, but the historic banking chamber has recently been converted into a cafe and art gallery, showcasing the work of his wife, printmaker Michaela Stoneman. Be sure to try the Bank Blend espresso.

THINGS TO DO NEARBY

Patea Beach
The top thing to do in Patea is to walk along the wild, black-sand beach; it's better suited to a stroll than a swim.

Tawhiti Museum
This small private museum in nearby Hawera houses amazingly intricate dioramas along with a bush railway and an indoor boat ride through candlelit historic scenes. *www. tawhitimuseum.co.nz*

CUSTOMS BY COFFEE SUPREME

39 Ghuznee St, Te Aro, Wellington;
www.coffeesupreme.com; +64 4 385 2129

◆ Food   ◆ Cafe
◆ Shop   ◆ Transport

Coffee Supreme is one of the southern hemisphere's speciality coffee trailblazers, and the Customs Brew Bar is its flagship, its showcase and the best place to drink its brews in Wellington. Customs opened in 2010 with a lovely wood-panelled fit-out that evokes a mid-20th century Scandi domestic space to match the retro brew methods that are the focus here (much of the beautiful timber was recycled from an old farmhouse that was owned by founders Chris Dillon and Maggie Wells). The aim at Customs Brew Bar is to reintroduce soft-brew methods to espresso-centric Wellingtonians, and there's a decent collection of filter gadgets – siphons, pots, percolators, Moccamasters – displayed on shelves around the walls.

On the coffee menu, nine single-origins are offered via

THINGS TO DO NEARBY

Te Papa Tongarewa – Museum of New Zealand
New Zealand's national museum and art gallery is filled with fascinating collections, including large holdings of Maori cultural treasures and spaces devoted to popular culture since Europeans arrived. *www.tepapa.govt.nz*

Mt Victoria Lookout
The 196m-high Mt Victoria lookout offers panoramic views of Wellington city and harbour, its suburbs and the Hutt Valley.

Six Barrel Soda Co
Fancy a break from coffee? Climb the stairs to this little hideaway looking over a grungy slice of downtown Wellington for a soda in inventive flavours like orange and dandelion or cherry and pomegranate. *www.sixbarrelsoda.co.nz*

Unity Books
New Zealand's best bookshop, with space dedicated to the country itself. *unitybooks.nz*

Fetco batch brew, V60, Chemex, cold-brew and, of course, espresso. A batch brew of a Costa Rica La Cruz might be clean and juicy, with hints of chocolate and mandarin sweetness, while a Honduras Yire makes a savoury, complex V60 filter. Espresso blends come from Coffee Supreme's Ratio series. Food on offer is minimal – cakes and slices from local suppliers – and while they push the filter brews, where better to sample Wellington's own, the flat white?

FLIGHT COFFEE HANGAR

119 Dixon Street, Wellington;
www.flightcoffee.co.nz; +64 4 830 0909

◆ Food   ◆ Cafe
◆ Shop   ◆ Transport

THINGS TO DO NEARBY

Katherine Mansfield House and Garden
The childhood home of one of New Zealand's most famous writers is a charming two-storey Italianate house built in 1887 and preserved in original style. *www.katherinemansfield.com*

Wellington Botanic Garden
This 25-hectare space hosts numerous plant collections, including an Australian garden and remnants of the New Zealand native forest that preceded the European settlement. *wellington.govt.nz*

Wellington Cable Car
New Zealand's only working funicular railway takes you from near the Botanic Gardens to the heart of the city at Lambton Quay, with spectacular views along the way. *www.wellingtoncablecar.co.nz*

Mount St Cemetery
Wind up the steep hills around Victoria University to the Mount St cemetery – one of Wellington's oldest, with great views of the city and harbour. *www.mountstreetcemetery.org.nz*

Flight Coffee Hangar is a buzzing timber and concrete space at the west end of Dixon Street, where it starts to climb one of downtown Wellington's steep surrounding hills. With former NZ barista champ Nick Clark among the owners, plenty of attention is paid to getting the basics right (a battery of grinders is calibrated for black, white and filter brews), but the care starts at the source: Flight's Helena Project is transforming a coffee farm in Colombia into a speciality coffee producer, working on every aspect of production, from planting to processing.

The best way to sample Flight's wares is via, er, a coffee flight: perhaps a taste-test of a single-origin as a short black, a flat white and a cold drip; or three flat whites with different origins. The Bomber blend makes a classic Kiwi espresso, with plenty of body and acidity; while a Fetco brew of Ethiopia Sidamo has honey sweetness and gentle floral flavours. The kitchen applies global influences to brunch, from a maple-bacon and fried egg butty or a smoked tofu salad with pumpkin hummus to the full Irish breakfast of bacon, egg, blood pudding, fried potatoes and soda bread.

HAVANA COFFEE WORKS

163 Tory St, Wellington;
www.havana.co.nz; +64 4 384 7041

◆ Food   ◆ Classes   ◆ Cafe
◆ Roastery   ◆ Shop   ◆ Transport

Havana's startling green art-deco building – once the headquarters of Firestone Tyres – brings a slice of 1950s cafe glamour to Wellington: the roastery is styled like a Latin American courtyard house, and the cafe is all wood-panelled and bar-mirrored, with old-school cafe chairs and marble-topped tables. Havana's philosophy is summed up as 'real trade' – dealing directly with farmers to source the six tonnes of green beans they roast here every week. The go-to coffee is Five Star blend – a dark roast that makes a short black which is syrupy and toasty to its chocolate-toned end. Filter brews come via Chemex, and the cafe features a guest coffee every week – for instance, the Nuclear Free blend from a farm on the slopes of a volcano in Vanuatu.

THINGS TO DO NEARBY

Pukeahu National War Memorial Park
The 300,000 New Zealanders who served (including 30,000 who died) in various wars are commemorated by this imposing art-deco carillon, the Hall of Memories and Tomb of the Unknown Warrior.
www.mch.govt.nz

Basin Reserve and New Zealand Cricket Museum
New Zealand's oldest cricket ground is built on land that was raised from a lake by the 1855 earthquake. The museum is open whenever a game – Test, first class, one-day or local – is on.
nzcricketmuseum.co.nz

INDEX

INDEX

INDEX

INDEX

ACKNOWLEDGEMENTS

Published in May 2018
by Lonely Planet Global Limited
CRN 554153
www.lonelyplanet.com
ISBN 978 1787 01359 9
© Lonely Planet 2018
Printed in China
10 9 8 7 6 5 4 3 2 1

Managing Director, Publishing Piers Pickard
Associate Publisher Robin Barton
Commissioning Editor Dora Ball
Editors Mike Higgins, Nick Mee, Yolanda Zappaterra
Art Direction Daniel Di Paolo
Layout Tina Garcia, Mariana Sameiro
Illustrations Jon Dicus, Jacob Rhoades
Image Research Regina Wolek
Print Production Lisa Ford, Larissa Frost, Nigel Longuet

Contributors: Kate Armstrong, Andrew Bain, James Bainbridge, Fleur Bainger, Robin Barton, Sara Benson, Oliver Berry, Abigail Blasi, Claire Boobbyer, John Brunton, Austin Bush, Kerry Christiani, Lucy Corne, Sally Davies, Peter Dragicevich, Carolyn Heller, Ashley Garver, Ethan Gelber, Bridget Gleeson, Valerie Greene, Carla Grossetti, Anthony Ham, Jacob Hanawalt, Paula Hardy, Matt Holden, Anita Isalska, Alex Kitain, Anna Kaminski, Patrick Kinsella, Sofia Levin, Stephen Lioy, Shawn Low, Rebecca Milner, Anja Mutic, Karyn Noble, Stephanie Ong, Brandon Presser, Kevin Raub, Brendan Sainsbury, Caroline Sieg, Helena Smith, Ashley Tomlinson, Jennifer Walker, Luke Waterson, Nicola Williams, Chris Zeiher
Thanks to James Ball, Erin Blok, Katie Coffee, Simon Hoskins, Flora Macqueen, Natalie Nicholson

STAY IN TOUCH lonelyplanet.com/contact

AUSTRALIA
The Malt Store, Level 3, 551 Swanston St,
Carlton, Victoria 3053 T: 03 8379 8000

USA
124 Linden St, Oakland, CA 94607
T: 510 250 6400

IRELAND
Digital Depot, Roe Lane (off Thomas St), Digital Hub,
Dublin 8, D08 TCV4

UNITED KINGDOM
240 Blackfriars Rd, London SE1 8NW
T: 020 3771 5100

Although the authors and Lonely Planet have taken all reasonable care in preparing this
book, we make no warranty about the accuracy or completeness of its content and,
to the maximum extent permitted, disclaim all liability from its use.

Paper in this book is certified against the
Forest Stewardship Council™ standards.
FSC™ promotes environmentally responsible,
socially beneficial and economically viable
management of the world's forests.